# Popular Trauma Culture

# Popular Trauma Culture

## Selling the Pain of Others
## in the Mass Media

ANNE ROTHE

RUTGERS UNIVERSITY PRESS

NEW BRUNSWICK, NEW JERSEY, AND LONDON

LIBRARY OF CONGRESS CATALOGING-IN-PUBLICATION DATA

Rothe, Anne
  Popular trauma culture : selling the pain of others in the mass media / Anne Rothe.
    p. cm.
  Includes bibliographical references and index.
  ISBN 978–0–8135–5128–9 (hardcover : alk. paper)—ISBN 978–0–8135–5129–6
(pbk. : alk. paper)
    1. Psychic trauma and mass media.   2. Holocaust, Jewish (1939–1945)—
In mass media.   I. Title.
  P96.P73R68   2011
  302.23—dc22                                                    2010049961

A British Cataloging-in-Publication record for this book is available
from the British Library.

Visit our Web site: http://rutgerspress.rutgers.edu

Manufactured in the United States of America

# CONTENTS

# PREFACE

$A$s it matters more who is speaking when scholarship extends beyond the theoretical and empirical to the ethical realm, let me briefly make my subject position explicit here. Having spent my first eighteen years in East Germany has made me critical of capitalism's many injustices but also appreciative of democracy, despite its flaws. The democratic ideal of freedom of thought, though never absolute, allowed me to think, speak, and write uninhibited by political pressures. Furthermore, the virtual absence of the Holocaust from East German collective memory, which I have critiqued elsewhere, has shaped my thinking on Holocaust commemoration, because it made me critically aware of the political appropriation of the past.

Another significant influence official East German memory had on me may be best conveyed via a story-within-a-story anecdote. My friend Eran mentioned one day that a fellow graduate student had asked to borrow his car while Eran went home to Israel for the summer. He had agreed but asked that the student from the former West Germany clean it inside and out before returning the car. When he did not appear keen to do so, Eran joked: "But don't you know, *Arbeit macht frei.*" My bewilderment at his clever but atypically unkind and ethically dubious comment was reinforced by knowing that Eran's father had survived Auschwitz. To my astonished question why he had never tried anything like this on me, Eran spontaneously replied: "It wouldn't have worked on you." Beyond having spent about a third of my life and the vast majority of my adulthood in the United States, I believe it is my East German upbringing that makes my thinking about Holocaust commemoration free from the oxymoronic sense of vicarious guilt that many (former) West Germans, even of the second and third postwar generation, still experience.

My critical stance toward official Holocaust memory was also influenced by the fact that I only learned about the small concentration camp, a satellite work camp of Neuengamme, that had existed outside my home town of Neustadt-Glewe, when I read John Roth and Carol Rittner's volume of Holocaust testimony *Different Voices* in Stephanie Hammer's Holocaust seminar. After some local history research, I found Lilli Kopecky, who had come to the camp on a death march from Auschwitz and was liberated there. Like myself at the time, Lilli was living in Los Angeles, and I regularly visited her for three years until I left for a postdoctoral research project in Israel. The conversations with Lilli have immeasurably contributed to my understanding of the Holocaust as lived experience and my sense of German collective identity. So has the chance encounter at a delicatessen in Haifa with another Auschwitz survivor who was liberated in Neustadt-Glewe and her generous invitation to visit her at home, where she shared her life story with me. These experiences have also made me aware that much official Holocaust commemoration, whether in the United States, Germany, or Israel, as well as some Holocaust scholarship in literary and cultural studies, anachronistically and unethically appropriate the actual survivors by transforming them into rhetorical figures.

There is a risk to publicly pondering one's subject position, as the brief reflections in this preface may be misused for an indiscriminate critique or even a blanket rejection of the argument developed in the book, instead of engaging in rational and empirically grounded scholarly debate over differences. I have nevertheless traced some of the experiences that shaped and reflect my subject position because it makes explicit some of the context within which my notion of ethics with regard to collective Holocaust memory and the representation of victimhood generally emerged. It also indicates that, while my critique is harsh at times, it is not callous but rooted in convictions that emerged in a decade-long process of self-reflection that was informed by the interactions between personal life and scholarship.

# ACKNOWLEDGMENTS

I gladly take this opportunity to gratefully acknowledge the many friends and colleagues who have helped this book along from inception to publication. Peter Blickle generously offered to read an earlier draft of the manuscript, and I remain immensely grateful for his generosity of spirit and enthusiastic encouragement over the past years. Guy Stern likewise thoroughly read the manuscript. Beyond that, I thank him as well as my other colleagues at Wayne State University for believing that I might some day grow into his shoes when they hired me upon his retirement. One day, Guy noted my shiny red sneakers, and remembering my earlier comment that his were big shoes to fill and would thus be the size of clown shoes on my feet, he joked that those were not his shoes. I greatly appreciate that I was encouraged by him and my colleagues at WSU—including Don Haase, Alfred Cobbs, Lisa Hock, Roz Schindler, Mark Ferguson, and Felicia Lucht—to "wear my own shoes." They helped me to develop my own research agenda rather than follow narrowly in Guy's footsteps or be restricted by my appointment in German-Jewish studies. While my research agenda differs from Guy's, he has been a role model both as a scholar and a person.

Wulf Kansteiner's theoretically and empirically erudite scholarship and his critical stance toward postmodern ethical relativity informed much of my thinking. His book *In Pursuit of German Memory: History, Television, and Politics after Auschwitz* sparked my interest in scholarly analyses of television programs and popular culture generally. Moreover, his critique of postmodern trauma theory and enthusiastic encouragement of my own reinforced my idea of writing a book that explores the ubiquity of the trauma concept in popular culture without recycling tropes from this still dominant discourse. I am also genuinely grateful for his exceptionally generous support in many a pragmatic matter.

My gratitude also goes to the anonymous reviewers of the manuscript for their time, effort, and constructive criticism. I would particularly like to thank one of them for a beautifully written and incisively argued review that was enthusiastically supportive to the extent of preemptively defending my arguments against just about any potential criticism. It also made explicit for me that I intuitively argue and indeed wrote the book "from an unapologetically Enlightenment perspective."

I would furthermore like to thank Atina Grossmann, Irene Kascandes, Leslie Morris, and Dorothee Wierling for the interest they expressed in my ideas at various conferences, and Stefanie Schüler-Springorum for her extensive support in both academic and personal matters. Many thanks also to Stephanie Hammer for teaching me the core ideas in Holocaust studies. For instance, she made me aware of the notion of collective identity by occasionally asking me, as the only German student in class, what I thought about a particular idea as a German. I have built my own research on the foundation I acquired in the graduate seminar Stephanie guest-taught at UCLA about a decade ago. When she gave me a copy of her book *Schiller's Wound: The Theater of Trauma from Crisis to Commodity*, she added a personal note that ended with the words "Now—here's to *your* book on trauma!" I hope she likes this one.

Karen Flint, Lori Lantz, and Eran Neuman have remained friends since grad school despite the distance between Detroit and Charlotte, Berlin, and Tel Aviv respectively. I specifically dedicate every "however" in this book to Eran since he once mentioned that this is his favorite word in English. And while the word "pink" probably does not figure in most scholarly manuscripts, it does make an appearance in mine and is dedicated to Lori because, as Olaf says, to her pink is not a color but an attitude. And after a recent stay with Karen, David, and Kerala in London, any mention of the city in the book and elsewhere now also serves as a reminder of this great time.

Let me also mention old and new friends and colleagues and thank them for formal and especially informal exchanges of ideas and stories at many conferences that I hope will continue for many years to come: Ulli Bach, Valentina Glajar, Yvonne Ivory, Susanne Kelley, Yulia Komska, Erin McGlothlin, Kerstin Müller, Caroline Schaumann, Joachim Schlör, Vera Stegmann, Susi Vees-Gulani, and Sebastian Wogenstein.

I am grateful to my PhD students Pauline Ebert and Juliana Mamou for both thinking independently and appreciating my advice, as well as being intrinsically motivated to write their dissertations. I am especially indebted to Pauline for her patience in waiting for my comments on her chapters. Her genuinely friendly, kind, and cooperative personality made the transition from *Doktormutter* to friend and colleague natural and easy. I am certain that Juliana will likewise soon complete an excellent dissertation.

My manuscript would not have become a book without Leslie Mitchner, the humanities editor at Rutgers University Press, and Marlie Wasserman, who serves double duty as the press director and editor in Holocaust and Jewish Studies. I am sincerely grateful to both of them. The book also greatly benefited from Rachel Friedman's editorial skills, which helped me to ruthlessly cut the manuscript in length by about a quarter, and in the process clarify the argument. Thanks also to Rachel for encouraging my tentative idea to reflect explicitly on my subject position. I would also like to thank Charles Annis for his thorough final editing of the manuscript.

I'm also grateful that Mark Ferguson and Louise Speed (and Sox) kept an eye on my house when I was away and helped in countless other pragmatic matters. And I owe apologies to my neighbors on Audubon Road who had to tolerate my front and back yard becoming ever more jungle-like over the past two years as the necessity of finishing the book before tenure review left time for little else. Last but certainly not least, I would like to thank my parents for supporting me in their own ways.

I am genuinely grateful for all of the encouragement even if I didn't always heed the advice but, *pace* Kant, plucked up the courage to use my own mind. The somewhat precarious decision, given the time constraints of tenure track, not to revise my dissertation but instead write a book from scratch was rewarded by the extensive interest in my manuscript among major American scholarly presses, six of which requested that I submit it for review. (That I remained committed to Rutgers University Press speaks to the exceptional support my project received there.) By writing a new book I could expand beyond the discursive constraints of the dissertation framework, generated after all during early graduate work, and thus develop a new research agenda that extends beyond both my home discipline of German studies and the canon that still dominates much literary studies scholarship to contemporary American popular culture. It also reflects my growing interest in ethical questions and will, I hope, contribute to the current ethical turn in cultural studies after some three decades of postmodern relativism.

# Popular Trauma Culture

# Introduction

## Oprah at Auschwitz

"We've become accustomed in American culture to stories of pain, even addicted to them. . . . In a culture of trauma, accounts of extreme situations sell books. Narratives of illness, sexual abuse, torture, or death of loved ones have come to rival the classic, heroic adventure as a test of limits that offers the reader the suspicious thrill of borrowed emotion."

–Nancy Miller and Jason Tougaw, *Extremities*[1]

The notion of popular trauma culture developed throughout the pages of this book can be captured in a nutshell by a brief discussion of three media events that exemplarily mark its emergence, culmination, and critique. The first is the trial of Adolf Eichmann in Jerusalem, which began on April 11, 1961.[2] Information about the trial was not only widely disseminated via radio, newspapers, and magazines, such as Hannah Arendt's famous reports for *The New Yorker* subsequently published as *Eichmann in Jerusalem*, but also and especially through the new medium of television. While this was the first trial filmed in its entirety, the television broadcasts focused on the testimony of Holocaust survivors and thus both reflected and reinforced the significance attributed to the witness accounts by the prosecution. However, as most survivors had no knowledge of crimes for which Eichmann could be legally held accountable, they did not function as eyewitnesses in the judicial sense, but were ascribed the new social function and identity of historical witnesses. Chief prosecutor Gideon Hausner and Israeli Prime Minister David Ben-Gurion wanted to use the trial to teach the world a history lesson.[3] Indicating his intuitive understanding of the new media discourse generated by television, Hausner cast survivors rather than legal experts as the core figures in the trial. As they were accompanied by dramatic displays of raw emotions, survivors' personal accounts of persecution were far more suitable for television than complex historical and juridical accounts of Eichmann's role in the "Final Solution."

The Eichmann trial not only introduced the significant notion that the genocide of European Jewry was a distinct and defining event in twentieth-century history, but it also constitutes the first key instance of popular trauma culture. It infused Western culture with the pain of others, to use Susan Sontag's famous phrase,[4] represented in historically and politically decontextualized narratives. They were constructed around a melodramatic conflict between absolute innocence and rank evil, which was embodied in the dichotomized flat characters of victim and perpetrator. According to the core story paradigm, the main character eventually overcomes victimization and undergoes a metamorphosis from the pariah figure of weak and helpless victim into a heroic survivor. As part of this transformation process, the victim-cum-survivor generates a witness testimony of the past traumatic experiences. The paradigmatic story line moreover recycles the Christian suffering-and-redemption trope of spiritual purification through physical mortification in trauma-and-recovery narratives and encodes a latently voyeuristic kitsch sentiment as the dominant mode of reception. Although the first day of the Eichmann trial proceedings thus symbolically marks the birthday of popular trauma culture, as cultural trends are generated through the mass media, its birthplace is the ephemeral space of the radio and TV airwaves rather than the Jerusalem courthouse.

The second exemplary media event in the genealogy of popular trauma culture, the *Oprah Winfrey Show Special* broadcast on May 24, 2006, signifies its most spectacular culmination to date. It depicts the host and Elie Wiesel at Auschwitz. After the fiasco of featuring James Frey's largely fabricated memoir *A Million Little Pieces*, in which he narrates his recovery from alcohol and drug addiction, in September 2005, Winfrey selected Wiesel's *Night* as the next text for her book club. As Adam Shatz, the literary editor of the *Nation,* put it sarcastically in the *LA Times*, what better way for Winfrey "to insulate herself from criticism over the Frey contretemps than to warm herself by the hearth of Holocaust remembrance?"[5] Shatz also noted that "Oprah is planning a trip to Auschwitz with Wiesel. . . . And yes, the pilgrimage to the camps will be filmed."[6] During their televised engagement in Holocaust tourism, Winfrey and Wiesel walk past the camp's iconic markers that have become so emblematic for the cultural memory of the Holocaust that the name of the camp provides its metonymy. The memorial site's surreal, otherworldly aura has been skillfully enhanced by the almost complete absence of other visitors at this usually heavily populated site, visited annually by about a million tourists, and by filming on a snowy day.[7] The thick snow generates an eerie light that blends the grounds into an equally milky-white sky. Although the show was filmed in color, it echoes the post-color black-and-white aesthetic of *Schindler's List* since, apart from Winfrey's colorful scarf and a pair of red shoes skillfully displayed atop the pile of shoes in the museum's exhibition, virtually all color is effaced by the peculiar quasi-black-and-white aesthetics generated by the white light outdoors.[8]

Simultaneously enveloped in and juxtaposed as two dark figures to the eerie, deadly still, and deserted white space, Winfrey and Wiesel are engaged in a conversation that generates a dissonant fusion between his quasi-religious understanding of the Holocaust as an incomprehensible mystery of suffering and redemption and her self-help platitudes of trauma and recovery. Film critic J. Hoberman's apt critique of *Schindler's List* as the ultimate "feel-good story about the ultimate feel-bad experience" thus likewise pertains to the *Oprah Winfrey Show Special*.[9] While Winfrey's immensely popular talk show reflected and reinforced trauma culture discourse, Roger Luckhurst's characterization of her as "the inaugurating figure of contemporary trauma celebrity"[10] pertains equally well to Wiesel, the other iconic representative of American trauma culture. He personifies the complementary discursive tendency of Holocaust sanctification to Winfrey's trauma-and-recovery kitsch. Functioning as "both priest and prophet of this new religion"[11] as which he practices Holocaust commemoration, Wiesel embodies victimhood and survivorship for a small, but culturally influential elite. They consume highbrow media like his more than forty books and the Arts and Leisure section of the Sunday *New York Times*, where they encounter Wiesel's Christ-like public persona of the eternally suffering victim and his regular sermons on the supremely significant and universally applicable, yet inherently incomprehensible, lessons of the unique Holocaust mystery.[12]

Winfrey and Wiesel not only engage in what John Lennon and Malcolm Foley have termed "dark tourism,"[13] but also up the trauma culture ante by filming their rendezvous at Auschwitz for mass consumption by American viewers whose socialization imparted little or no knowledge onto them about the Holocaust as historical event.[14] Reflecting and reinforcing dominant American Holocaust discourse, their televised sentimental journey through Auschwitz does not inform viewers about the complex socio-political history of the "Final Solution," but rather constitutes a search for mystical revelations and uplifting self-help messages. According to Adam Shatz, it transforms "the Holocaust into another recovery narrative."[15] The *Oprah Winfrey Show Special* thus both enacts and signifies that popular trauma culture has incorporated and transformed the American Holocaust discourse out of which it initially emerged.

Despite the continued prominence of both Holocaust kitschification and sanctification, they no longer constitute the only modes of representation. Mel Brooks's 1968 film *The Producers*, its successful 2001 transformation into a Broadway musical, and its 2005 re-adaptation into a new movie; Tova Reich's 2007 satirical novel *My Holocaust*; and the 2004 episode "The Survivor" of Larry David's *Curb Your Enthusiasm* series critique American Holocaust pieties via satire and parody. A scene from the latter metonymically marks another core moment in the genealogy of popular trauma culture, namely its most concentrated critique to date. The episode, which I will later discuss in greater detail, parodies both the representation of the Holocaust as a quasi-sacred event, a veritable Holycaust, and the made-in-Hollywood trivialization of the genocide as Hollycaust in tear-jerking blockbusters, as well as the interaction of both modes of Holocaust emplotment with American culture. The most spectacular scene from the episode ensues when a dinner-table conversation turns into a shouting match between Solly, a fictional Holocaust survivor who in appearance and behavior constitutes the ultimate antithesis to Wiesel's public persona, and Colby, a former participant in the popular reality series *Survivor*. They fight over who had to defeat greater obstacles, suffered more, and thus constitutes the preeminent "survivor." The scene ridicules via satiric exaggeration and parody emblematic components of popular trauma culture: the clichéd nature of dominant American Holocaust representations, the ubiquitous but ethically and epistemologically untenable notion of Holocaust uniqueness and preeminence,[16] the excessive, and unethical because inherently competitive claims to victim status, and the vast metaphoric extension of the survivor position.

These three exemplary media events indicate that narratives of victimization and survival, trauma and recovery are anything but restricted to scholarship in postmodern trauma theory and the select examples from the literary and filmic canon that constitute its limited empirical corpus.[17] According to the alternative paradigm proposed here, it is precisely the question that trauma studies scholarship has left out that ought to be explored, namely how the ubiquitous notion of trauma functions in contemporary culture. And since cultural trends are generated via the interaction of vast audiences and the mass media products they consume, it is the representation of traumatizing experiences in popular culture that must be analyzed.[18] The notion of trauma widely disseminated via the self-help industry, which is reflected and reinforced by other popular culture products, describes a psychological reaction to an experience in which a seemingly omnipotent perpetrator inflicts extreme violence on a helpless victim. Because the latter's psychological suffering continues long after the physical pain subsided, self-help literature teaches its many consumers that in order to overcome traumatizing experiences and transform weak victims into heroic survivors, the traumatic memories must be narrated.

According to Bruno Latour, a concept succeeds based on its degree of associative power to bind otherwise heterogeneous ideas, that is, the extent to which it functions as a discursive knot.[19] Expanding Latour's argument from the natural sciences to representation at large and popular culture in particular, I suggest that the trauma concept functions as a discursive knot in contemporary culture due to its vast associative powers of generating interactions between disparate ideas. In other words, the discursive knot generated by the trauma concept provides the dominant mode of emplotment—the basic narrative structure and core set of characters—for representing such diverse experiences as child abuse, Holocaust survival, war combat, terminal illness, and addiction in contemporary Western culture. However, the media spectacles of popular trauma culture remove these experiences of victimization and suffering from their socio-political contexts by reducing them to their smallest common denominator of a body in pain. They proclaim that, no matter what happens, whether genocide or child abuse or lesser evils, there will always be a happy ending when good wins over evil, victims become survivors, and perpetrators are punished, thus teaching consumers that the socio-economic status quo need not be changed through political action. Mass media emplotments of the pain of others are thus not only unethical because they transform traumatic experiences into entertainment commodities but also because they are politically acquiescing and covertly reinforce the oppressive hegemonies of late-modern capitalism that have generated, or at least enabled, the victimization experiences. My understanding of popular culture thus bears some family resemblances to the Frankfurt School critique of mass culture and the rejection of gothic and sentimental novels for their politically anesthetizing capacity in the so-called German and British reading debates of the late eighteenth century.[20]

The analysis of popular trauma culture developed throughout the book is structured as follows: In part one, I analyze how the currently dominant plot formula, set of characters, and core tropes for representing victimhood and suffering emerged in American Holocaust discourse. The genealogy of popular trauma culture includes an analysis of the transition in rhetoric from testimony to so-called victim talk and of the survivor figure's rise to hero status. It furthermore encompasses critiques of the political appropriation of Holocaust memory in American culture and of the Holocaust envy signified by claims of vicarious victimhood. Part one concludes with a critique of teary-eyed kitsch sentiment encoded as the dominant reception mode into the narratives that embody popular trauma culture.

As daytime TV talk shows and the popular literature genre of misery memoirs currently constitute the preeminent genres for depicting the pain of others as mass media spectacles, they are explored in parts two and three respectively. Like the witness testimony given at the Eichmann trial that signaled the advent of trauma culture, the accounts of victimization and violence, pain and suffering generated on talk shows are widely disseminated via television.[21] First-generation shows like *Phil Donahue* and *Oprah Winfrey* represented personal experiences of extremity as individual melodramas in the inherently de-politicized manner paradigmatic for self-help discourse. Subsequently, the platitudes and clichés of pop psychology were supplemented by the modern-day freak show spectacles of second-generation shows like *Ricki Lake* and *Jerry Springer*. The so-called trash talk shows parodied the trauma kitsch of their predecessors as trauma camp and replaced the sentimental and inherently condescending pity encoded into the first-generation shows as their dominant reception mode with the non-empathic ridicule of *Schadenfreude*. Despite the significant differences between pop-therapeutic and trash talk shows, the latter are likewise politically acquiescing because they cast the status quo as the sane and safe Other to their freak show dystopia.

Part three turns to the depiction of victimization experiences as spectacles of suffering in misery memoirs. Although they currently constitute the largest growth sector in book publishing worldwide and have been widely discussed in the international press, this is the first scholarly analysis of this popular literature genre. I further extend the analysis to fictional, and therefore fake, misery memoirs and the scandals they generated when exposed, because forgeries signify which objects are considered most valuable and hence significant in a given culture. As the dominant subjects of fake misery memoirs are child abuse and the Holocaust survival of children, part three concludes with exemplary analyses of Anthony Godby Johnson's and JT LeRoy's fake autobiographical narratives of horrific child abuse as well as Misha Defonseca's and Binjamin Wilkomirski's likewise forged memoirs of Holocaust survival by young children. Although all four texts and the scandals surrounding them have been widely reported in the press, none but the last has been previously discussed in literary scholarship.

The epilogue extends the analysis of popular trauma culture by critiquing the dominant, but ethically flawed, reception mode encoded into mass media representations of victimhood and suffering. These popular culture products incite audiences to engage in fantasies of witnessing the pain of others. The book concludes with an exemplary analysis of Katharina Hacker's 2005 novel *Eine Art Liebe* (A Love of Sorts). The German author reimagines Saul Friedlander's famous memoir *Quand vient le souvenir* (*When Memory Comes*) in fictional form so her strongly autobiographical narrator can engage in a fantasy of witnessing the Holocaust by listening to the testimony of Friedlander's fictional alter ego. The epilogue thus not only returns to Holocaust discourse, bringing the exploration of popular trauma culture full circle, but it also expands the realm of analysis beyond American popular culture to indicate that trauma culture is neither a purely American phenomenon nor solely generated via the mass media.

# PART ONE

# Popular Trauma Culture

## Generating the Paradigm
## in Holocaust Discourse

"The Holocaust—once it became its own archetype and entered the public imagination as an independent icon—also became a figure for subsequent pain, suffering, and destruction."

—James Young, *Writing and Rewriting the Holocaust*[1]

Popular trauma culture emerged when the genocide of European Jewry was incorporated into the collective memory of the United States because American Holocaust discourse generated the dominant paradigm that would subsequently be employed to represent the pain of others in the mass media. The Holocaust was transformed from an event in European history into a core constituent of American memory, not only because it became the core marker of American-Jewish identity via the dubious notion of hereditary or vicarious victimhood, but also and especially because it was appropriated politically on a national level. After the popular stage and film adaptations of Anne Frank's diary in the 1950s, American Holocaust discourse shifted in focus from victims to survivors with the television broadcasts from the Eichmann trial and the rise of Elie Wiesel to preeminent Holocaust representative. And despite the wide spectrum of Holocaust representations between commercialization and sanctification, stories of survival have dominated over depictions of death ever since. The new narrative mode of witness testimony generated at the Eichmann trial and disseminated widely via radio and television broadcasts was quickly adopted beyond the legal realm. It was not only employed to represent the genocide itself, but also became an archetype for emplotting diverse experiences of victimization. Silvia Plath's figurative use of Holocaust imagery in particular foreshadowed the rise of Holocaust discourse to paradigmatic status for representing historically unrelated suffering.

However, unlike Plath who borrowed Holocaust language to express her own interminable suffering, representations of the pain of others in the mass media culminate in happy endings of survival and redemption. The protagonist's testimony, which may be overtly or covertly expressed in the inherently competitive rhetoric of victim talk, is cast in sync with self-help doctrine as indicative that the increasingly clichéd metamorphosis from victim into survivor has been accomplished. The survivor figure, who imbues the unethical Social Darwinist notion of the survival of the fittest with the quasi-sacred aura of the Holocaust, rose to cultural dominance at the same time that the American ideal of pursuing individual success and happiness gave way to a sense that life was a constant struggle for survival. Overcoming victimization—increasingly termed survival, even if the victim's life was not threatened—thus replaced traditional notions of accomplishment and heroism. While the heroes of old altruistically risked their own lives to save another's, the objective of the modern-day antihero is simply to survive.

Popular trauma culture thus recycled the quintessentially American rags-to-riches tale and the Christian suffering-and-redemption plot in Holocaust-and-survival narratives, which in turn provided the paradigm for trauma-and-recovery stories. As Jacob Heilbrunn recently wrote in the *New York Times*, "the further the Holocaust recedes into the past, the more it's being exploited to create a narrative of redemption."[2] After all, when the Holocaust is emplotted for mass consumption, Nancy Miller and Jason Tougaw argued, the representations must enable audiences "to take pleasure in—or at least be comfortably moved by—the Holocaust as spectacle."[3] And this teary-eyed sentimentality would be encoded into popular culture products at large as their dominant mode of reception because it enabled the transformation of the pain of others into bestselling mass media commodities. Or as Lauren Berlant put it, the "production of tears where anger or nothing might have been more urgent" happened with the "coming to cultural dominance of the Holocaust and trauma as models for having and remembering collective social experience."[4]

# 1

# Holocaust Tropes

"As the Holocaust moved from history to myth, it became the bearer of 'eternal truths' not bound by historical circumstances."

–Peter Novick, *The Holocaust in American Life*[1]

The Holocaust has been so thoroughly integrated into American national memory that, according to Gary Weissman, "as a term, 'the Holocaust' suggests not only the Jewish genocide but its Americanization, not only the event but the attempt to name or represent it."[2] Located among the core monuments to American history, the U.S. Holocaust Memorial Museum was opened in 1993 in the nation's capital, and its operating expenses—originally to be raised by private donations—have been largely taken over by the federal government. U.S. presidents have urged their constituents to preserve Holocaust memory and official remembrance ceremonies are held annually in the Capitol Rotunda and by the American military. The Holocaust is also a mandatory subject on the high school curricula of many American states.[3]

The genocide was furthermore kept in the public sphere by news reports on related contemporary subjects: Between 1977 and 1978, there was a controversy over the right of a handful of American Neo-Nazis to conduct a march in Skokie, Illinois.[4] On an official visit to West Germany in 1985, President Ronald Reagan attended a commemoration ceremony with Chancellor Helmut Kohl at the Bitburg cemetery, where not only Wehrmacht soldiers, but also SS men are buried. Beyond the participation in the memorial service itself, Reagan generated a widely reported public relations fiasco by remarking that "German soldiers buried in the Bitburg cemetery were victims of the Nazis just as surely as the victims of the concentration camps."[5] A year later, the Nazi past of Kurt Waldheim, the former UN secretary-general and new president of Austria, was widely publicized, and the question was raised whether he should be placed on the American watch list of Nazi criminals and thus barred from entering the United States.[6] Subsequently, another controversy emerged over Pope John Paul II's reception of Waldheim at a time when the latter was a pariah throughout Europe.[7] Another point of controversy involving the Catholic Church was

9

the presence of a Carmelite convent at the Auschwitz site. It remained in the news because the promised relocation of the convent was continually postponed for several years. In 1987, another trial of a Nazi criminal in Jerusalem was widely broadcast on American television. However, while John Demjanjuk, who had been extradited from the United States to Israel, was found guilty of being a particularly brutal camp guard in Treblinka, the verdict and death sentence were overturned in 1993 by the Israeli Supreme Court.[8] The Holocaust was furthermore kept in the news by ongoing debates over Swiss banks' reluctance to pay out the funds in "dormant accounts" of Holocaust victims and the revelation that the Nazi gold that the Swiss banks laundered included dental fillings of concentration camp prisoners.[9] Most recently, there was headline news about the restitution of five Gustav Klimt paintings that had been confiscated by the Nazis to an American descendant of the Austrian-Jewish owner, who sold them in 2006 for more than $327 million.

American Holocaust discourse is intrinsically intertwined with the extensive oeuvre and omnipresent public persona of Elie Wiesel, "who acts as a self-appointed spokesman-of-sorts for the survivor generation," as Tim Cole put it.[10] Wiesel widely disseminated the notion that the genocide of European Jewry constitutes a unique event and an unknowable mystery that can nevertheless teach America universal lessons. However, it was particularly the representation of the Holocaust in the mass media that disseminated the subject widely. The most important products generated by what Norman Finkelstein dubbed the "Holocaust industry"[11] include the stage and screen adaptations of Anne Frank's diary in the 1950s, the 1978 Holocaust TV mini-series, Roberto Benigni's 1998 commercially and critically successful film Life Is Beautiful, and Roman Polanski's likewise acclaimed 2003 movie The Pianist. However, most important was Steven Spielberg's 1993 blockbuster Schindler's List. Its premier was perfectly timed in the same year that the Holocaust museum in Washington, DC, opened. Not only Jerry Seinfeld's sitcom parents urged their son to watch Schindler's List, but President Bill Clinton, public officials nationwide, and Oprah Winfrey asked their fellow Americans to watch it as their civic duty.[12] Most recently, Mark Herman directed the film adaptation of John Boyne's bestselling children's novel The Boy in the Striped Pajamas. Also released in 2009, director Stephen Daldry adapted German law professor and crime author Bernhard Schlink's novel Der Vorleser (The Reader) for the screen after the novel had become an international bestseller when it was featured on Oprah Winfrey's talk show in 1999.

As Nancy Miller and Jason Tougaw aptly observed, "the unprecedented success of Holocaust suffering marketed for mass consumption and popular entertainment seems to know no limits."[13] And A. O. Scott recently commented in the New York Times that "for American audiences a Holocaust movie is now more or less equivalent to a western or a combat picture or a sword-and-sandals epic."[14]

Except that, given what Jacob Heilbrunn described as their "saccharine prom-ises of redemption,"[15] Holocaust movies made in Hollywood are more likely than other films to win an Academy Award. As the actress Kate Winslet, "playing herself" on the British sit com *Extras*, remarked, "I've noticed that if you do a film about the Holocaust, you're guaranteed an Oscar."[16] While her remark evokes the Best Actor awards given to Roberto Benigni for *Life Is Beautiful* and Adrien Brody for *The Pianist*, winning Best Actress herself in 2009 for her role in *The Reader* turned her quip into a quasi-prophecy. And the famous line that "there's no business like Shoah business" cited by a character in Philip Roth's *Operation Shylock* indicates not only the continued significance of the Holocaust as a subject for the American film industry, but also its thorough integration into American culture.[17]

## Holocaust Lessons in American Values

Although the Holocaust is ubiquitous in U.S. politics and culture, and polls reg-ularly show that vast numbers of Americans consider it an important subject, Americans are by far the least informed with regard to factual knowledge about the historical event, compared to their French, British, and German contempo-raries.[18] While some 95 percent of Americans claim to have heard the term "Holocaust" and 85 percent maintain that they know what it means,[19] "38% of American adults and 53% of high school students either do not know or offer incorrect answers to the question: 'What does the term "the Holocaust" refer to?'"[20] Moreover, only 21 percent of Americans possess even such basic information as knowing "that the Warsaw ghetto has a connection to the Holocaust."[21] It is thus as an ahistorical myth, rather than as a historically spe-cific event, that the Holocaust has been adopted into the national memory of the United States, or as Tim Cole put it, "myth has replaced reality, and indeed myth had become more important than reality."[22]

In fact, the ignorance about Holocaust history was a necessary prerequisite for, and in turn reinforced by, the adoption of the genocide of European Jewry into American national memory. It was precisely this lack of historical knowledge that enabled emplotting the Holocaust based on melodrama's good-versus-evil dichotomy and casting the United States as Nazi evil's innocent Other to minimize America's own past and present crimes. Given its status as critically self-reflective and empirically substantiated scholarly discourse, histori-ography thus constitutes an inherently antithetical counter-discourse to the transformation of the Holocaust into an American myth. According to Roland Barthes, myth "abolishes the complexity of human acts" and "gives them the simplicity of essences" because "it does away with all dialectics" and "organizes a world which is without contradictions."[23] It also deceptively claims to be "not . . . an explanation but . . . a statement of fact"[24] to hide its own status as only one possible mode of representation and thus suppress counter-narratives. Myth is therefore inherently hegemonic. In fact, Barthes characterized it as "the language of the oppressor."[25] The notion that the Holocaust as myth constitutes an ideological construct "whose central dogmas sustain significant political and class interests"[26] is central to Norman Finkelstein's polemical indictment of the American Holocaust industry.

In the process of mythification, as the Holocaust was transformed from an event in European history into an American cultural memory, it was ascribed eternal truths and universal lessons. According to a core doctrine of American Holocaust discourse, the genocide of European Jewry is both a unique event in human history and inherently incomprehensible.[27] Nevertheless, unlike any other atrocity, or even any other historical event, we are to believe that the Holocaust can teach us universal lessons, paradoxically, not despite, but precisely because of its uniqueness and incomprehensibility.[28] It is because of these supposed universal lessons that Americans should learn more about Hitler's Jewish victims than, say, about Stalin's Soviet victims or Pol Pot's Cambodian victims.

While American Holocaust discourse was prefigured in the 1950s stage and screen adaptations of Anne Frank's diary and entered the public sphere with the televising of survivor testimony from the Eichmann trial in 1961, the term "Holocaust" itself only became a household name with the 1978 broadcast of the *Holocaust* TV series. It aired after the Watergate scandal, the Vietnam War, and racial violence, all of which signaled to many Americans an increasing fragmentation of their society and the erosion of traditional American values. It was the longing for simple moral certainties in an increasingly complex and divided late-capitalist society that led many Americans to embrace the dichotomous moral universe of *Holocaust*.[29] "Whether someone was politically liberal, moderate, or conservative," Robert Wuthnow wrote, "that person was more likely to be interested in the Holocaust if he or she perceived serious problems with the moral order."[30] However, "it was the Holocaust as symbol of ever-present evil rather than the Holocaust as historical event that was of interest to persons troubled about the moral fabric."[31] As Michael Berenbaum, the former director of the U.S. Holocaust Memorial Museum, put it, "'people don't know what good or evil are, but they are certain about one thing: the Holocaust is absolute evil.'"[32] Raul Hilberg similarly wrote that the Holocaust allowed Americans "to know the difference between good and evil."[33] While Americans may not be able to agree on much else today, they can join together in deploring the Holocaust. The genocide of European Jewry was, then, adopted as a cornerstone of U.S. national memory because, cast as ultimate evil, it was dubiously appropriated in providing a lowest common denominator for American values. In other words, the Holocaust serves the core social function in "the fundamental tale of pluralism, tolerance, democracy, and human rights that America tells about itself,"[34] of enabling the United States to celebrate and reinforce its own traditional values by showing their negation.[35] Or as John Mowitt put it, "in relation to it 'we' know with a certain certainty where we stand."[36]

Defining the Holocaust as absolute evil in quasi-religious, rather than historical, terms teaches America untenable lessons, such as good and evil are both absolute and hence clearly distinguishable. Ascribing to the Holocaust the status of principal reason that the United States fought in the Second World War allowed an understanding of it in melodrama's simplistic moral certainties as the last just war. Furthermore, casting American soldiers as having heroically defeated the ultimate evil of Nazism—while minimizing the significant contributions of the Allies, particularly the Soviet Red Army—enabled the United States to define itself as the ultimate virtuous Other to Nazi evil. The Holocaust was thus turned into the benchmark against which all other events would be assessed. When compared to the Holocaust, the forceful seizure of the New World and the destruction of Native American life, slavery and segregation, the nuclear bombing of Japan, and the Vietnam War pale in comparison precisely because the Holocaust has been defined *a priori* as ultimate evil. The Holocaust was, then, adopted into American national memory because it could be unethically appropriated as an exculpatory screen memory to evade responsibility for the crimes perpetrated throughout American history.[37] As Peter Novick put it, "the repeated assertion that whatever the United States has done to blacks, Native Americans, Vietnamese, or others pales in comparison to the Holocaust is true—and evasive." And while a serious and sustained encounter with America's own crimes "might imply costly demands on Americans to redress the wrongs of the past, contemplating the Holocaust is virtually cost-free: a few cheap tears."[38]

Moreover, as Christopher Lasch argued, when the notion that American lives were dominated by the pursuit of happiness gave way to the sense that they were governed by an insidiously traumatizing fight for the survival of the fittest, narratives of the Holocaust experience were ascribed the capacity to teach Americans survival lessons.[39] However, applying supposed Holocaust survival lessons to mundane, if highly stressful, American life is untenable. Despite the unethical exploitation and oppression of the vast majority to generate profits for a minute minority inherent in the economic system of capitalism, equating this with the slave labor and extermination of Holocaust victims is ahistorical and unethical.[40] This notion not only belittles their suffering but, in sync with psychotherapeutic discourse, it also anesthetizes the justified frustration with the American way of life, instead of leading to concerted efforts to effect political changes. As the ethical dilemmas and political choices faced by Americans today are categorically different from those of Holocaust victims, Peter Novick writes, "lessons for dealing with the sorts of issues that confront us in ordinary life, public or private, are not likely to be found in this most extraordinary of events."[41] Paradoxically, it is based on the Holocaust's supposed uniqueness and incomprehensibility that it was ascribed universal lessons, or, as Tim Cole put it, that it became "a bottomless 'lucky dip' which can mean all things to all people."[42] Phillip Lopate likewise scathingly critiqued American Holocaust discourse because it "has a curious double property of being both amazingly plastic—able to be applied to almost any issue—and fantastically rigid, since we are constantly being told that the Holocaust is incomparable, a class by itself, *sui generis*, not to be mixed up with other human problems or diluted by foreign substances."[43]

Representations of the Holocaust are moreover consumed because of the dominant, if dubious, notions that suffering generates spiritual purification and that moral enlightenment can be gained not only from one's own immediate experience, but also through the vicarious experience of others' suffering via media consumption. According to Peter Novick, "it is accepted as a matter of faith, beyond discussion, that the mere act of walking through a Holocaust museum, or viewing a Holocaust movie, is going to be morally therapeutic" and hence that "multiplying such encounters will make one a better person."[44] Philip Gourevitch also sarcastically noted this paradigmatic notion of popular trauma culture in his review of the U.S. Holocaust Memorial Museum. As he put it, the museum is apparently "meant to serve as an ideological vaccine for the American body politic" because "a proper dose of Holocaust," we are to believe, "will build up the needed antibodies against totalitarianism, racism, [and] state-sponsored mass murder."[45]

While the legacy of the Holocaust could be taken as the global responsibility to end and prevent all persecution and atrocities, the ubiquity of the Holocaust in the American public sphere has not generated such a political awakening. While some Holocaust museums may host special exhibitions informing visitors of current human rights violations, they rarely suggest concrete action beyond charitable donations. Likewise, audiences of Holocaust movies and memoirs are not asked to engage politically in the present. After all, the Nazis were defeated long ago, and the surviving victims are no longer persecuted. For instance, although the frequently cited number of one to one-and-a-half million Jewish children killed in the Holocaust has prompted many a sentimental tear, it has had no effect on the fact that as many children die worldwide annually of the effects of malnutrition and preventable diseases. In fact, American Holocaust discourse is inherently apolitical. This is also indicated by the fact that the neo-conservative critics, who attacked the addition to the Western literary canon of minority narratives constructed around collective experiences of victimization during the so-called Culture Wars of the 1990s, saw no need to criticize Holocaust studies.[46] And while establishing the Holocaust as the ultimate embodiment of evil is unethical in itself because it minimizes all other instances and forms of oppression, victimization, and atrocity, it also lessens the probability of individual and collective political action to end current and prevent future human rights violations.

## The Jew-as-Victim Trope

Holocaust discourse also generated the problematic conflation of Jewish identity with victimhood. Although the victim Anne Frank has long been replaced by the survivor Elie Wiesel as the paradigmatic Holocaust figure in American culture, the Jew-as-victim trope introduced into the public sphere by the screen and stage adaptations of her diary and reinforced by the television broadcasts from the Eichmann trial, has had a long discursive afterlife. Transformed from signifying empirical Holocaust victims into a rhetorical figure, it has been employed to designate a wide range of individuals and groups who experienced victimhood and oppression.

The Jew-as-victim figure populates feminist writings from Simone de Beauvoir's reference to "Jewish character" to Betty Friedan's provocative accusation that suburban 1950s American housewives were living in comfortable concentration camps and Naomi Wolf's recent evocation of the Holocaust to emphasize how severe and prevalent eating disorders are among American women. It has furthermore been employed to highlight the politically liberatory potential of Otherness from Hanna Arendt's notion of Jews as "conscious pariahs" and Jean-Paul Sartre's "authentic Jew" to Jean-François Lyotard's "the Jews."[47] Moreover, Paul Celan cites Russian poet Marina Tsvetaeva's line that "all poets are Jews" and Nelly Sachs wrote that "all human beings who suffered became Jews."[48]

However, the Jew-as-victim trope was most prominently employed to signify suffering unrelated to Holocaust history in the later poetry of Silvia Plath, particularly in the infamous lines from "Daddy": An engine, an engine./ Chuffing me off like a Jew./ A Jew to Dachau, Auschwitz, Belsen./ I began to talk like a Jew./ I think I may well be a Jew."[49] The Eichmann trial had coincided with her own hardships, which included a miscarriage, the infidelity of her husband, Ted Hughes, their subsequent separation, and her electroshock therapy that eventually led to her suicide in 1963.[50] Given the prominence of the trial in the mass media and the spectacular and unimaginable nature of the events recounted in detail in the witness testimony, Plath came to know and express her own pain in this new language. For her, the Holocaust did not primarily constitute a distinct historical event, but a discourse that provided radically new but widely understood images that she could use to articulate her own agony.[51]

The dominant notion among literary critics that Plath's ahistorical use of Holocaust imagery is unethical[52] likewise pertains to the Jew-as-victim figure in feminism, existentialism, and postmodernism, despite the fact that it served to advocate collective emancipatory projects. It also and especially applies to the ubiquity of Holocaust tropes in popular culture, because the redemptive narratives serve to transform the pain of others into politically anaesthetizing mass media commodities. Transforming empirical Holocaust victims into a rhetorical figure is moreover unethical because it effaces the actual victimization experiences of real, non-metaphoric Jews.

## Holocaust Envy

Although the Holocaust is ascribed the capacity to teach Americans universal lessons, paradoxically, it is also cast as a unique event in history. "It is not enough that the Holocaust was dreadful," Phillip Lopate critiqued this untenable idea, "it must be seen as *uniquely* dreadful."[53] The earliest record of the ahistorical claim that the Holocaust was a singular, and therefore incomparable and incomprehensible, event are the proceedings of the 1967 symposium on "Jewish Values in the Post-Holocaust Future."[54] The notion of Holocaust uniqueness emerged in a discussion among Emil Fackenheim, George Steiner, Richard Popkin, and Elie Wiesel in which the word "unique" was used more than twenty times.[55] However, the uniqueness claim was not generated based on Holocaust historiography. Not only were none of the participants historians, but the genocide was only on the verge of becoming a viable historiographic subject.[56] Rather, it emerged by way of religious chosenness in a debate of Jewish philosophy and theology about post-Holocaust values.

The idea that the Holocaust was a unique event is not only nonsensical but also unethical because, as Peter Novick writes, it inevitably constitutes a demand for preeminence.[57] He provocatively argues that the notion of uniqueness signifies that "your catastrophe, unlike ours, is ordinary; unlike ours is comprehensible; unlike ours is representable"[58] and even marks a claim to "permanent possession of the gold medal in the Victimization Olympics."[59] Phillip Lopate similarly rejects the privileged status of the Holocaust in the "pantheon of genocides"[60] because it "diminishes, if not demeans, the mass slaughters of other peoples (or, for that matter, previous tragedies in Jewish history)."[61]

When merged with the idea that to compensate them for their suffering, victims are entitled to benefits in the present,[62] the uniqueness-cum-preeminence claim entitles Holocaust survivors to maximum compensation. Or, in Norman Finkelstein's uncharacteristically understated words, "*unique* suffering ... confer[s] unique entitlement."[63] Reinforced by the moral superiority ascribed to Holocaust survivors *pace* Wiesel because their suffering had purified and sanctified them, Holocaust survival was transformed into the ultimate moral capital in the present. Since in contemporary culture communal identities are based "almost entirely on the sentimental solidarity of remembered victimhood,"[64] resentment arose among other groups that the Holocaust had become the central symbol of oppression and atrocity in American culture and the benchmark against which other atrocities were judged (and found lacking).[65]

The most common defense against the assertion that the claim of Holocaust uniqueness-cum-preeminence is unethical has been the counter-charge that it was in fact others who were behaving unethically by appropriating Holocaust language and imagery.[66] Wiesel declared at the 1967 symposium that "'Negro quarters are called ghettos; Hiroshima is explained by Auschwitz; Vietnam is described in terms which were used one generation ago'"[67] and that this should constitute a reason for transforming the Holocaust experience from a source of shame into one of pride. Subsequently, however, he would consider such analogies as illegitimate appropriations occasioned by what critics have variously termed Holocaust envy,[68] survivor envy,[69] or memory envy.[70] According to Novick, Wiesel even claimed that "'they are stealing the Holocaust from us.'"[71] The sentiment was echoed by Maurice Messer, a fictional Holocaust survivor with an "embellished" heroic past in Tova Reich's satire *My Holocaust*. He complains about a group of New Age hippie visitors at the Auschwitz memorial site that "'they're trespassing on mine Holocaust!'"[72] Most effective, however, in the defense of the moral capital of Holocaust preeminence is the accusation that denying Holocaust uniqueness constitutes a form of Holocaust denial.[73] Nevertheless and despite the oxymoronic fallacy, overtly claiming uniqueness and covertly preeminence of the suffering endured by one's own group has become paradigmatic in trauma culture. As a character in Reich's satirical novel put it: "We at United Holocausts shall always be mindful of our debt to the pioneering work of the Jewish people in the creative and conceptual uses of victimhood and survivorship and Holocausts. . . . You are the model that our equally special and equally unique and equally equal Holocausts aspire to and strive to emulate."[74]

## Vicarious Holocaust Victimhood

In addition to the political appropriation of the Holocaust to minimize the crimes in American history, the unethical transformation of empirical Holocaust victims into metaphors via the Jew-as-victim trope, and the untenable claim of Holocaust uniqueness-cum-preeminence, the genocide has also been used to redefine American-Jewish identity. As the integrating ethos of American idealism was increasingly replaced by the particularism of identity politics, Jewish selfhood was likewise reconstructed around difference. However, increasing secularization and intermarriage meant that religious belief and practice could no longer function as the dominant identity marker. And after the Israeli victory in the Six-Day War and the beginning of the occupation of Palestinian territories in 1967, Zionism likewise lost much of its unifying pull.[75] Reinforced by the dominant zeitgeist of generating group loyalties around experiences of victimization, American-Jewish identity was thus not only increasingly transformed from a religious into an ethnically based sense of self, but also largely constructed around the Holocaust. As Ian Buruma put it, "when Jewishness is reduced to a taste for Woody Allen movies and bagels, or Chineseness to Amy Tan novels and dim sum on Sundays, the quasi authenticity of communal suffering will begin to look very attractive."[76]

For instance, a 1989 American Jewish Committee survey indicated that while only 46 percent of American Jews considered practicing Jewish rituals important, 85 percent found Holocaust commemoration significant.[77] And in the 1998 Annual Survey of American Jewish Opinion, remembrance of the Holocaust was likewise "chosen as 'extremely important' or 'very important' by many more than synagogue attendance, Jewish study, working with Jewish organizations, traveling to Israel, or observing Jewish holidays."[78] The new American-Jewish "civic religion,"[79] of "Holocaust and Redemption"[80] essentially substituted *Holocaust* and *Schindler's List* for Torah and Talmud. Religious rituals and traditions were likewise replaced with new practices, from "twinning" adolescents with a Holocaust child victim at bar and bat mitzvahs, quasi-pilgrimages to camp memorials,[81] and proudly wearing yellow stars on Yom Hashoah on college campuses.[82] The Jew-as-victim trope thus came to dominate American-Jewish identity and, as Peter Novick critiqued, constitutes "our 'epistle to the gentiles' about what it means to be Jewish."[83]

Embracing the Holocaust as the preeminent marker of American-Jewish identity is based on the epistemologically and ethically untenable notion of vicarious Holocaust victimhood. Gary Weissman argued that individuals who claim vicarious victim status actually exhibit a paradoxical longing to witness the genocide themselves. He emphatically dubs them "nonwitnesses" and suggests that they consume and/or produce countless representations of the Holocaust, including scholarship, to imagine themselves as its victims in ahistorical horror fantasies.[84] As Alain Finkielkraut self-critically admitted, along with his own imaginary Holocaust victimhood went "deep ignorance" about the history of the genocide.[85] Holocaust historiography is not simply irrelevant to the nonwitness, but, given the indebtedness of historical scholarship to self-critical and rational analysis, it is inherently antithetical to Holocaust fantasies. Hence lack of detailed knowledge in Holocaust history is a necessary condition for the fantasies.

Daniel Schwarz, for instance, writes in his study of Holocaust literature, aptly entitled *Imagining the Holocaust*: "I dream of myself within shtetls, camps and confined circumstances, as a participant in the very world I am writing about. I awake in a cold sweat from dreams of being deported."[86] He continues the story of his fantasized Holocaust victimhood, claiming that "we see ourselves in these ghetto places, these streets. In our nightmares, we are deported and suffer the horrors of these camps."[87] In order to authorize his fantasy Schwarz thus expands his own usurpation of the victim position by ascribing it to other Holocaust scholars or even all Jews when he attributes similar nightmare visions to an unspecified "we." And while Ian Buruma emphatically rejects such fantasies, he also self-critically attests to the power of their pull. He admits that, during his visit to the Auschwitz site, he too gave in to such "smug and morbid thoughts" as these: "But for the grace of God, . . . I would have died here too. Or would I? An even more grotesque calculation passed through my mind: How did I fit into the Nuremberg laws? Was I a *Mischling* of the first degree, or the second? Was it enough to have two Jewish grandparents, or did you need more to qualify for the grim honor of martyrdom?"[88] He furthermore wrote: "I am not the child of Holocaust survivors. My mother was Jewish, but she lived in England, and no immediate relations were killed by the Nazis. And yet even I couldn't escape a momentary feeling of vicarious virtue, especially when I came across tourists from Germany. They were the villains, I the potential victim."[89]

Some nonwitnesses even ahistorically imagine the Holocaust into contemporary America. Norma Rosen, for instance, claims that "for a mind engraved with the Holocaust, gas is always that gas. Shower means their shower. Ovens are those ovens." Her fantasy culminates in a Holocaust kitsch image par excellence, "a train is a freight train crammed with suffocating children."[90] According to Michael Bernstein, Rosen "qualifies this grisly description with the scarcely less overwrought acknowledgement"[91] that "of course this does not always happen. Some days the sky is simply blue and we do not wonder how a blue sky looked to those on their way to the crematoria."[92] However, this disclaimer reinforces rather than lessens the claim that more than half a century after its end and thousands of miles away from its site, an event she did not experience dominates her ordinary American life. And Vanessa Ochs even imagines herself in a hypothesized Holocaust in the near American future: "When I move to a new town, I give great thought to whom, among my gentile friends, I might entrust my children, should that ever become necessary."[93] Aviva Cantor likewise generates a Holocaust fantasy set in the immediate American future and, like Schwarz, generalizes her own fantasies to authorize the usurpation of the victim position: "Every conscious Jew longs to ask her or his non-Jewish friends, 'Would you hide me?'—and suppresses the question for fear of hearing the sounds of silence."[94] Leslie Brody echoes Cantor's claim and ascribes her own fantasy of vicarious Holocaust victimhood to supposed numerous others, like both Cantor and Schwarz, when she writes: "Many Jews report that the unspoken question they ask themselves when interacting with non-Jews is 'Would she or he have saved me from the Nazis?'" And she confesses that "I have asked myself this question innumerable times" because the hypothesized answer constitutes "the ultimate standard by which to measure trust in a non-Jewish person."[95]

Although the notion of vicarious Holocaust victimhood has become a core constituent of American-Jewish selfhood, the victim-by-proxy claim has also found a number of vocal critics. While Gary Weissman predominantly analyzed the epistemology of nonwitnesses engaging in fantasies of witnessing the Holocaust, Zygmunt Bauman, Michael Bernstein, Alain Finkielkraut, Phillip Lopate, and Peter Novick extended their critiques to the ethics of claiming vicarious victim status. The notion of vicarious Holocaust victimhood expresses the claim that the status of ultimate righteousness,—which is ascribed to Holocaust victims via the untenable assertions that suffering extreme violence ennobled them and that the Holocaust was the preeminent atrocity in history—even constitutes a hereditary trait of Jewish identity. As overt anti-Semitic discrimination has ceased in the American present, the subject position of Holocaust victim was figuratively extended to generate a particularist American-Jewish identity in sync with identity politics. However, the victim-by-proxy claim is not only ahistorical but also self-aggrandizing as nonwitnesses give in to what Finkielkraut described as "the pleasurable temptation of claiming the victim's exemplary prestige as one's own."[96] Extending Holocaust victim status figuratively via the trope of vicarious victimhood is also unethical because it appropriates the persecution and death of the real victims. In other words, it transforms the pain of others into the moral capital of the nonwitness, or as Bauman put it, into "a signed-in-advance and *in blanco* certificate of moral righteousness."[97]

According to Michael Bernstein, "once victimhood is understood to endow one with special claims and rights, the scramble to attain that designation for one's own interest group is as heated as any other race for legitimacy and power."[98] As the Holocaust fantasies of Ochs, Cantor, and Brody indicate, non-Jews are collectively and permanently ascribed the ahistorical position of vicarious perpetrator or, at best, bystander. In the Holocaust fantasy universe, they function as the Other against which nonwitnesses can establish themselves as "representatives of the Just,"[99] as Finkielkraut put it. Consequently, Bauman admonishes, "the others, the non-Jews, emerge as one-dimensional as the Jews appear in the vision of their haters."[100] And Bernstein not only argues against "regarding hallucinations like Rosen's as in any way a fitting memorial to the murdered"[101] but also rejects any "urge to establish one's credentials as an eternal victim in order to claim an unassailable moral high ground."[102] He even asserts that "too sharp a sense of one's own victimization can easily lead to a compensatory urge to tyrannize over others, and those convinced of their unique victimhood are quite likely to prove tyrants both to themselves and to others if given the chance."[103]

The identity politics notion of victim-based group identities, the trauma culture zeitgeist "of an almost clinically excessive identification with the suffering of others,"[104] and the omnipresence of Holocaust melodramas in the mass media engendered the claim to vicarious victimhood. Nevertheless, it constitutes an appropriation of the pain of others for the nonwitnesses' gain. And while the suffering from the collective memory of the Holocaust expressed by Schwarz, Rosen, Ochs, Cantor, and Brody seems genuine, casting it as analogous to the suffering of Holocaust victims is indefensible. According to George Steiner, no "human being other than an actual survivor ha[s] the right to put on this death-rig"[105] and Alain Finkielkraut admits to "draping myself with the torture that others underwent."[106] Merging their metaphors, the Holocaust fantasies of nonwitnesses could be conceptualized as a kind of discursive death-rig drag put on by those who can only "remember by fiat of imagination"[107] in order to "slip . . . into an identity belonging to others."[108] However, an epistemologically sound and ethically responsible form of Holocaust memory is based on acknowledging that a "fundamental chasm exists between me and the history of my people," as Finkielkraut writes, and it requires "before all else, this negative gesture: to not appropriate the difference."[109] Despite the fact that it is illogically based on the Wieselesque uniqueness-cum-preeminence doctrine, not to mention its empirical and ethical indefensibility, the notion of vicarious Holocaust victimhood generated a paradigm on which other groups would model their own hereditary claims to victim status. Zygmunt Bauman's acerbic critique of proxy claims to Holocaust victim identity can thus be generalized: Anyone claiming hereditary victim status is "basking in the fame of his ancestral martyrs without paying the price of the glory" and thus "living on a borrowed identity—as martyrs by appointment, martyrs who never suffered."[110]

# 2

# Victim Talk

"We compete with one another as to who is the most damaged. Whoever can most fully explain his biography, his weaknesses and defeats, his suffering, and his complexes as a series of wounds inflicted upon him by society deserves the crown of victimhood."

–Peter Schneider, *Couplings*[1]

The subject position of victim constitutes an instance of what philosophers call human kinds and distinguish from natural kinds. Unlike natural kinds, like thunderstorms or bacilli, human kinds do not exist independently of the knowledge we create about them because, as Ian Hacking writes, "they come into being hand in hand with our invention of the categories labeling them."[2] For instance, Michel Foucault argued in the *History of Sexuality* that, while male-male and female-female sexual acts existed prior to the invention of the category of homosexuality, the people engaging in them were not homosexuals. Analogously, the broadcast of testimony from the Eichmann trial radically transformed the meaning of victimhood, introduced the social roles of witness and survivor into the public sphere, and disseminated these newly generated human kinds widely. While people had of course suffered, died from, or survived both natural disasters and manmade catastrophes before, they neither thought of themselves nor were they perceived by others in these categories, which became paradigmatic in trauma culture. Furthermore, while our knowledge about natural kinds changes over time, the changing knowledge does not have any direct effect on them, only the human actions based on new knowledge does, such as killing bacilli with vaccines.[3] Human kinds, however, are directly influenced by the knowledge created about them because "the available classifications within which [people] can describe their own actions and make their own constrained choices,"[4] Hacking explains, create "new ways for people to be."[5] While "people classified in a certain way tend to conform to or grow into the ways they are described," he furthermore argues, "they also evolve their own ways, so that the classifications and descriptions have to be constantly revised."[6] In other words, human kinds not only evolve as categories over time like natural kinds because our knowledge about them changes. They also develop because something collectively agreed upon as a truthful statement will change the very individuals "about whom it was supposed to be the truth."[7] This cycle generates a continuous interactive feedback loop.

In imagined communities, such new ways for people to be are not only generated through the immediate social interaction between individuals, but also and especially by the interaction of consumers and media products. Hence, the identities of victim, survivor, and witness rose to cultural dominance in the Western public sphere with the radio and TV transmission of testimony from the Eichmann trial. The rise of the victim-cum-survivor figure to the status of trauma culture's ultimate moral authority and antihero was reinforced by the identity politics notion that minority group loyalties were generated around past and/or present victimization. As claims to the newly appreciated position of victim became ubiquitous in American culture, they were increasingly expressed in an egocentric and inherently competitive rhetoric Martha Minow dubbed victim talk.[8]

However, there is a danger in criticizing the public voicing of victimization experiences. Telling personal stories of victimization can be both therapeutically beneficial for the victim and essential as public testimony to provide a balance to the abstractions of politics and historiography. Moreover, many forms of oppression, discrimination, and persecution continue, and those who were victimized in the past have often been silenced. The critique that will be offered here therefore pertains not to the discourse of largely altruistic testimony, which primarily seeks to commemorate non-surviving victims and warn others to prevent their victimization. Instead, it is directed at self-serving victim talk or, more precisely, at the transformation of the former into the latter. It thus significantly differs from the vindictive ridicule of voicing victim experiences widely disseminated through the print journalism, book publications, and television appearances of neo-conservative intellectuals. Although their so-called anti-victimist discourse actually constitutes a version of victim talk, anti-victimists polemically attacked the ubiquity of claims to victim status in American culture.

The rise of the victim figure to antihero status generated significant changes in the understanding of victimhood and suffering. Although the semantically wider notion of suffering does not require that the experience was caused by a perpetrator, it was increasingly conflated with victimhood. Last but not least, popular trauma culture also altered our understanding of perpetration. Traditionally, perpetrator designated someone who gratuitously caused another to suffer by inflicting physical pain, often sanctioned and protected by socio-political and economic hegemonies. However, the vast bureaucracies of advanced capitalist societies have made the human agencies responsible for facilitating large-scale but covert victimization—through unemployment, poverty, and the exploitation of man and nature—impenetrable and only rarely

attributable to individuals. Consequently, the perpetrator role has been generalized and tends to be attributed to abstract entities like life, society, the government, or, if you are politically left-minded, the inherently inhumane economic
order of capitalism. However, anthropomorphizing such abstract entities serves
to hide the actual perpetrators so that claims for recognition and compensation
cannot be addressed to them and are therefore made to society at large.
Moreover, it ensures that the status quo that generated the insidious victimization inherent in the capitalist, patriarchal, ethnocentric, and hetero-normative
hegemony remains unquestioned.

## Victimhood and Suffering

There are two traditions of understanding suffering in contemporary Western
culture. According to Susan Sontag, the modern one "regards suffering as something that is a mistake or an accident or a crime. Something to be fixed. Something
to be refused."[9] As the consumer and entertainment industries promised ever
greater worldly pleasures and the self-help industry proposed the pursuit of
happiness as the ultimate life goal, we have come to "understand anything that
threatens our happiness—real and potential—as a form of suffering."[10] As we
also increasingly believe that we live "in an era when happiness and well-being
are official expectations of the great majority,"[11] Joseph Amato writes, the idea
"that suffering is an inevitable part of human experience"[12] was replaced with
"the utopian notion that there should be neither pain nor suffering in human
life at all."[13]

When suffering was no longer taken to constitute a common human experience, it was ascribed the capacity of signifying mental illnesses. The semantic
transformation of suffering reflected and reinforced the rise of psychiatric
discourse to cultural significance and the consequent steady increase of behaviors and psychological states conceptualized as symptoms of a likewise ever-
increasing number of mental disorders. With its pathologization, suffering was
conceptually separated from the experience of physical pain, and consequently
its temporal boundaries were likewise removed. In other words, the experiences
of physical pain and suffering are no longer believed to necessarily coincide.
Especially after the introduction of Post-Traumatic Stress Disorder into the 1980
edition of the *Diagnostics and Statistics Manual of Mental Disorders*,[14] suffering
acquired the meaning of a belated and long-term psychological state.

Although contemporary Western culture thus largely understands suffering
as pathological, it simultaneously still honors the pre-modern Christian notion
that suffering caused by a body in pain purifies the soul and sanctifies the
sufferer. This tradition has influenced both American Holocaust memory and
trauma culture at large to the extent that victims are revered as modern-day
quasi-saints and suffering is invested with redemptive value and reinterpreted

as sacrifice. While both notions are paradigmatically embodied by Elie Wiesel's public persona as Christ figure,[15] the latter is moreover reflected in the problematic choice of the term "Holocaust," which is derived from Greek via late Latin and signifies a burnt sacrificial offering, to designate the genocide of European Jewry.

Beyond the revival of the Christian notion of suffering in American Holocaust discourse, the transformation of sufferers into saint-victims[16] became dominant in Western culture because of the ethical imperative that senseless suffering is unjust, particularly when gratuitously inflicted. Not only many Holocaust survivors, but victims generally, often find it intolerable to think that their suffering and survival were arbitrary, and thus they reinterpret suffering into a sacrifice and attribute metaphysical meaning to their survival.

While popular trauma culture thus reflects both the pathologization and the sanctification of suffering, it also transformed its meaning by conflating suffering and victimhood. Put differently, popular trauma culture can not only be captured in a nutshell through yet another paraphrase of Descartes's famous line as "I suffer, therefore I am," but also and especially by extending the phrase into "I suffer, therefore I am a victim." However, the equation of victimhood and suffering constitutes a logical fallacy: While all victims suffer, not everyone who suffers is a victim, because some forms of suffering are not the result of victimization. A victim is someone whose suffering was caused, either intentionally or accidentally, by another.[17] In other words, unlike the more inclusive notion of suffering, the concept of victimhood requires that there be a perpetrator. Hence, when we casually speak, for example, of cancer or earthquake victims, we anthropomorphize the disease or disaster because the suffering was not caused by a human agency. Bernard Giesen argued with respect to earthquakes that only if at least some information about the quake and the risk to human lives had been available, yet insufficient or no warning was given, that is, if the deaths and injuries are at least in part based on human action, is the term "victim" justified.[18] His argument can be extended to individuals who suffer from the pain caused by physical illness. Only if the illness was caused or exacerbated by another, for instance through misdiagnosis or mistreatment by doctors, is a sick person a victim. However, the claim to victim status by individuals whose suffering was not caused by a human agent reflects the need of all who suffer to see their suffering, if not lessened, then at least recognized.

While suffering and victimhood are thus fallaciously conflated in trauma culture, the categorical distinction between both notions is evident in a core Western discourse that precedes trauma culture by centuries, namely the visual representation of suffering in art. According to Susan Sontag, the "sufferings most often deemed worthy of representation are those understood to be the product of wrath, divine or human," that is, suffering intentionally inflicted by an agency. However, "suffering from natural causes, such as illness or childbirth, is scantily represented in the history of art" and suffering "caused by accident, virtually not at all."[19] However, as the encounters with suffering not caused by a perpetrator that used to constitute a normal part of daily life in pre-industrial society—birth, death, insanity, and illness—were removed from the everyday and relegated to special institutions in modern societies,[20] the pain resulting from gratuitously inflicted violence came to dominate the idea of what causes suffering.

Both its iconography in Western art and the history of everyday life in the modern period indicate a clear epistemological distinction between suffering and victimization that is effaced in popular trauma culture. However, while it is logically fallacious, the conflation of victimhood and suffering may be justified ethically because it reflects the moral imperative to respond and seek to alleviate *all* suffering.[21]

## The Epistemology and Ethics of Victim Talk

Based on the ancient ethical injunction that the rich help the poor and the strong aid the weak,[22] the innocently wronged deserve attention and sympathy, which are valuable attributes in an increasingly attention-taxed culture of survival-of-the-fittest egotism.[23] Moreover, according to current notions of ethics, to right the wrongs and reestablish the equilibrium of justice victims should be compensated for their suffering.[24] This might entail pecuniary reparation, as West Germany accorded Holocaust survivors, or indirect benefits of preferential treatment, as the American affirmative action program grants minorities. Past or present suffering therefore turns the victim not only into a wronged but an owed party. Since perpetrators tend to be either impossible to establish or incapable of righting their wrongs, requests for attention and compensation are usually addressed to society at large.

While the notion that victims deserve empathy and assistance is widely accepted, the question of whether society or only the perpetrator is responsible for helping victims and righting injustices is ethically complex. Michael Bernstein, for instance, argued that "because it is so dismissive of temporal development and historical context, any ideology that endows victimhood with a singular authority to make claims upon others who were not themselves the agents of the injury, strikes me as morally incoherent."[25] However, because individual perpetrators in late-capitalist bureaucracies can either not be determined or are unable to compensate their victims, holding society at large accountable, based on the ideal of solidarity and the categorical imperative of aiding all in need, seems equally valid.

This epistemological and ethical ambivalence is also reflected in the recourse victim talk takes to therapeutic discourse. Based on the notion that not only the victims' bodies but also their psyches were damaged, therapeutic discourse defines them as genuinely ill. While this legitimates their need for help and grants victims support for their recovery, it also ascribes them the pathological status of mental infirmity. Victim talk not only defines victims as chronically sick, damaged, weak, and helpless people, but also stipulates that the victimization experience determines their essence, thus confining their notion of self to this social role. Anyone who departs from this narrowly circumscribed position—for instance, by making his or her testimony public in order to engender political changes rather than restricting it to the semi-private realm of therapy—does not fulfill the role expectations and risks losing the benefits of victim status. Victim talk moreover depoliticizes victimization because it solely demands retroactive compensation but does not proactively advocate large-scale political changes to prevent it.[26]

Victim talk particularly recycles the tropes of popular psychology generated by the self-help industry. It not only includes the justified notion that victims did not cause, and therefore cannot be held accountable for, their victimization, but also the dubious idea that they can abdicate responsibility for their present dysfunctions because they are pathological symptoms.[27] As the self-help industry incited consumers to solely "blame external sources—a virus, sexual molestation, chemical warfare, satanic conspiracy, alien infiltration—for psychic problems," in the last two decades of the millennium American culture became a "hot zone of psychogenic diseases."[28] Peter Novick argued that victim talk rose to such preeminence precisely because Americans were "attracted to explanations that make clear that our troubles are someone else's fault, that we are blameless."[29] After all, "in this hectic, chameleon-like, deregulated, and unpredictable world of privatized loners," as Zygmunt Bauman put it, "one is indeed greatly relieved if at least the blame for one's troubles can be shifted onto something other than one's own shoulders."[30] For instance, after the so-called recovered memory movement rose to a preeminent branch of self-help psychology in the mid-1980s, for the next decade it incited women to re-conceptualize their discontent with patriarchal oppression as suffering caused by purported experiences of repressed sexual child abuse.[31] In its extreme version, sometimes dubbed the 'abuse excuse,' victim talk even advocates that individuals victimized in the past cannot be held accountable for any present criminal acts. According to Joseph Amato, criminals "were welcomed into the field of victims" based on the ethically and epistemologically dubious argument that their crimes constituted "proof that they themselves, not the victims of their crimes, were the true victims of the system."[32]

While it is doubtful whether the abdication of individual responsibility for seeking to overcome suffering and taking responsibility for one's own present actions is therapeutically beneficial, it is clearly unethical, because it excuses antisocial and even criminal behavior. Moreover, the latter notion indicates that, while the subject positions of victim and perpetrator are cast as dichotomous in victim talk and conflated with good and evil, the matter is more complex. From a strictly synchronic perspective, victims and perpetrators indeed occupy exclusive and opposing positions, such as torturer and tortured or child abuser and abused child. However, a diachronic perspective, like the history of Stalinist persecution in the Soviet Union, illustrates that the roles of victim and perpetrator are not necessarily absolute and dichotomous.

Although the gratuitous infliction of violence constitutes the current notion of evil incarnate and victims are ascribed the status of ultimate moral authority based on the notion that suffering ennobles, the conflation of victim and perpetrator with good and evil is too simplistic. At least since the introduction of the trauma concept by Jean-Martin Charcot, Pierre Janet, and Sigmund Freud more than one hundred years ago,[33] we know that the Christian notion of spiritual purification through physical mortification is unsupportable, at least in the case of extreme and gratuitous violence. Despite the widely held belief that "as once the upper classes, especially the nobility, defined the good, now victims—the downtrodden, the oppressed, the humiliated—were equated with the good,"[34] traumatizing violence does not imbue victims with permanent innocence and goodness. A. B. Yehoshua thus writes with regard to the Holocaust: "We must bear in mind that our having been victims does not accord us any special moral standing. The victim does not become virtuous for having been a victim. Although the Holocaust inflicted a horrific injustice upon us, it did not grant us a certificate of everlasting righteousness. The murderers were immoral; the victims were not made moral. To be moral you must behave ethically. The test of that is daily and constant."[35] Zygmunt Bauman even argued that not only are victims not necessarily morally superior to non-victimized others, but that they are not even "guaranteed to be morally superior to their victimizers."[36] After all, they may take as the core lesson of their victimization the idea that humankind is divided into victims and perpetrators and that to avoid victimization one must become a victimizer.[37] Joseph Amato shares Bauman's ethical critique of infusing victimization experiences with redemptive value and transforming victims into quasi-saints, and he even suggested that nothing "guaranties that today's victims won't be tomorrow's victimizers."[38]

Moreover, "if victims' stories premised on subjective experience are all we have," Martha Minow wrote, "then counterclaims of victimhood obtain as much authority without enabling any possible evaluation of the relative scale or seriousness of competing claims."[39] By reducing all victim claims to the smallest common denominator of a politically and historically de-contextualized body in pain, victim talk conflates such diverse experiences as concentration camp imprisonment, rape, war combat, child and spousal abuse. As such, it blurs the distinctions between degrees of harm, leveling "all suffering to the same undifferentiated plane of equal seriousness and triviality."[40] Consequently, Minow argued, "competing claims either cancel one another out or trivialize some claims by equating them with much more minor harms."[41] Expanding this notion, Alyson Cole suggested that every claim of victimization can be contested by two equally troubling counter-claims, a denial ("No, you're not!") or a trump ("No, I'm the real victim here!").[42]

Since victims have little or no other resources to contend for power in an increasingly global capitalist competition, testimony degenerated into victim talk because they have to translate their suffering into a "moral currency"[43] and seek to attain a primary rank on the "meritocratic scale"[44] of victimhood. And since in capitalism the commodity value of any entity is determined by the ratio of supply and demand, the competition over victimhood's moral capital not only requires establishing one's own right to the victim position but also denying it to others in order to keep supply low and demand high. In the victim talk world, people thus "exchange testimonials of pain in a contest over who suffered more," Minow writes.[45] They generate what Zygmunt Bauman dubbed a "pecking order of pain" reminiscent of the rivalry among the tuberculosis patients in Thomas Mann's *Magic Mountain*, "who quickly established their own hierarchy of prestige and influence measured by the size of their pulmonary caverns."[46] The inherently competitive rhetoric of victim talk thus generated infinite blame game cycles of figurative finger-pointing and shouting matches—literalized on talk shows like *Jerry Springer* and parodied in the "Survivor" episode of *Curb Your Enthusiasm*—in which everyone seeks to out-suffer competing claims in an effort to attain preeminent victim status. Consequently, American politics and culture degenerated into "a competition for enshrining grievances," in which "every group claims its share of public honor and public funds by pressing disabilities and injustices"[47] and hence even "the most banal causes adopt, exploit, and thus cheapen the moral rhetoric of suffering owed."[48]

## The Victim Talk of Anti-Victimists

As scholars like Martha Minow, Zygmunt Bauman, Joseph Amato, and Michael Bernstein have demonstrated, there are substantial epistemological and ethical reasons for rejecting both the ubiquitous claims to victim status paradigmatic for trauma culture and the victim talk rhetoric employed to express them. However, their theoretically and empirically sophisticated and ethically responsible arguments must not be confused with the highly polemical, empirically questionable, and unethical attacks generated in the neo-conservative discourse of the American political Right in the early 1990s. The latter simplistically mistook victim talk solely to express identity politics positions associated with the liberal Left and hence feared it undermined their patriarchal and hetero-normative WASP hegemony. According to Alyson Cole, the so-called anti-victimists dismissed, ridiculed, and condemned virtually all claims of victims for attention, sympathy, and compensation. They argued that the United States had become a *Nation of Victims* whose never-ending whining generated a *Culture of Complaint*, as the titles of Charles Sykes's and Robert Hughes's prominent anti-victimist monographs respectively proclaim.[49] In vast numbers of newspaper articles[50] and trade-press publications, which also prominently include Alan Dershowitz's *The Abuse Excuse: And Other Cop-Outs, Sob Stories, and Evasions of Responsibility*, they sought to de-legitimize the vast majority of victim claims.[51]

The neo-conservative critics re-named victims "victimists" and called themselves "anti-victimists." Evoking Social Darwinist notions, they cast victimists as pathetic losers in the struggle over the survival of the fittest, who blame everyone but themselves and particularly the anti-victimists for their own failures and ineptitudes, and guilt others into providing them with unmerited privileges with sappy tales of fabricated, or at least exaggerated, suffering. And although they themselves engage in far more aggressive polemics, anti-victimists bemoan the hostile and accusatory tone of victimist claims. Anti-victimists thus reverse the roles of victim and perpetrator: Re-named victimists, victims are cast as the true villains, whose excessive and unjustified claims victimize the alleged perpetrators, particularly the anti-victimists, who are thus revealed to be the true victims.[52]

In anti-victimist discourse, "true victimhood is defined in opposition to victimism," Alyson Cole writes, and "a victim is 'true' because the victimist is evidently a bogus victim"[53] and true victims can be differentiated from victimists based on personal qualities: They are noble victims who endure their suffering with dignity and refrain from complaining or other unbecoming public displays of weakness. They do not exploit their victim status or use it as an excuse for their personal failures and incompetence. They are reluctant about assuming victimhood, even rejecting the status altogether. They claim victimhood as an individual status even if they experience victimization as a member of a group. Their victimization occurs in the present rather than the past. But the most important virtue of true victimhood is innocence. The victims' innocence must not only be complete and incontrovertible in that they have in no way contributed to their injury, but they must also be morally upright and pure by neo-conservative standards.[54]

However, as the core embodiments of the true victim in anti-victimist discourse are the aborted fetus, the crime victim, and especially the white, middle-class man who suffers unjustly from identity politics' supposed reverse discrimination, most of the core characteristics of true victims actually do not pertain to any of them. It would, for instance, be nonsensical to claim that aborted fetuses endure their suffering with dignity and do not make excessive claims to the moral capital of victimhood. And as anti-victimists are predominantly white, upper middle-class men, they not only ascribe true victimhood to themselves but, given the ubiquity and aggressive polemic of anti-victimist discourse, they also do not fulfill their ideal of true victims to modestly refrain from voicing their victimhood.[55]

While anti-victimists demonize victimhood, seeking to suppress, negate, and erase most victim claims, ironically they employ victim talk rhetoric themselves and thus participate in the phenomenon they criticize. Not only do they engage in polemics far worse than those of which they accuse the victimists, but while they lament the proliferation of victim claims, anti-victimists nevertheless devise new groups of true victims. Foremost in the pantheon of true victims are the aforementioned casualties of supposed reverse discrimination "who have been ostracized, censored, and punished in other ways by political correctness, affirmative action, hate speech codes, and similar manifestations of injurious victim politics."[56] With the exception of aborted fetuses and crime victims, anti-victimists thus reject all claims to victim status but their own, in order to generate an optimal ratio of minimal supply and maximal demand for the victim position they first and foremost ascribe to themselves. As such, they participate in precisely the inherently competitive victim talk discourse they so ostentatiously reject. Moreover, they present the same distorted, dichotomous perspective of society that they attribute to victimists, namely that it is "fundamentally and irreconcilably divided between victims and victimizers," only that in the anti-victimist depiction the roles are reversed.[57] And while they criticize victimists as blaming others for their own shortcomings and misfortunes, their apparent remedy for the ubiquity of victim talk is more victim talk and blaming, namely of victimists.[58]

# 3

## American Survivors

"'I am your mother,' she said, though she should have said: 'I'm the one who survived.' But that would be a line from a modern American novel."

–Hanna Krall, "The One from Hamburg"[1]

The inflation of claims to victim status and their expression in the epistemologically and ethically flawed victim talk rhetoric significantly changed the meaning of victimhood. The victim figure was increasingly understood not only as a saintly antihero but, reviving Social Darwinism's unethical tenet, also perceived as a weak loser in the fight for the survival of the fittest. Alison Cole argued that the victim became such a key figure in American culture precisely because of its "very susceptibility to diverse, indeed, opposing, interpretations and applications" as they "facilitate contestation and render keywords pregnant with meaning."[2] However, because popular trauma culture is emplotted according to the simplistic good-versus-evil structure of melodrama, it requires unambiguous characters. In order to disambiguate trauma culture's antihero, the victim figure was increasingly replaced by the survivor since the latter is defined solely in positive terms.

The transition from the victim to the survivor as the core character in popular trauma culture had been prefigured in Holocaust discourse. Initially, all Holocaust victims, including survivors, were infamously accused of having gone like sheep to the slaughter and cast as pitiful and despised pariahs. While those murdered were thus blamed as partially responsible for their killing, their deaths were also ascribed redemptive qualities. Victims were thus cast in contradictory terms as naïve, weak, and helpless losers in the struggle for the survival of the fittest, and at the same time, as innocent quasi-saints. Holocaust survivors were not only considered abject outsiders, but also demonized as collaborators, who had only been able to save their own lives at the expense of others. Because survivors were defined in entirely negative terms, the dominant notion was that the best had perished, despite the ambivalence in defining the victim position.

The Eichmann trial and the replacement of Anne Frank by Elie Wiesel as America's preeminent Holocaust representative radically transformed the understanding of victims and survivors. While the earlier dichotomy between victims and survivors was retained, the values ascribed to each position were reversed. The trial positively differentiated survivors from victims for the first time by imbuing only the former with the new social function of juridico-historical witness. Elie Wiesel's quest to transform the Holocaust from a source of shame into one of pride solidified the differentiation, because it was not the externally imposed Holocaust victimhood but the accomplishment of its survival that constituted the source of pride.[3] While Wiesel's effort to de-stigmatize survivors is laudable, his strategy is unethical. The transformation of Holocaust survival into an exceptional achievement not only covertly evoked Social Darwinism, but it was also attained at the discursive expense of the murdered victims. Although the victim figure continued overtly to be cast as quasi-saint, covertly it functioned as the survivor's weak Other who died for lack of survival skills.

Donald Downs argued that "America began to define itself, at least in part, as a nation of 'survivors.'"[4] However, in order for many Americans to redefine themselves from victims into survivors, the understanding of the latter term had to undergo another change in meaning. In Holocaust discourse, "survivor" increasingly came to signify not only survival of the genocide, but also and especially the fact that one's life was no longer dominated by the victimization experience. And it is the latter meaning that dominates in popular trauma culture, where "survivor" designates not necessarily, or even primarily, someone whose life was threatened, but rather someone who has overcome post-traumatic suffering. Recasting survival as the ultimate achievement in American Holocaust discourse and, metaphorically expanded, into signifying victimhood overcome in trauma culture at large, replaced traditional notions of accomplishment and heroism: "We are becoming heroes again," Anatole Broyard wrote, but "not the old heroes of myth and fable, not supermen, but heroes of the minimal, heroes of survival."[5]

## Holocaust Survivors and Witnesses Testimony

Although bearing witness constituted the core motivation for the considerable number of archival projects and Holocaust diaries compiled as the genocide was unfolding,[6] it was only with the Eichmann trial that Holocaust testimony reached a wide audience. Moreover, as the subject position of historical witness was generated at the trial, experiential knowledge of victimization was ascribed social significance, and Holocaust survivors were transformed from shunned pariahs into revered antiheroes, as their survival came to signify perseverance and strength, success and accomplishment. Most immediately indicative of this shift was the fact that both the prosecutor's and the judge's office were "being bombarded with hundreds of requests from people who wished to testify."[7]

While the Eichmann trial was conceptualized as a large-scale history lesson, the genocide of European Jewry was not represented as a complex sociopolitical event, but rather as the sum total of the individual experiences expressed in survivor testimonies.[8] It thus introduced the notion that the past is best understood via testimony, rather than through the analytical and self-critical discourse of professional historians. Hannah Arendt remarked at the time that most of the witnesses did not posses "the rare capacity for distinguishing between things that had happened to the storyteller more than sixteen, and sometimes twenty, years ago and what he had read and heard and imagined in the meantime."[9] This view became dominant in early Holocaust historiography. Lucy Dawidowicz, for instance, argued that that survivor accounts must be categorically excluded as primary sources from Holocaust historiography because they are based on imperfect observation and flawed memory. According to Dawidowicz, testimony is also "full of discrepancies" and "distorted by hate, sentimentality, and the passage of time" as well as by the inclusion of "hearsay, gossip, rumor, assumption, speculation, and hypothesis."[10] However, this critical view remained marginal in the public sphere, because the mass media embraced the contrary idea that witness testimony constitutes the optimal resource for understanding the past. In fact, the witness figure and the narrative mode of testimony have come to occupy such a prevalent position in Western culture since the Eichmann trial that Annette Wieviorka described this as the era of the witness.

The interrelated advance of the survivor-witness and the testimonial genre to cultural prominence was significantly reinforced by Elie Wiesel's rise to the "most influential interpreter of the Holocaust as sacred mystery" in American culture.[11] Best known as the author of *Night*, the most famous and continuously bestselling Holocaust memoir in the United States, he generated a vast oeuvre of more than forty books and countless newspaper articles and public speeches. Besides extensively practicing testimonial writing, Wiesel also promotes it through laudatory commentary. For instance, he famously and rather self-aggrandizingly proclaimed that, as "the Greeks invented tragedy, the Romans the epistle, the Renaissance the sonnet, our generation invented a new literature, that of testimony."[12] However, Wiesel's promotion of witness testimony is coupled with the demotion of historical scholarship. He declared that "any survivor has more to say than all the historians combined about what happened"[13] and argued with regard to "the scholars and philosophers of every genre," that "Auschwitz, by definition, is beyond their vocabulary."[14] The notion that the witness rather than the historian constitutes the prime Holocaust interpreter was inadvertently confirmed by Hill and Wang, the trade press that published Tom Segev's *The Seventh Million*, when they printed a favorable statement about the book by Wiesel on its front cover. The press thus employed Wiesel's interpretative authority as Holocaust survivor as an endorsement for the provocative scholarly study of Israeli Holocaust memory.

Wieviorka, however, emphatically rejects this culturally dominant assignment of superior authority to the Holocaust witnesses rather than to the historian, and of testimony over historiography as the primary mode of representing the past. She considers this to be most strongly promoted by the Shoah Visual History Foundation. Unlike the video testimonies collected for the Yale Fortunoff Archive, which were intended to supplement the necessary abstractions of Holocaust historiography, the Shoah Visual History Foundation claims to provide an "exhaustive picture of the life of Jewish communities in the twentieth century."[15] However, even if the omniscient claim is limited geographically to European communities and temporally to the Holocaust, witness testimonies would "at most be able to draw a picture of how the survivors remembered their communities fifty years after their destruction."[16]

Although Holocaust testimony provides information about the individual experience of this core event in twentieth-century history, it clearly cannot replace Holocaust historiography. Testimony is often factually imprecise and at times even inaccurate. And individual life stories cannot encompass large-scale, collective aspects, such as the social, economic, and political circumstances of the late Weimar Republic, which facilitated the rise of Nazism, or the ubiquity of eugenicist ideas in early twentieth-century Western culture. Furthermore, as testimony represents the speaker's often horrifically brutal victimization, it lacks the distance and self-critical stance of the historian to the subject matter. And its typical tripartite structure of before-during-after is problematic because the notion of a "before" leads to anachronisms and teleology, while the idea of "after" defines the Holocaust as the decisive life experience for every survivor and casts it as a quasi-religious second myth of collective Jewish origin.[17]

Testimony certainly has a significant therapeutic potential for reestablishing the survivors' dignity and validating experiences that many of them had feared would not be believed. However, as Wieviorka emphatically asserts, "the concentration camp experience does not confer any prophetic talent" to the survivor.[18] She even questions its social function: "What is there to testify about then? What knowledge do the survivors possess—because they must certainly possess some knowledge? What does the audience expect from testimony? Is a story of atrocity supposed to inoculate us against future atrocity?"[19] She underpins her provocative questions by citing her mentor, Holocaust survivor and psychoanalyst Anne-Lise Stern, who similarly challenged Holocaust discourse: "We are expected, we are urged to testify 'before it is too late,'" Stern explains, "yet, what knowledge do they hope to gain? What deathbed confession, what family secret, do they expect to hear? Where is all this listening to survivors leading, whether by those who have had little education or by those who are overeducated?" Aptly summarizing the omnipresent Holocaust commoditization, she answers: "Toward sound bites, I fear, which future generations will play with and enjoy. It's happening already."[20] Alexander von Plato has likewise cautioned that Holocaust video testimonies will be used by docutainment producers only in brief segments since, in today's media landscape, "talking heads" have minimal entertainment value.[21] The function of such testimony sound bites is to authorize the media product, because in the era of the witness, it is no longer primarily the authority of the historian's professional brand name that is employed to signify the factual accuracy of documentaries.[22]

## Holocaust Survival as Triumph

Although the shift from the victim to the survivor as the preeminent Holocaust representative began in the sphere of early Israeli political culture, when only the latter was ascribed the status of historical witness at the Eichmann trial, subsequently the figure of the Holocaust survivor was predominantly "made in America." The transition initiated at the trial was reinforced, more than anything, by Elie Wiesel, America's "emblematic survivor"[23] and—at least until the 1993 premier of *Schindler's List*—also its most important public interpreter of the Holocaust. He introduced what would become the pillars of his Holocaust divinations, and consequently of collective American memory, at the aforementioned 1967 *Judaism* symposium, where he developed the following argument: "Why then do we admittedly think of the Holocaust with shame? Why don't we claim it as a glorious chapter in our eternal history? . . . It is still the greatest event in our times. . . . Everything today revolves around our Holocaust experience. Why then do we face it with such ambiguity? Perhaps this should be the task of Jewish educators and philosophers: to reopen the event as a source of pride, to take it back into our history."[24] The transition from the shame of victimhood to the pride of survival became a core doctrine in American Holocaust discourse. Beyond Wiesel's extensive oeuvre, it is prominently represented in the differences between casting Holocaust witnesses as damaged victims and successful survivors, respectively, in the two most important video testimony projects: The Yale Fortunoff Archive and the Shoah Visual History Foundation.

The Yale Fortunoff Archive was established in the wake of the *Holocaust* mini-series to counter its kitsch-sentimental representation and give victims the opportunity to voice "their sense of being isolated forever from the world and from their relatives by an extreme experience."[25] The interviews were generally conducted in a darkened and minimally furnished interview room, which reinforced the bleakness of the interviewees' atrocity narratives and the unbridgeable differences between the witness and the audience. The Fortunoff

Archive videos thus cast the witnesses as victims who occupy a time-space dislocated from contemporary American life.

Conversely, the aesthetics employed by the Shoah Visual History Foundation, established in the wake of *Schindler's List*,[26] "is based on the desire to show 'ordinary people,' people who have returned to 'normal.'"[27] The interviews are typically set in the survivor's home and culminate in a scene in which survivors are joined by their family to evoke middle-class normalcy and mundane life as well as suggest a continuity of Jewish generations. Showing survivors surrounded by Western comfort and loving families essentially gives their Holocaust stories a happy, redemptive ending.[28] And by emphasizing the typical elements of American life stories—overcoming persecution; emigration to the promised land; becoming successful, self-made immigrants—the interviews represent Holocaust survivors as ordinary Americans. Unlike the traumatized victims of the Fortunoff interviews, they are cast the proud and accomplished survivors Wiesel envisioned in 1967.

Changing the Holocaust from an occasion of shame into one of pride required that survival was stressed over death and that the meaning of survival be radically altered from signifying collaboration to marking an exceptional accomplishment. While the collective demonizing of survivors as ruthless collaborators was both historically and ethically wrong, elevating them to modern-day heroes, saints, and prophets is likewise wrong, as it is ahistorical and was only possible at the expense of the non-surviving victims. Wiesel's notion that survivorship designates a status that was earned and could therefore constitute a source of pride reinforced the dubious elevation of survivors over victims that began with the ascription of witness status solely to survivors at the Eichmann trial.[29] Casting Holocaust survival as an achievement requires stigmatizing victims by casting their death as due to their lack of the necessary skill and will to survive.[30]

American Holocaust discourse thus not only obliquely echoes the ethically exceptional reality of the camps, where the *Muselmann*, that is, the prisoner who had given up the fight for survival, was despised as pariah, but also reiterates the notion of the survival of the fittest. The most pronounced version of the latently Social Darwinist Holocaust survivor figure was put forth by Terrence Des Pres. He argued that "survivors refused to accept the definition of themselves as victims" and that their "recalcitrance" lay in their "refusal to be determined by forces external to themselves."[31] The narrator of Tova Reich's satire of American Holocaust discourse aptly summarizes its infusion with Social Darwinist survivalism as follows:

> Survival of the fittest. . . . In this world if you survive, you win, and if you win, you're good. . . . If you don't survive, you lose. If you lose, you're nothing. . . . Why had they survived? Luck, it was luck, they said.

But they didn't believe it for a minute. It was the accepted thing to say, so as not to insult the memory of the ones who hadn't survived, the ones who, let's face it, had failed. . . . The real truth, they knew, was that they had survived because they were stronger, better—fitter. Survival was success.[32]

## TV Survivors

As more and more people felt like hapless victims threatened by the vast unresolved problems of late capitalism, the American ideal of pursuing individual success and happiness gave way to a sense that life was a constant struggle for survival.[33] It was in this cultural climate that Americans began to look to the Holocaust for survival lessons. However, conceptualizing American life as akin to genocide is grossly ahistorical and obscures the socio-economic causes of present victimization and suffering as well as the idea that they can be addressed through collective political action. It also does anything but minimize survival anxiety.

Nevertheless, progressive political groups like the peace movement and the environmental movement took survival as their slogan, and a vast range of popular culture artifacts and other consumer products began to invoke the concept: Gloria Gaynor asserted in her 1978 hit that "I will survive," a Los Angeles radio station advertised itself as "your survival station for the eighties," and Samsonite's largest briefcase in the mid-eighties was called "the Survivor."[34] The growing genre of self-help literature exploded when it took up the survival trope and designated everyone a fighter in the struggle over the survival of the fittest, from the housewives of Betty Canary's *Surviving as a Woman* to the neo-conservative misogynists of Edgar Berman's *A Survival Guide for the Bedeviled Male*.[35] The notion of survival thus became increasingly metaphorical as its meaning changed from defeating life-threatening danger to overcoming any form of suffering or even supposed "reverse discrimination." However, at the same time, the media also depicted victimization and violence in ever more spectacular detail, for instance in such popular disaster movies as *Earthquake*, *The Poseidon Adventure*, and *The China Syndrome*, and *Memoirs of a Survivor*.[36] Victimhood and survivorship also dominated TV daytime talk shows, and in the 1990s the subject even generated entire new popular literature subgenres such as incest novels and misery memoirs.[37] In the new millennium, representations of survivors on American television are ubiquitous and highly diverse. They range from the extreme metaphorical extension of the concept on the reality show *Survivor* to the horror spectacles of the semi-documentary series *I Survived*, and from Elie Wiesel's Holocaust tourism to the Auschwitz site on the *Oprah Winfrey Show Special* to the satire of the American obsession with survivors on *Curb Your Enthusiasm*.

Pseudo-validated as survival lessons, each hour-long episode of *I Survived* narrates and partly reenacts as spectacular melodramas three unrelated experiences of Americans who survived life-threatening ordeals. In the pilot, which aired in April 2008 on the Biography Channel, a woman recounts being raped, shot, and left for dead by an intruder in her home; a man remembers being caught in a deadly blizzard; and two boys recollect the hours after they survived a plane crash while rescue workers tried to find them in the wilderness. Subsequent episodes include accounts of a brutal attack by a hitchhiker, being stranded on a barren island, the sinking of a ferry boat, a vicious assault by a neighbor, capture and multiple rapes by a stranger, simulating death for hours after being shot by a boyfriend, and a savage attack of a store owner by robbers. While the depicted experiences are diverse, the overall narrative structure of each episode is formulaic: Solely based on victim testimonies, they are narrated as voice-over of partial reenactments staged by actors and as video testimonies filmed before a dark background that echoes the aesthetics of the Yale Fortunoff Holocaust video testimonies but employ more extreme close-ups. Paradigmatic for the representation of victimhood in trauma culture, the testimonies are constructed as apolitical personal tragedies, or rather melodramas, and their predictable narrative structure blends the three disparate individual stories in each episode into what Ian Buruma called "a kind of soup of pain."[38] The episodes are furthermore unified by thematic similarities: One of the three segments involves a women being physically, and often sexually, attacked by a man. Victims are more frequently assaulted by strangers than by someone they know. And gratuitously inflicted violence far outweighs life-threatening situations caused by technological malfunction or natural catastrophe.[39] *I Survived* reflects and reinforces America's continued fascination with autobiographical stories of horrific victimization cast as spectacles of suffering that began almost half a century ago with the Eichmann trial.

However, television not only encourages the dubious fascination with the survivor figure, but has also become the medium of its critique. The American "cult of survival"[40] was most prominently ridiculed through satire in the aforementioned episode of the HBO series *Curb Your Enthusiasm* entitled "The Survivor."[41] The show was produced by *Seinfeld* co-creator Larry David, who is also its lead character. It merges the two most successful TV genres, the sitcom and the reality show, mocking both. While scripted like a sitcom, the show is filmed in a pseudo-documentary style, which gives the viewer the impression of voyeuristically observing someone else's real and anything-but-sitcom-ideal life. And unlike the thirty-something sitcom stars with the bland girl/guy-next-door good looks of shows like *Friends*, Larry David is in his late fifties, largely bald with remnants of unkempt white hair, unfashionably bespectacled, and rather grumpy, unsympathetic, argumentative, egotistical, and rude. Like reality show characters, he "plays himself" while all other characters and the plot are fictional. "The Survivor" episode from the fourth season, which aired in 2004, constitutes the most scathing critique of American trauma culture to date. It mocks not only the omnipresence and vast metaphorical expansion of claims to survivor status and the aggressively competitive victim talk rhetoric in which they are voiced, but also the role that American Holocaust discourse plays in popular trauma culture.

The central and most spectacular scene of the episode ensues from a misunderstanding. Larry assumes that the man whom his rabbi wants to bring to Larry's dinner party and describes as "a survivor" is a Holocaust survivor. Believing that he would like to meet another Holocaust survivor, Larry asks his father to bring his friend Solly "who's also a survivor." At the party, Larry realizes that the rabbi did not invite a Holocaust survivor but a young man named Colby, who was a participant in the reality show *Survivor* and wanted to meet Larry because he is "a huge fan of *Seinfeld*." At the dinner table, Colby starts bragging (or testifying?) about the dangers he encountered in the Australian Outback, where the second season of *Survivor* took place. When Solly, the fictional Holocaust survivor, feels the preeminence of Holocaust suffering challenged and starts testifying (or bragging?) in an equally contentious and exaggerated manner to his camp experience, a shouting match ensues over who suffered more and thus constitutes the preeminent survivor.

The hyperbolic scene critiques American Holocaust discourse by recycling its tropes in de-familiarized fashion: The fictional Holocaust survivor is short, fat, bald, egocentric, and obnoxious and thus depicted as antithetical to trauma culture's romanticized survivor figure, paradigmatically embodied by Elie Wiesel. Solly furthermore vastly exaggerates Holocaust suffering, claiming that he did not eat for months and experienced 42 degrees below zero in the camp. He also expresses his testimony in the loud, aggressive, and competitive rhetoric of victim talk. However, the clichéd nature of Holocaust tropes is most provocatively parodied when Colby counters each of Solly's claims of deprivation with an analogous one. While Solly evokes the extreme cold, starvation, insufficient clothing and shoes, and lack of all markers of civilization in the camps, Colby claims equal if not greater suffering due to extreme heat, limited availability of snacks, enforced wearing of flip flops, and—indicating the absence of civilization—the unavailability of gyms in the Australian Outback.

The use of the singular in the episode title "The Survivor" parodies the composite American survivor figure as it merges the vastly different subject positions of a fictional Holocaust survivor and a reality TV show participant. As the dinner table quarrel between Solly and Colby reveals significant similarities not only in the victim talk rhetoric both men employ, but also in the arguments they construct, the scene reinforces the title's critique of American Holocaust discourse itself and its role in trauma culture. Both "survivors" violate the romanticized survivor figure by their aggressive competition over preeminent suffering and survivor status, which culminates when both repeatedly shout at each other "I'm a survivor." The scene critiques both victim-talk rhetoric and the role that claims to Holocaust preeminence play in its generation by hyperbolically literalizing it as a shouting match evocative of trash talk shows like *Jerry Springer*. Moreover, as both Colby and Solly invoke the survival of the fittest when they each stress that it was their physical fitness that helped them "survive," the scene parodies the infusion of American Holocaust memory and trauma culture at large with Social Darwinist ideas. Last but not least, as both men express their respective claims of triumphing over preeminent suffering directly through or in analogy to Holocaust tropes, the scene criticizes both the oversaturation of American culture with formulaic Holocaust narratives and their figurative use in narratives of overcoming difficulties.

The "Survivor" episode also criticizes through satire, parody, and hyperbole the trivializing ubiquity of victim claims, the vast metaphoric extension of survival, and the appropriation of Holocaust discourse in American culture in three other scenes: Larry grossly exploits collective Holocaust memory when he tries to make amends with his stereotypically obnoxious shiksa mother-in-law for a snappy comment he made by assuming vicarious Holocaust victim status. Ridiculing the appropriation of the genocide, he claims that the argument between Solly and Colby made him emotionally vulnerable because it had evoked in him "what happened to my people." And when Larry's rabbi self-servingly evokes historically significant victims, he models his own vicarious victim claim on the notion of hereditary Holocaust victimhood but extends it beyond the self-aggrandizing misappropriation of the genocide in American-Jewish culture to American culture at large. In the same conversation with Larry in which he asks whether he could bring "a survivor" to dinner the next day, he also claims that his late brother-in-law was a victim of historical significance because "he died on September 11th." Only after Larry's repeated questioning does the rabbi explain that his brother-in-law actually died in a traffic accident in uptown Manhattan and his death was thus unrelated to the World Trade Center attack. The rabbi nevertheless continues to invoke the historical significance of 9/11 for the death of his brother-in-law, even beyond this conversation. Subsequently, he is deeply offended by Larry's casual use of the phrase "let's roll," the famous last words of one of the passengers who brought down the third hijacked plane in Pennsylvania, because it supposedly defiled the memory of his late brother-in-law. The "Survivor" episode culminates by ridiculing the vast metaphoric extension of survival in American culture even further when Larry finds himself evacuated from a Los Angeles hotel after a very minor earthquake, which endangered no one, and has a brief chance encounter with Colby, who remarks "Hey, we survived."

# 4

---

# Trauma Kitsch

"Kitsch causes two tears to flow in quick succession. The first tear says: How nice to see children running on the grass! The second tear says: How nice to be moved, together with all mankind, by children running on the grass!"

–Milan Kundera, *The Unbearable Lightness of Being*[1]

The ubiquity of victim talk, the increasingly metaphorical claims to victim and survivor status, and American Holocaust discourse have begun to be critiqued in scholarship. Moreover, these core elements of popular trauma culture have recently been parodied and satirized in literary texts like Tova Reich's *My Holocaust* and on television shows like Larry David's *Curb Your Enthusiasm,* which are much more widely consumed, and therefore more influential in shaping cultural trends, than scholarship.

Despite the recent presence of such critical voices, melodramatic Holocaust-and-redemption kitsch continues to generate highly commercial media products. It was prefigured in the American mythification of Anne Frank and fully emerged with the *Holocaust* mini-series. And more recently, it was successfully employed in *Schindler's List* and *Life Is Beautiful* on the high-brow end of the spectrum as well as *Sophie's Choice* and *The Boy in the Striped Pajamas* on the low-brow end. Reinforced by the self-help industry and exemplified by the queen of trauma kitsch, Oprah Winfrey, daytime TV talk shows also reveled in depicting victimization experiences as redemptive trauma-and-recovery tales. Last but certainly not least, the commercially most successful literary subgenre of misery memoirs, which depict horrific victimization as titillating melodramatic spectacles, encode kitsch sentiment as their dominant mode of reception. As the pain of others was transformed into commercially successful entertainment commodities by being emplotted as kitsch-sentimental melodrama, an exploration of how kitsch and melodrama function in popular trauma culture will conclude its genealogy.

The kitsch concept originates in mid-nineteenth century German *Biedermeier* culture and has been explored through the distinct approaches of mass culture theorists and popular culture scholars. Mass culture theorists define kitsch as a style derivative and imitative of higher art styles that it reduces to banal, trite, and predictable formulas and stock motifs.[2] They not only consider kitsch radically inferior to the creativity and innovation of the high culture object it imitates and indicative of bad taste, but also take it to constitute a forgery because it seeks to pass off an imitation for an original. As a cheaply mass-produced product lacking craftsmanship and artistic refinement, they define kitsch as symptomatic of mass culture.[3] The popular culture approach to kitsch rejects that model and proposes that the kitsch objects of popular culture reflect as much creativity as the products of highbrow culture and that, therefore, the distinction between high and low art forms is without grounds.[4] Sam Binkley's astute analysis of kitsch follows mass culture theory with regard to the characteristics of kitsch and popular culture studies in dispensing with the traditional hierarchical framework. He argues that kitsch neither exhibits the same innovative, avant-garde features as high art nor does it constitute its failed, inferior version, but rather that kitsch should be understood on its own terms, because it reflects its own distinct aesthetic:[5] It celebrates banality and advocates continuity, conformity, and routine. It proposes simple moral truths that are repeated over and over and reduces complexity by relying on well-rehearsed formulas, clichés, and conventions. Moreover, kitsch transvalues its anti-innovative aesthetic into signifying authenticity, modesty, sincerity, and frankness, and—assuming a pseudo-democratic posture of naïveté and anti-elitism—asserts that it is both representative of the essence of human nature and universally comprehensible.[6]

It can thus be argued with Avishai Margalit that kitsch is not only an aesthetic but an ethical category. Central to his argument is the idea that kitsch "distorts reality by turning the object (or event) represented into an object of complete innocence," which is constantly being menaced by its dichotomous Other of evil incarnate.[7] Margalit furthermore maintains that the ontological innocence ascribed to the kitsch object is central to its reception because it enables and even enforces the troublesome ease with which consumers align themselves with the subject position of total innocence.[8] Marita Sturken similarly argues that "most kitsch conveys a kind of deliberate and highly constructed innocence" and relates this feature of kitsch objects to their reception as it dictates a predetermined and thus manipulative emotional response. Luc Boltanski describes the dominant mode of reception encoded in kitsch artifacts as the "sweetness of being moved to tears" when "a certain joy is mixed with sadness"[9] and Sam Binkley similarly characterizes it as "a teary eye and a lump in the throat."[10] Like Sturken, Binkley considers the sentiment that kitsch artifacts evoke in consumers to be manipulative. It not only reduces the intricacy of human emotions to melancholy and nostalgia, but also incites the audience to indulge in the pleasure of their own sentimental arousal and thus represses the alternative reception mode of critical distance.[11]

Both Margalit and Sturken invoke the reflections on kitsch sentiment as an economy of the second tear in Milan Kundera's *The Unbearable Lightness of Being*. Whereas the first tear indicates a genuine emotional response of sorrow, kitsch sentiment is expressed by the second tear. It does not emerge from direct involvement with the object of feeling, but rather constitutes a derivative response, a meta-tear shed upon the perception of the first one that signifies the audience's reveling in their own emotional arousal.[12] Analogously, Boltanski argued that the mediated and therefore distant suffering of others can be perceived by either an altruistic or a selfish gaze. The altruistic gaze is "motivated by the intention to see the suffering ended" and gives rise to the genuine emotional response of sorrow that Kundera captured through the metaphor of the first tear. And akin to Kundera's disingenuous second-tear response, Boltanski argues that there is also "a selfish way of looking which is wholly taken up with the internal states aroused by the spectacle of suffering: fascination, horror, interest, excitement, pleasure."[13] Unlike Kundera, who understands kitsch sentiment as derivative of the genuine emotional reaction, Boltanski thus considers the altruistic and the selfish modes of reception mutually exclusive, and Margalit analogously reinterprets Kundera's notion of second-tear-jerking kitsch sentimentality. According to Margalit, an artifact actually constitutes kitsch in its purest form when it evokes the second tear without the first—when the audience's emotional response is entirely disingenuous and narcissistic.[14]

The cultural climate in which the desire for kitsch thrives was generated by what Anthony Giddens termed modern society's disembedding institutions and practices.[15] Embeddedness describes the forms of sociability characteristic of premodern societies, when existential questions were bracketed by shared beliefs and traditions that provided a sense of ontological security. However, modern society's "unprecedented choices in consumer goods, ethical outlooks, and life plans" uprooted individuals "from the 'protective cocoons' that flood social interactions, cultural outlooks, and experiences with cohesive meanings, and tie daily life to fundamental patterns of trust and reassurance."[16] As life's uncertainties not only vastly increased but were no longer balanced by enduring conventions and convictions, modernity gave rise to a sense of omnipresent but intangible threat. The late-modern zeitgeist is characterized by the notion that life in the increasingly global world of techno-capitalism is insidiously victimizing and even traumatizing. And kitsch, Binkley argues, "works to re-embed its consumers, to replenish stocks of ontological security, and to shore up a sense of cosmic coherence in an unstable world of challenge, innovation, and creativity."[17] The mass media thus rely on the kitsch aesthetic to emplot the pain of others because its clichés and conventions, tropes and formulas, stock plots and set pieces generates a sense of repetitiveness and familiarity with the represented violence. As Andy Warhol put it, "when you see a gruesome picture over and over again, it doesn't really have any effect."[18] And Marita Sturken observed along the same lines that after she sat through the commemorative reenactment of the Oklahoma City bombing a few times, it lost its shock impact and came to seem mundane.[19] As the mass media moreover rely on melodrama's plot formula for representing victimization and suffering, the trauma kitsch ubiquitously generated in popular culture conveys a sense of comfort, because it asserts that no matter what happens—whether genocide or child abuse or lesser evils—good always wins over evil, and the world is predictable and safe.

Trauma kitsch narratives ostensibly represent an apolitical world. However, by omitting the socio-economic contexts of oppression, victimization, and violence by representing these quintessentially political subjects as individual tragedies, trauma kitsch covertly reinforces the power structures that have created the represented injustices. In conveying the message that teary-eyed sentimentality constitutes an adequate and sufficient reaction, they suppress the critical reception from which political action can arise. Moreover, trauma kitsch and its covert message of political acquiescence is not only restricted to the entertainment commodities of the mass media, but even permeate something as seemingly progressive as American cancer activism. According to Barbara Ehrenreich, the American breast cancer movement suppresses women's political agency not only by infantilizing them through such kitsch objects as pink teddy bears, but also by inciting, even enforcing, the popular psychology doctrine of positive thinking. Although there is no empirical evidence for the purported healing function of positive thinking, it continues to be espoused by the self-help industry as the cure-all solution to the problems of late-capitalism, from poverty and unemployment to potentially terminal illness. However, the kitsch master narrative suppresses what should be an orchestrated anger at and collective political action against what Ehrenreich calls the Cancer Industrial Complex, which promotes profitable drug treatments over costly research into prevention and particularly research into environmental causes of cancer.[20] What matters, then, is precisely what kitsch leaves out.[21]

The ubiquitous mass media representations of the pain of others as trauma kitsch elicit an escapist and politically acquiescing mode of reception because they represent all forms of injustice and oppression, violence and suffering as melodrama. According to Peter Brooks, in its "effort to make the 'real' and the 'ordinary' and the 'private life' interesting,"[22] melodrama infuses the quotidian with the sublime. However, in the post-sacred era, the sublime no longer signifies solely the sacred, but also the supremely evil, and melodrama thrives on the simultaneity of extreme situations, events, and emotions and the ordinary world of the every-day. Melodrama, Brooks furthermore writes, indulges in "strong emotionalism; moral polarization and schematization; extreme states of being, situations, actions; overt villainy, persecution of the good and final reward of virtue; inflated and extravagant expression; dark plottings, suspense

[and] breathtaking peripety."[23] Trauma kitsch particularly evokes gothic melodrama, which is "preoccupied with nightmare states, with claustration and
thwarted escape, with innocence buried alive and unable to voice its claim to
recognition" and "with evil as a real, irreducible force in the world, constantly
menacing outburst."[24] In the melodramatic tales of popular trauma culture,
suffering is gratuitously inflicted by a perpetrator figure, who evokes the Gothic
villain, on the innocent victim, who echoes the maiden-in-distress and is thus
inherently infantilized and feminized. The relentless pursuit of the ontologically
innocent by rank evil constitutes the dark secret of gothic melodrama, of which
the mundane world is—or at least pretends to be—ignorant.

As a genre, melodrama originated in post-revolutionary France and
"expresses the anxiety brought by a frightening new world in which the traditional patterns of moral order no longer provide the necessary social glue."[25]
In other words, it reflects the disembeddedness of the modern individual and
the insecurities and anxieties of the new post-secular age of the enlightenment
into which the French Revolution catapulted not only France, but also Britain
and the German states. Analogously, as the dominant mode of emplotment of
the pain of others in the mass media today, melodrama echoes the trepidations
and angst brought about by a world in which mundane life is increasingly
experienced as not only disembedded but as insidiously traumatic. As a late-
eighteenth-century genre, melodrama strove "to find, to articulate, to demonstrate, to 'prove' the existence of a moral universe" at a time when modernity
challenged both pillars of the premodern age, the monarchy and the church.[26]
It became "the principal mode for uncovering, demonstrating, and making
operative the essential moral universe in a post-sacred era."[27] The genre "represents both an urge toward resacrilization and the impossibility of conceiving
sacralization other than in personal terms," which is why good and evil are
personalized, that is, embodied by characters lacking in psychological complexity because they represent quasi-allegorical absolutes.[28] When "Good and Evil
can be named as persons," Brooks writes, "evil is villainy; it is a swarthy, cape-
enveloped man with a deep voice."[29] And good is represented by the innate
innocence ascribed by Christian tradition to childhood and virginity, which the
Romantics merged into the figure of the maiden-in-distress.

These dichotomous flat characters still populate today's kitsch-sentimental
emplotments of the pain of others as melodrama. The victim figure not only
remains associated with women and children but victimization is widely perceived as emasculating. And the current two paradigmatic embodiments of
ultimate evil are hyper-masculine: The sexually child-abusing father figure is
omnipresent on made-for-TV movies and in such popular literary subgenres
as incest novels and misery memoirs, while the de-historicized Nazi figure is
prominently represented in commercial cinema like *Schindler's List*, *Sophie's
Choice*, and *The Night Porter*.

As both dramatic genre and mode of emplotment, melodrama enacts the optimistic belief that good wins over evil as the victim is redeemed and the villain is punished. However, the overt optimism expressed in the redemptive-happy endings is undermined by the fact that the vast majority of the plot casts innocence as constantly threatened by seemingly omnipotent evil, which lurks everywhere under the surface of mundane life. The simultaneous overt optimism and covert angst may explain the addictive capacity that made such hot commodities not only of Gothic novels but also of today's trauma kitsch as depicted in misery memoirs and daytime TV talk shows. As audiences seek more and more reassurance that, despite appearances to the contrary, all will be well in this late-modern world, they look, ironically, in all the wrong places. Despite its optimistic endings, the kitsch-sentimental melodramatic emplotments of the pain of others actually reinforce the consumer's sense of omnipresent but intangible danger that is paradigmatic of trauma culture.

Scholars like Nancy Miller and Jason Tougaw, as well as James Young, have noted in passing that the incorporation of the Holocaust into American national memory has "produced a discourse—a set of terms and debates about the nature of trauma, testimony, witness, and community" and generated a new plot archetype.[30] However, existing scholarship has not analyzed how the core elements of particularly American Holocaust discourse—the characters, plot structure, dominant rhetoric, and inscribed mode of reception—have been employed to represent the pain of others in popular culture, as I seek to do in this study. In the following chapters I will thus extend my analysis and ethical critique beyond the appropriation of the genocide to minimize American crimes and define American-Jewish identity and beyond its commoditization by the entertainment industry to the portrayal of victimhood and suffering in the mass media for which Holocaust representations provide the framework.

# PART TWO

# Television

## Watching the Pain of Others on Daytime Talk Shows

"On the one hand, television has contributed to the breakdown of the barriers of citizenship, religion, race, and geography that once divided our moral space into those we were responsible for and those who were beyond our ken. On the other hand, it makes us voyeurs of the suffering of others, tourists amid their landscapes of anguish. It brings us face-to-face with their fate, while obscuring the distances—social, economic, moral—that lie between us."

–Michael Ignatieff, "Is Nothing Sacred? The Ethics of Television"[1]

Like the televised witness testimony from the Eichmann trial that signaled the advent of popular trauma culture, the dominant contemporary narratives of victim-hood and suffering are autobiographical, relayed orally in a manner of heightened emotions, and broadcast on television, most prominently on daytime TV talk shows. First-generation programs like *Phil Donahue* and *Oprah Winfrey* employed and further disseminated the core elements of popular trauma culture established in American mass media representations of the Holocaust: the lead characters of victim, survivor, witness, and perpetrator; the dominant rhetoric of testimony-cum-victim-talk; the melodramatic good-versus-evil plot structure; and the dominant reception mode of kitsch sentiment.

Second-generation talk shows like *Ricki Lake* and *Jerry Springer* parody the testimonial rhetoric and popular psychology tropes of first-generation programs. They reinvented the carnival freak show for the television age and increasingly merged the trauma culture figures of victim and victimizer into the deviant freak. Trash talk shows ridicule the increasing rivalry for victim status emblematic of trauma culture by inciting participants to enact the inherently competitive rhetoric of victim talk as shouting matches and physical fights. Moreover, they ridicule the reception of first-generation shows by transforming trauma kitsch into trauma camp, as they unethically invite the ironically distanced and therefore unempathic camp gaze as the appropriate reaction to the freak show spectacles that they stage the participants' conflicts as. Last but not least, they implicitly echo the appropriation of the Holocaust in American culture and politics as they likewise reinforce traditional American values by showing their negation.

Although the gaudy freak shows of trash talk and the kitsch sentimentality of the pseudo-therapeutic first-generation programs differ vastly from one another, both versions of talk TV indicate that victimhood is increasingly performed as spectacle, ascribed commodity status, and sold to consumers for its dubious entertainment value. They also share the politically anaesthetizing character of other popular trauma culture embodiments, as they generate knowledge that is inherently conformist and reinforces existing power relations.

Initiated by the American reception of the Eichmann trial broadcasts, popular trauma culture thus continues to be made in America and on TV. Television constitutes "an intrinsic and determining element of our cultural formation"[2] because it not only functions as the dominant communicator of information[3] but even determines what constitutes knowledge and what kind of world exists.[4] According to Neil Postman, "The number of hours the average American watches TV has remained steady, at about four and a half hours a day, every day" even since the advent of personal computers and the internet, and "by age sixty-five, a person will have spent twelve uninterrupted years in front of the TV."[5]

Television continues to function as a significant, if largely inadvertent, site of knowledge construction and social learning. It informs the frameworks we employ to order and interpret our own lives and the lives of others. Comparable in its social impact to the invention of print or the creation of the internet, television is "rewriting our cultural scripts, altering our perceptions, our social relationships and our relationships to the natural world."[6] As the socio-economic conditions of late capitalism isolate individuals, we increasingly turn to the hyper-real time-space of televisual simulations to make sense of the world. Consequently, the possibility of corrective feedback from our own immediate perception of social interactions in non-mediated reality is minimized.[7] The extent to which television shapes reality was aptly demonstrated by Wayne Anderson, who reported in an op-ed piece in the *New York Times* in August 1996 that half of the students in his astronomy class at Sacramento City College believed in "a government conspiracy to conceal UFOs, and cited television programs as evidence."[8]

The American broadcasting system is required by the 1934 Communications Act to offer "a space where debates, serious news stories, labor issues, economic concerns, and cultural events" could be disseminated widely "to inform citizens in order for them to be valuable participants in democratic government."[9] However, this idealist mission has been largely neglected, because television programming has been created almost entirely by media corporations that actively participate in and benefit from the market economy. Therefore they have an interest in reinforcing the oppressive hegemony that both generates and masks the vast disparities in social wealth and the distribution of power emblematic of late capitalism.

Furthermore, the monopoly of a small number of media conglomerates "leads to politically and economically imbalanced media, for as ownership is concentrated, small independent media are reduced, and real choice and debate are diminished."[10] Commercial television thus inhibits criticism of capitalism as foundational discourse and of its current practices because it marginalizes and displaces alternative voices.[11] Because programming is first and foremost a commodity in the almost entirely commercial American media system, audiences are primarily addressed and defined as consumers rather than as citizens. However, despite the advent of pay-per-view, programming is predominantly not sold directly to audiences, but instead serves to attract maximum numbers of viewers. They are in turn sold in lots of a thousand in the form of ratings—themselves transformed into a commodity—as potential product consumers to advertisers who buy time slots during programming breaks.[12] As commercial television "must both sell products and reinforce the ideological positions of the dominant culture,"[13] programming is based on the two core principles of attracting maximum audiences and not offending advertisers.

The autobiographical narratives of overcoming suffering and victimhood broadcast on first-generation daytime talk shows like *Phil Donahue* and *Oprah Winfrey* therefore constitute predominantly "a media commodity that has a use value based on its sensationalism and drama" and "circulates within the relations of media competition to boost ratings."[14] Beyond the commercial nature of television, the structural constraints of first-generation talk shows were those of the narrowly normalizing and inherently depoliticizing disciplinary master narrative of popular psychology. As therapeutic discourse and practice has taken over aspects of organized religion, it functions analogously to Marx's critique of religion as the opium of the masses. By employing popular psychology as their framework for containing guests' diverse stories, talk shows reinforced its cultural significance and anesthetized any notion that political change was both necessary and possible. They proposed solely individualized solutions, namely therapeutic intervention, to such intrinsically political problems as addiction, racism, unemployment, poverty, homophobia, child and spousal abuse, single and teen motherhood, and crime. The programs did make many problems of ordinary people, particularly minorities, better known by letting women, people of color, working-class people, gays, lesbians, and transgenders publicly talk about the challenges they face in everyday life. However, while the inequality and oppression based on class, ethnicity, gender, and sexual orientation that generated many topics of first-generation talk shows are lived at a personal level,[15] the shows obscured the fact that political action can alter the underlying structures by casting the guests' problems as grounded solely in individual pathology and interpersonal dysfunction. Although first-generation talk shows claimed to empower the oppressed, disenfranchised, and marginalized and to practice the identity politics notion of making the personal political, they actually promoted the idea that individuals can and need to change nothing but themselves. In sync with therapeutic discourse and practice at large, they engaged in the contrary practice of transmuting political problems into interpersonal conflict and individual dysfunction.[16] In short, pop therapeutic talk shows promoted the notion that "I'm ill, I've been abused, I need recovery" precisely to suppress the competing interpretation that "I'm angry, I'm oppressed, my oppression is based on structural inequities that I share with others, with whom I must work to change society."[17]

The shows' overt ideology of democratic populism masked the fact that they promoted conformity to the white, hetero-normative, patriarchal, bourgeois hegemony and that they commoditized minorities by transforming their victim testimony into spectacular entertainment products.

The excessive and inherently depoliticized exposure of the personal continued on second-generation talk shows like *Ricki Lake* and *Jerry Springer* that were created in the early 1990s. However, the individualized conflicts were no longer predominantly narrated by the innocently wronged victim-cum-survivor, with the perpetrator largely absent. Instead, the ever more spectacular arguments were increasingly enacted by individuals hardly distinguishable as victim or perpetrator, in profanity-riddled shouting matches and physical fights. The new generation of daytime talk shows replaced popular psychology with a revival of the carnival freak show and ridiculed the excessive emotions and kitsch sentiment of *Oprah* and *Donahue* through parody and encoded the camp gaze as their own dominant mode of reception. Although the camp gaze constitutes a reception mode characterized by ironic distance, it does not signify a critical stance towards the show's commercial exploitation of socio-economic and ethnic minorities as freak Others. On the contrary, while these televised freak shows differ vastly from the psycho-babble of the first-generation shows, they still individualize inherently socio-economic problems. However, they no longer even advocate sentimental pity, but rather ironic bemusement and contemptuous ridicule as the appropriate reaction to the pain of others. And while trash talk shows appeared to challenge the dominant order by permitting the spectacular violation of rules, analogous to the suspension of dominant norms at the old-time carnival, they actually reinforced the status quo as both normal and, given that it was only violated by freak Others, even desirable. Representing the pain of others as camp spectacle on second-generation talk shows, then, strengthened the hegemonic status quo as the sane and safe Other to the freak show dystopia.

# 5

## Talking Cures

"In our culture of recovery . . . everyone gets to claim that she's survived some holocaust of family life, everyone gets to testify. . . . I never really wonder anymore why people want to talk about themselves for nearly an hour in front of millions of strangers. . . . I do wonder at the eagerness and pride with which they reveal, on national television, what I can't help thinking of as intimacies—sexual and digestive disorders; personal conflicts with parents, children, spouses, lovers, bosses, and best friends. I wonder even more at the intensity with which the audience listens."

–Wendy Kaminer, *I'm Dysfunctional, You're Dysfunctional*[1]

On Monday, November 6, 1967, at 10:30 A.M., Phil Donahue made TV history at a local station in Dayton, Ohio, by creating a new television genre: the daytime talk show. He dispensed with the typical band and, microphone in hand, left the stage to talk to the audience and, even more radically, decided that, since he was unable to get the rich and famous to come to Dayton, he would feature ordinary people as guests.[2] *The Phil Donahue Show* opened with the Catholic-turned-atheist Madalyn Murray O'Hare, who discussed her campaign to eliminate prayer in public schools. On Tuesday, a group of bachelors talked about what kind of women they found attractive. Wednesday featured an obstetrician and showed a film of a baby's birth. On Thursday, the funeral industry was discussed. And the week wrapped with a debate about the appropriateness of anatomically correct dolls as children's toys.[3] While these subjects are "a far cry from the disclosures of the nineties, in which ministers confessed to pedophilia and women confessed that they had slept with their daughter's boyfriends," in 1967 they created quite a stir.[4]

By 1978, the show was in national syndication with some eight million viewers every weekday and had the largest audience share in its time slot in 68 percent of the market.[5] By the time it went off the air in 1996, *Donahue* had made the personal, if not political, then at least public—and certainly spectacular.

The subjects *Donahue* featured over the years have become exemplary for the genre: marriage, family, adultery, promiscuity, artificial insemination, abortion, penal implants, diverse sexual practices, homosexuality, gay and lesbian parents, sex bias crimes, date rape, child and spousal abuse.[6] The interpersonal stories told on daytime talk shows thus sensationalize the extraordinary aspects of ordinary life through the sex-and-violence formula that dominates the commodities of popular culture. In fact, talk shows became the central site within mainstream American media for constructing and circulating knowledge about sexuality. The first-generation shows—which include *Phil Donahue*, *Oprah Winfrey*, *Sally Jessy Raphael*, and *Geraldo Rivera*, all of which went into national syndication in the 1980s—engaged in a highly successful symbiotic relationship with popular psychology. Consequently, the sexual stories they broadcast were couched in the dichotomy of normal versus abnormal and increasingly related to violence and dysfunction.[7] Participants were coached to discuss sexual deviance in the traditions of the juridico-religious confession of the sinner-victimizer and the juridico-political witness testimony of the victim-cum-survivor. Confession and testimony would establish the truth, educate the public, and generate the cathartic relief that supposedly follows from telling what, in the lingo of the recovery movement, are called "toxic secrets." The narratives follow the trauma-and-recovery paradigm: "There is always a suffering which gives the tension to the plot; this is followed through a crisis or turning point or epiphany where something has to be done"—a silence must be broken and a toxic secret be revealed—"and this leads to a transformation—a surviving and maybe a surpassing."[8] As the sexual stories told on talk shows are predominantly about deviance and victimization, sexuality is largely construed as dangerous and violent, forbidden and secretive.

While Phil Donahue inaugurated the daytime talk show genre, Oprah Winfrey further popularized it. Known as "the queen of talk," she first worked as a news anchor for about a year, but was considered inadequate for the position because she frequently ad-libbed and became noticeably upset when reporting on natural and manmade disasters. Winfrey was pulled off the air after she wept on camera while interviewing a woman who had lost her seven children in a house fire. Since she had a six-year contract with the Baltimore television station, she was asked to co-host their morning show, *People Are Talking*, and that was where she found her ideal TV show format. Even though it shared the time slot with *The Phil Donahue Show*, *People Are Talking* became a ratings success after Winfrey joined. In 1984 she went to *AM Chicago*, and her own show was in nationwide syndication by 1986. In 1991 *The Oprah Winfrey Show* was the highest-rated talk show in the history of American television. By 1993, it had an audience of some fifteen million viewers every weekday, drawing 55 percent more viewers than *Donahue*, its closest competitor at the time.[9] The show also became a highly successful business venture and "by 1994 revenues from *Oprah* had reached $180 million."[10] The success of *The Oprah Winfrey Show,* named like all daytime talk shows after the host, largely derives from Winfrey's rapport with audiences. Unlike Phil Donahue and Sally Jessy Raphael, whose bespectacled and besuited appearance evoked the distanced authority of the expert, Winfrey created a more intimate style, based on her ability to obscure her position of authority as host, celebrity, and media mogul with a $50 million annual income.[11] Dressed in the subtly more upscale version of her audience's attire that made her a style icon, she posits herself as a typical American woman in her beliefs and experiences, and thus positions herself as a representative of the audience. Embodying Whitney Houston's "I'm Every Woman," one of the show's theme songs over the years, Winfrey constructed her everywoman public persona so successfully that the *New York Times* explicitly referred to her by this label.[12] And she evokes her pseudo-ordinariness frequently on the show: "When I first heard about this, like everybody, I wondered what the big deal is . . ." or, at her most self-aggrandizing, "The question we all have, I am speaking for the audience here and the audience around the world listening to you. . . ."[13] While she thus takes up the subject position and discursive stance of the audience, Winfrey reinforced her everywoman public persona by also frequently putting herself in the position of her guests seeking therapeutic advice from an expert.

Audiences learned, on their respective shows, that Donahue had a conflicted relationship with Catholicism, that Rivera had hidden his Hispanic minority status to make it in television and had been a womanizer, and that Raphael had experienced the rape of her mother as a child, that she had suffered unemployment and poverty as an adult, and that her daughter died of a drug overdose.[14] However, it was Winfrey who became the master in orchestrating personal disclosure and in turning her own suffering into the cultural capital of authenticity.[15] Although her intimate revelations seemed spontaneous, they were timed with an astute business sense, right before the sweeps periods—the time when the viewer ratings that determine the pricing for the next season's advertising slots are calculated—because they would inevitably increase the ratings. As she "continually called on her personal experience as a source of evidence,"[16] Winfrey became famous for her spectacular confessions and testimony: born out of wedlock to a teenage mother as the result of a "brief encounter," she experienced both dire poverty and sexual abuse as a child, became a promiscuous teenager, was addicted to cocaine, and had a gay half-brother who died of AIDS. Despite her everywoman persona, then, Winfrey's own life history is anything but ordinary, and aptly embodies the highly successful paradoxical talk show genre formula of extraordinary ordinariness.

Her battle with weight evolved into a leitmotif of the show, staged in dozens of programs on weight control, dieting, and exercise.[17] On one program, Winfrey famously wheeled onto the stage a little red wagon piled high with the sixty-seven pounds of animal fat that corresponded to her most recent weight loss. On others, including one titled "The Pain of Regain," she read from her diary, which revealed her frustration, self-hate, and pain with her ballooning weight in intimate and gory detail.[18] The Oprah Winfrey Show cast weight and body shapes not only predominantly as a women's issue but also solely in therapeutic terms of overcoming a personal problem. The discussions thus ignored gender inequality, unhealthy beauty standards for women, and the fact that diet and exercise habits are largely socio-economically determined.[19] Supported frequently by self-help gurus like Geneen Roth, author of When Food Is Love and Feeding the Hungry Heart, Winfrey promoted core recovery movement doctrines: weight is not only or even primarily a physical problem, but rather a symptom of emotional problems, and thus overeating indicates a misguided substitute for (self-)love and (self-)acceptance.[20] It also constitutes an addictive behavior analogous to alcohol and drug dependence and is likewise predominantly caused by a dysfunctional childhood and the subsequent lack of self-esteem.

Recovery rhetoric in general provides the ideological framework for The Oprah Winfrey Show and holds together such diverse topics as love, romance, monogamy, betrayal, adultery, womanizers, sex, pornography, teenage pregnancy, the biological clock, lesbians, child abuse, incest, domestic violence, suicide, depression, obesity, addiction, ugly people, celebrity mothers, and ministers who sinned.[21] Eliminating their socio-economic contexts, the show casts the diverse problems of ordinary people solely in the tropes and formulas of the recovery movement: caring and sharing, the dysfunctional family, childhood trauma, codependence, the healing process, getting in touch with the inner child, toxic secrets, the healing power of talk, and of course self-esteem.[22] Even in her discussions with celebrities, Winfrey focuses on personal and emotional issues. In her 1993 interview with Michael Jackson, for example, she focused on his childhood and present emotional state. And as audiences became mesmerized by these often highly emotional and spectacular televisual simulations of the talking cure, Eva Moskowitz argues, that they "fundamentally reconstituted public debate, making stories of addiction, denial, and recovery the story of America."[23]

The phenomenal success of The Oprah Winfrey Show encouraged a wave of others. Sally Jessy Raphael premiered locally in 1983, was syndicated nationally in 1985, and by 1993 had achieved the third-highest audience ratings for daytime talk shows, after Oprah and Donahue.[24] While Sally likewise employed the rhetoric of the recovery movement and the self-help industry, the host also claimed with pride "that she started the first 'family feuds.'"[25] The show thus prefigured the even more sensationalist campy freak show spectacles of Ricki Lake and Jerry Springer that would become so successful in the 1990s.

Geraldo Rivera, who launched his syndicated talk show nationally in 1987, only a year after Oprah had gone national, went even further in the direction of tabloid journalism by presenting social deviants as fascinating freaks. The show even had a production unit who combed the back streets of New York and developed programs based on its contacts with drug addicts, pimps, prostitutes, and criminals, who not only functioned as sources but frequently also as guests.[26] While employing a thin veneer of therapeutic altruism and empathy, the show became infamous for its sensationalism, and Rivera was dubbed "the prince of sleaze." Many of the show's features would become paradigmatic for the second generation of daytime talk shows. *Ricki Lake*, for instance, borrowed the men-are-dogs leitmotif from *Geraldo*.[27] And while Rivera reduced the use of experts to the absolute minimum necessary for the therapeutic guise, the post-1990s shows largely dispensed with the expert all together. Further upping the emotional ante, Rivera introduced both so-called hate groups—a subject subsequently taken up particularly by *Jerry Springer*—and on-air physical violence to the talk show universe. In 1988, only a year after his show started, this potent mix resulted in the now legendary program about racism, when Rivera had his nose broken and face bruised in the fight between black activist Roy Innis and white supremacists, and the image of Rivera's bandaged face appeared on the cover of *Newsweek*.[28]

This chapter explores first-generation talk shows, particularly *Phil Donahue* and *Oprah Winfrey*, as core embodiments of popular trauma culture. The programs reflect the rise in claims to victim status as the ultimate moral capital and the consequent transformation of testimony into victim talk. As claims multiplied and victims were increasingly defined in the negative terms of Social Darwinism, talk shows sought to demonstrate that victims could be transformed into survivors. In order to do so, the programs employed popular psychology discourse, particularly the twelve-step programs of the recovery movement, as well as the quintessentially American narrative of the self-made man who overcomes difficulty and emerges victorious and successful, a narrative that had also determined the dominant understanding of Holocaust survival in the United States. Furthermore, talk shows echoed and reinforced the significance ascribed to the testimony of victims-cum-survivors and the relative insignificance of the perpetrators that has dominated popular trauma culture since it was introduced with the Eichmann trial. Although perpetrators figure in the guests' victim stories, they rarely appear in person on the programs. First-generation talk shows also invite trauma culture's paradigmatic mode of reception, which likewise emerged in American Holocaust discourse, namely the teary-eyed sentimentality of kitsch that enabled the transformation of the pain of others into mass media spectacles.

My subsequent analysis critiques the politically acquiescing notion that talking about victimization solely within the parameters of therapy or its simulation on talk shows is a necessary and sufficient reaction that, in the language of the recovery movement, ensures the transformation of victims into survivors.

The discussion furthermore relates the increasingly dominant notion in American Holocaust memory that survivors, rather than historians, constitute the primary source for information about the genocide to the relationship between the experiential knowledge of the victim-cum-survivor and the professional wisdom of experts on talk shows. I conclude with a discussion of testimony and confession as the discursive modes employed by victim and perpetrator, respectively, to speak about victimization, which have been insufficiently differentiated and even conflated in scholarship on talk shows.

## Televising Therapeutic Talk

The rise of popular psychology to cultural dominance since the 1980s was aided by the ideology of American individualism, which defines people as free agents of their actions and destiny and suppresses the role of social institutions, economics, and power structures.[29] The American obsession with psychological well-being infused everyday life with what Eva Moskowitz dubbed a "lust for the therapeutic"[30] through self-help books, advice columns in women's magazines, recovery movement support groups, and of course daytime TV talk shows.[31] And according to James Nolan, it also enabled the expansion of the therapeutic gospel into social institutions from schools and hospitals to prisons, courts, and even churches.[32] The great variety of realms that have been shaped by therapeutic discourse furthermore includes the economic sphere of capitalist enterprise.[33] And when Bill Clinton famously declared in 1992 "I feel your pain," it had also reached the highest echelons of the political sphere.[34]

While psychotherapy—whether the traditional dialogue between therapist and client or the revelatory self-talk in groups advocated by the recovery movement—may be experienced as helping and healing, it nevertheless constitutes a form of disciplinary power.[35] Therapeutic discourse legitimates the existing order as normal. It exercises covert social control by advising individuals to police themselves in the name of mental health and to adapt and acquiesce to the hegemonic structures and institutions of the status quo rather than to change their environments. It advocates conformity by pathologizing difference as deviance and depoliticizes discrimination and oppression by addressing them solely on the individual and interpersonal level as the results of psychosocial dysfunction. The discourse of popular psychology not only cultivates social subjects who imagine their lives solely in therapeutic terms, but instead of celebrating human potential, it stresses psychological vulnerabilities. It declares virtually everyone as suffering from one dysfunction or another and hence in need of psychological intervention.[36] The troubling result is that therapeutic subjects are so caught up in self-examination that they are unable to perceive and therefore do not seek to change the larger socio-economic causes of what they subjectively experience as personal problems.[37]

Particularly the recovery movement, which became dominant in the 1990s, encroached upon the private sphere by creating a cultural climate wherein disclosure was not only embraced and encouraged, but also enforced, because in recovery discourse anything not shared is a secret and all secrets are toxic. It transformed the notion of therapy from a talking cure to a life-long survival mechanism, which generated an unprecedented proliferation of therapeutic talk. Or, as Mimi White put it, "the therapeutic ethos is an incitement to talk, to talk constantly, of oneself to others."[38] And since, according to recovery doctrine, someone who admits to an addiction or other dysfunction is a hero, it radically altered the notion of appropriate levels and topics of disclosure.[39] The recovery movement, then, generated ubiquitous and ever more intimate public disclosures, particularly of violent and often sexual victimization experiences. The trauma-and-recovery stories were widely disseminated, not only in the three million support groups modeled on the twelve-step program of Alcoholics Anonymous and attended by some 40 percent of Americans,[40] but also and especially on television talk shows.

*Donahue* had introduced Americans to ordinary people's extraordinary stories, but it was *The Oprah Winfrey Show* that popularized the public performance of victimization, dysfunction, and recovery. With *Oprah* leading the way, talk shows became the TV genre that disseminated popular psychology widely as it provided their overall interpretative framework and some two thirds of programs dealt explicitly with psychotherapeutic subjects.[41] Talk shows could so seamlessly embrace the notion of talk's quasi-mystical cure-all powers because they likewise constitute "a cultural form whose substance and purpose is the production of talk."[42] Talk shows simulate the supposed empathy and nonjudgmental acceptance that guides both the hierarchical dialogue of individual therapy and the group therapy that grew out of the countercultural consciousness-raising and was subsequently reinvented for the mainstream as recovery groups. The tradition of one-on-one therapy is reflected in the presence of a so-called expert on the show, usually the author of a self-help book seeking publicity, who may or may not have had any formal training in either clinical psychology or psychiatry. The group therapy tradition is evoked by the studio audience's participation in the discussion by asking questions and providing their own testimony or confession.

Historically, the emerging bourgeoisie contained all of what it rejected in the notion of madness and through this act of disavowal construed it to serve as the negative foil against which bourgeois culture could define itself as sane and normal. Like the performances of insanity staged in asylumns, most famously, by Jean-Martin Charcot at the Salpêtrière in Paris, and the physical anomalies displayed in dime museums like P. T. Barnum's and in carnival freak shows, talk shows exploit a fearful curiosity about the unknown. Justified by a veneer of public education, grassroots democracy, and therapeutic benevolence, they stage difference from the white, middle-class, male and hetero-normative status quo as deviance, which engenders a fear of nonconformity in audiences. Despite their claim to the contrary, talk shows thus do not enact differences in gender, class, race, and sexual orientation to dispel prejudicial misconceptions and promote tolerance and acceptance, even if this was the core motivation for some of the participants to appear as guests on the show.[43]

Talk shows encode a mode of reception characterized by a potent mix of kitsch-sentimental pity masquerading as empathy, mesmerized fascination, and fearful disgust that reaffirms the spectator's subject position as the sane and normal antithesis of this spectacular parade of Otherness. While the Othering of guests was amplified in trash talk shows like *Jerry Springer* and *Ricki Lake*, it was also enacted on pop-therapeutic shows like *Donahue* and *Oprah*. However, first-generation programs oscillate between casting guests along trauma culture's victim/victimizer dichotomy and merging their subject positions into the pathological Other of therapeutic discourse. Talk shows moreover reinforce the hegemonic notion of normalcy through its embodiment in the figures of host and expert.[44] Last but not least, talk shows reinforce the status quo because they convey the notion that conformity signifies normalcy when they transform victims into survivors and other deviants into individuals whose appearance and behavior no longer transgress the norm.

Despite the focus on individual and interpersonal problems and the absence of their political contexts, talk shows and popular psychology at large are anything but apolitical enterprises. As mass media products, they are principally institutions of dominant power. Hence, the knowledge they produce and seek to naturalize into common sense truths serves to maintain the socioeconomic hegemonies that made them multimillion-dollar enterprises. In order to establish their own as the dominant mode of signification, talk shows must suppress alternative viewpoints, particularly those that aim to change socioeconomic conditions rather than teach the disenfranchised how to cope with oppression and injustice. Even *Donahue*, the most political and liberal show, discounted structural change and advocated working within existing structures.

In their relentless personalization of social conflict, daytime talk shows rely on two core strategies, topical frames and the use of tags. Topics set the parameters for who appears on the show and what can and cannot be talked about. Their ideological character is necessarily covert, but becomes clearer when the conflicts stated in show titles as individual or interpersonal are hypothetically recast in a socio-economic context. For example, an *Oprah* program on "Couples Who Fight over Money" could be retitled "Money, Power, and Gender" or "Gendered Inequality within the Economy."[45] Tags containing the guests' first names and short characterizations of their "issues" are displayed on screen when they are first introduced and repeated intermittently. They likewise obscure the structural determinants within which the respective individual problems and interpersonal conflicts originate. For example, "Jean—wants her husband to get a job" casts as solely interpersonal such inherently socio-economic subjects like unemployment and economic gender inequality, which is reflected in both unequal pay for men and women and asymmetrical power relations in families.[46]

Despite their claims of altruism, public education, and participatory democracy, first-generation talk shows instead reflect and reinforce the disciplining practice of modern psychology:[47] They reinterpret the democratic ideal of the sovereign individual as a victim pariah and/or pathological Other and transmute "conflicts that originate in the material conditions of a society marked by structural inequalities of social power"[48] into individual anomaly and interpersonal conflict. They further the incessant encroachment of the private sphere, because they incite, even enforce, relentless therapeutic talk based on the notion that it will cure all problems.

## Experts and Witnesses Talking

Talk shows reflect the dominant trauma-culture notion that authority for interpreting the past is predominantly grounded in the experience of witnesses. However, these shows also honor the traditional idea that the knowledge of learned experts is superior to that of laypersons.

While guests are known only by their first names, to ensure anonymity and create tele-intimacy, this practice also infantilizes them. And since experts are referred to and addressed by their titles and full names, their position and knowledge are established as superior. The discursive dominance of experts is also subtly established by the fact that, while viewers sometimes hear only the guest's voice as the camera pans reactions of audience members, experts are always visible when they speak.[49] Their preeminence is further enhanced by the fact that, while there are several guests, there is generally only one expert on each program. Their position of knowledge-power is moreover demonstrated by their use of the pseudo-scientific rhetoric of popular psychology at large and of the recovery movement in particular. Most immediately, however, experts are recognizable as representatives of bourgeois hegemony by their professional attire. Juxtaposed to the casual and often unflattering clothing, hairstyle, and makeup of many guests, the experts' appearance indicates their superior class status and educational level. This demonstrates that they are in a position of power to diagnose problems and impose their professional wisdom as cure-all solutions. Moreover, while guests are represented as people with deficiencies, the presence of the experts signifies their competences. The relation between expert and guest is, then, inherently defined as one of superior to inferior. Guests have problems, engage in personal disclosures, and are cast as inept and helpless, while experts provide solutions and answers in the quasi-objective professional rhetoric that largely omits personal information. Experts also remain virtually unchallenged, because the implicitly understood rules of the program prohibit guests or audiences from questioning its underlying assumptions, including expert authority. And although hosts often demonstrate their own omnipotence by interrupting not only guests but also experts or by redirecting the subject of the conversation, they do not question the professional authority of the expert. After all, the experts' function is to validate the shows as therapeutic and educational, and thus the program narrative tautologically imbues them with the authority to do so.[50] Experts wield significant power as they are authorized to define before an audience of millions what constitutes normal or abnormal behavior. Cast in the pseudo-altruistic role of professional helpers who competently sort out the guests' interpersonal problems, experts tend to not only criticize them in a subtly condescending manner, but also participate in the program's ideological mission of generating solutions that are limited to the therapeutic realm and thus reinforce the socio-economic status quo.

Talk shows thus reflect the fact that, as Anthony Giddens argued, expert knowledge is an instrument of power and its omnipresence and persistent invasion of the personal sphere are defining features of technologically advanced, consumer-oriented, anxiety-laden Western society.[51] And Michel Foucault criticized expert commentary as "a type of discourse that has the aim of dominating the object" because "by supplying commentary, one affirms a superior relation to that object."[52] The history of critcizing expertise as a form of dominance can even be traced to Immanuel Kant, who cautioned that one ought not to abdicate thought and reason to the experts.[53] While he famously urged his readers to have the courage to use their own minds and think for themselves, late-modern, techno-capitalist, bureaucratic societies are so thoroughly organized and guided by highly specialized expert systems that most of our daily life is placed under the authority of technical and professional knowledge.[54] When ordinary people became increasingly dependent on the technical skills of certified experts, as Kant well knew, the latter became serious power wielders, if not—to paraphrase the title of Jethro Lieberman's book—modern-day tyrants.[55]

Modern individuals have turned over to the respective experts "the power to make legal, medical, aesthetic, social, even religious decisions"[56] for them. Experts have also taken hold of our daily lives and defined us as incapable of making meaningful decisions without their professional guidance.[57] Even in such personal matters as regulating our emotions and organizing relationships and family life, we are told by vast numbers of mental health professionals—psychiatrists, psychotherapists, counselors, clinical psychologists, clinical social workers, and life coaches—that we cannot do without their advice. They justify the imposition of their expertise onto more and more people by claiming that many, if not most of them, are unable to engage in fulfilling or even functional personal lives without professional assistance.[58] This "monumental increase in the psychologization of modern life," as James Nolan put it, is reflected in the vast increase of both mental health professionals and mental disorders.[59] In the United States, the former exceed the number of librarians, firefighters, mail carriers, dentists, or pharmacists and are outnumbered only by police and lawyers, but by less than two to one in either instance.[60] And between 1980 and 1990 the number of disorders catalogued in the American Psychiatric Association's *Diagnostics and Statistics Manual of Mental Disorders* (*DSM*) increased by almost 300 percent.[61] The use of mental health professionals in the role of expert and the simulation of both individual and group therapy as the organizing paradigm on first-generation talk shows reinforced this cultural trend.

Although talk shows evoke the notion that expert discourse has superior explanatory power, they also reflect the antithetical trend, dominant in popular trauma culture, of a growing distrust in and challenge to expert knowledge in favor of witness testimony. Frequently seating experts in the audience rather than on stage with the host and guests formally identifies them as equal group members rather than superior interpretative authorities. They are also given significantly less overall air time than either guests or host and interrupted by the host more frequently than are the guests. *The Oprah Winfrey Show* of April 14, 1994, about depression and the use of antidepressants, illustrates the notion that witness testimony is equal, if not superior, to expert knowledge. The expert, Dr. Peter Breggin, a leading scientist in biochemistry and psychophar-macology, criticized the widespread use of antidepressants. This resulted in the emotional outburst of many audience members who testified to their experi-ence of depression, confessed their use of antidepressants like Prozac, and praised their benefits. It remains unclear whether this confrontation had been planned in advance by placing an unusually large number of antidepressant users in the audience, or to what extent production staff incited them to dis-agree with the expert before the show or during advertising breaks. In any case, so powerful is the belief in the authenticity of personal experience, partic-ularly of suffering, that the audience members believed that they knew more about the causes of depression and the neurological effects of antidepressants than a leading scientist. And although a second expert, also critical of wide-scale antidepressant use, had the last word in the discussion as the credits rolled, the program established testimony as equal, if not superior, to expert discourse.[62]

The notion that the experiential knowledge of ordinary people generally, and victims in particular, supersedes the professional knowledge of experts is also reflected in the highbrow discourse of American Holocaust memory, as video testimonies, particularly those collected by the Shoah Visual History Foundation, represent survivor-witnesses rather than historians as the pri-mary authority on the genocide. This belief was, moreover, widely dissemi-nated though the self-help industry. For instance, Laura Davis and Ellen Bass prominently stated in *The Courage to Heal*, the bestselling "bible" of the recovery movement: "We must reaffirm that survivors of child sexual abuse are the true experts on their experience. . . . We need to remember that our greatest understanding comes not in listening to professionals, but to the survivors themselves."[63]

The fact that the preeminence of lay testimony over professional expertise was asserted by the two most prominent experts in the recovery movement is rather ironic. More important, it indicates that, although popular psychology discourse sometimes casts expert analysis and witness testimony as antagonistic— as on the *Oprah* show about antidepressants—they are actually symbiotic. The collaboration of experts and witnesses is necessary, because they each rely on the other to authorize their respective representations of victimhood and suffering. Most talk show experts employ both everyday language and the pseudo-scientific rhetoric of popular psychology, with which many guests are in turn familiar from watching other talk show programs, reading self-help books, and attending recovery groups. Therefore experts and witnesses speak largely the same language. And in the talk show universe, the message of the programs is ultimately determined by the host, whose omnipotence trumps the authority of either the guests' witness testimony or the experts' professional expertise.[64] On talk shows, both expert discourse and witness testimony are, then, contained by the overall program narrative. This narrative reflects the inherently counter-oppositional and politically acquiescing therapeutic paradigm for understanding the self and its interaction with the world that dominates popular trauma culture.

And on a more general note, the hegemonic status of much expert discourse, rightly criticized by Kant, Foucault, and Giddens, among others, does not imply that the common-sense knowledge of laypersons, including memories of victimhood, is inherently counter-hegemonic. On the contrary, according to Antonio Gramsci, common sense describes ideas that are taken for granted by the majority, and thus reflect conformity, and provide a unifying master narrative that reinforces the current power structures.[65] Although experts have an inherent interest in reinforcing the socio-economic structures and belief systems that grant them their privileged status, unlike the pseudo-expertise of self-help gurus, scholarly discourse always contains the potential to be critical of dominant ideas, structures, and institutions, not least because its commodity status is negligible.

## Talk as Testimony and Confession

First-generation talk shows enact the autobiographical traditions of testimony and confession. Confession traditionally describes the confidential dialogue between a confessor and a confessee. The confessor is conventionally cast as a guilty but repentant sinner who accuses himself of having engaged in non-sanctioned behavior, including taboo thought. The confessee, or interlocutor, was traditionally a priest but today is more often a therapist, who has been ascribed the capacity to absolve and heal. While confession is overtly cast as an altruistic act on the part of the confessee for the sake of the confessor's soul or mental health, Michel Foucault famously argued that it covertly constitutes a coercion that serves to discipline indocile bodies and minds.[66] According to his much-cited characterization, confession "unfolds within a power relationship, for one does not confess without the presence (or virtual presence) of a partner who is not simply the interlocutor but the authority who requires the confession, prescribes and appreciates it, and intervenes in order to judge, punish, forgive, console, and reconcile."[67] Foucault furthermore argued that, while the discursive power resides not "in the one who knows and answers, but in the one who questions," confession "produces intrinsic modifications in the person who articulates it: it exonerates, redeems, and purifies him; it unburdens him of his wrongs, liberates him, and promises him salvation."[68] And since the obligation to confess is deeply ingrained in Western consciousness, "we no longer perceive it as the effect of a power that constrains us" but, on the contrary, believe that "confession frees"[69]

The act of confessing is regarded as cathartic and therapeutic because it has been ascribed the mystical power of spiritual transformation.[70] This notion was adapted and widely disseminated by the self-help industry and especially the recovery movement, which defined confessional speech as healing because it unburdens the speaker of supposedly toxic secrets.

While their subject matter varies, the secrets of confession are inherently of an intimate, and often a sexual, nature. In fact, according to Foucault's classic analysis, "from the Christian penance to the present day, sex was a privileged theme of confession" as confessional speech joined truth and sex "through the obligatory and exhaustive expression of an individual secret."[71] The dominance of sexuality as the subject of confessional speech has been prominently enacted in the first decade of the new millennium on *Jerry Springer*, *Maury Povich*, and *Montel Williams*, as these talk shows primarily broadcast the sexual secrets of their guests. However, the realm of sexuality explored is largely conventional and heterosexual, and the conflicts primarily arise from cheating, contested paternities, and unusual couplings (for example, a grandmother who slept with her granddaughter's boyfriend).

Foucault furthermore argued that in the nineteenth century the ritual of confession was adapted according to the parameters of science and transposed from the religious to the therapeutic realm.[72] As the latter expanded its sphere of knowledge-power beyond victimizers and other sinners to victims, it dubiously merged the subject positions of victim and victimizer into the pathological Other and their respective illocutionary acts into therapeutic talk.[73]

The fusion of confession and testimony was facilitated by the fact that they share a number of characteristics. Both constitute autobiographical narratives that are traditionally presented orally and narrate behavior that is not sanctioned by convention and has therefore not been communicated to others. According to both the religious and the therapeutic understanding, this motivated silence constitutes a secret that must be revealed, and hence both realms reflect the incessant invasion of the private and intimate sphere for the decided purpose of disciplining indocile individuals. Furthermore, given the therapeutic incitement to talk and the intimate nature of the subject matter, Foucault's notion that in confession "one goes about telling, with the greatest precision, what is most difficult to tell"[74] likewise pertains to testimony. And while the truth that emerges in confession "is corroborated by the obstacles and resistances it has had to surmount in order to be formulated,"[75] analogously the high degree of emotion displayed in testimony is commonly taken to signify both an inherent difficulty in expressing experiences of victimization and suffering and the subjective truth of the testimony.

Last but not least, the increasing fusion of confession and testimony was facilitated by the fact that both speech acts have signifying power in the religious and the juridical spheres. Both repentant sinners and legal defendants confess their respective offences. In fact, the subject positions of sinner and defendant and the religious and juridical practice of confession were merged in juridico-religious torture. According to Foucault, "when it is not spontaneous or dictated by some internal imperative, the confession is wrung from a person by violence or threat" and hence torture has accompanied confession like a shadow.[76] Testimony is likewise employed in both legal and religious contexts. Witnesses testify in the court of law, and, in the tradition of American Christian fundamentalism, testimony also has religious significance. As Jane Shattuc writes, "the original religious sense of the practice means the public testimony given by Christian witnesses to Christ and his saving power. Within evangelicalism the act of standing up and speaking one's religious experience is a social obligation—done without regard for personal safety and comfort."[77]

The conflation of the confessional and the testimonial narrative modes was reflected in the mistaken designation in both academic and popular contexts of first-generation programs as confessional talk shows. However, this categorization only pertains to the post-1990 trash talk programs, which discarded recovery rhetoric to a greater (*Ricki Lake* and *Jerry Springer*) or lesser (*Maury Povich* and *Montel Williams*) extent and primarily broadcast the spectacular confessions of victimizers. The secrets disclosed on first-generation shows were primarily the testimony of victims. Furthermore, Foucault's argument that "confession has spread its effects far and wide," permeating the realms of "justice, medicine, education, family relationships, and love relations,"[78] pertains equally, if not more so, to testimony. Today, it is not primarily perpetrators and other sinners who confess their own crimes and sins, but, as the popularity of first-generation talk shows and misery memoirs indicates, it is victims who testify to their own suffering and the sins and crimes of others. In short, we have not only become a singularly confessing society, as Foucault argued,[79] but in the era of the witness we have also created a culture of testimony.

Despite their similarities, testimonial and confessional narratives also exhibit significant differences, which their dubious conflation obscures. Not only was testimony introduced into the public sphere much more recently, but the two different speech acts can also be distinguished according to whose interest they primarily serve. Confession is overtly self-serving in both religious and therapeutic contexts, as the admission of non-sanctioned behavior provides cathartic relief to the confessor, who remains largely unaware of confession's covert disciplinary function. And while in the juridical context confession also serves the public interest as it contributes to the conviction of the defendant, confession is motivated by self-interest, namely to reduce the severity of the punishment. Testimony, however, is predominantly given for the altruistic purpose of doing public good. In the legal context, where the concept originates, testimony both serves the conviction of the perpetrator and provides a public warning to prevent the repetition of a similar crime and hence the potential suffering of other victims. Testimony has only come to be understood as also serving the speaker when it was dubiously merged with confession by ascribing to it confession's characteristic of cathartic relief through revealing secrets and the curative capacity of therapeutic talk.

Testimony and confession furthermore differ with respect to their generation of truth claims. Witnesses know and can testify before the public to the subjective truth of their experience, which constitutes the privileged notion of truth in trauma culture. However, truth in confession is established interactively because, according to Foucault, it is not taken to reside "solely in the subject who, by confessing would reveal it wholly formed" but is rather established "in two stages: present but incomplete, blind to itself, in the one who spoke, it could only reach completion in the one who assimilated and recorded it."[80] Testimony and confession also differ because witnesses need a large audience for their words to constitute testimony while confessors only require an individual interlocutor. Most important, however, the merging of both modes in therapeutic discourse obscures the fact that they constitute the speech acts of individuals who occupy the distinct subject positions of victim and victimizer. While the rhetoric of testimony-cum-victim-talk is paradigmatic for first-generation talk shows, the post-1990s trash talk shows are dominated by the even more spectacular confessions of individuals who are no longer defined according to the trauma culture binary of victim and perpetrator but rather merged into the figure of the freak Other.

# 6

## Trauma Camp

"I was hired to be a ringleader in a circus."

—Jerry Springer, on *Larry King Live*[1]

$M$ass culture products like popular literature, commercial cinema, and television programs exhibit a propensity for formulas because media corporations seek to duplicate profitable formats. The attempt to repeat the success of the talk shows hosted by Phil Donahue, Sally Jessy Raphael, Geraldo Rivera, and particularly Oprah Winfrey thus gave rise to a second wave of shows in the early 1990s. As popular psychology constituted the organizing paradigm for first-generation shows, guests were inherently defined as dysfunctional Others, who confirmed the viewer's normalcy. Moreover, at times they exhibited a penchant for spectacle, such as the propensity for drag queens on *Geraldo* or *Oprah*'s little red wagon of animal fat. Even Phil Donahue, who is considered the most progressive and serious host, dressed up in a skirt for a program on drag and in a bald "wig" for a show on baldness.[2] He also produced a program on infantilism which "opened with the adult male panelists dressed as infants and shown sitting in a crib, high chair, and playpen"[3] and another show on "children with progeria, a disfiguring disease that 'ages' children, turning eight- and nine-year-olds into tiny, hunched men and women."[4] Despite the pseudo-scientific rhetoric and claim to public education, sometimes even the first-generation programs presented freak spectacles.

The new shows, including *Ricki Lake* and *Jerry Springer*, further upped the ante when they replaced "the wacky transvestites, the bizarre tales of incest, the tearful AIDS victims" with the even more spectacular characters from America's "trailer parks and ghettos," as Richard Zogling put it in a *Time* article.[5] Although the second-generation shows largely discarded the popular psychology tropes of their predecessors in favor of trash talk spectacles, they still employed a token number of therapeutic clichés, particularly the toxicity of secrets, to disguise the exploitative parading of freaks, and because parody shares some features with the ridiculed original. The new shows reinforced the reduction of interpersonal conflict to sexual matters and confirmed the idea that sexuality is the primary subject of confession because of the average nine disclosures per show five were of a sexual nature. However, four of the participants' revelations still "revolved around an addiction, compulsion, disorder, or health issue" and thus evoked therapeutic and testimonial speech.[6] Furthermore, Ricki Lake invoked therapeutic rhetoric when she repeatedly used the formulaic phrase "We're here to help you," while both Lake and Springer concluded their shows with a pop psychology platitude, termed "final thought" on *Springer*. Last but not least, the so-called ambush disclosure constitutes a sensationalist extension of the therapeutic doctrine that secrets are toxic. It became a staple on the new shows until the taping of *Jenny Jones* on March 6, 1995 when a guest, Jon Schmitz, was "ambushed" with the revelation that his secret admirer was another man, Scott Amedure, and three days later, Schmitz killed Amedure.[7]

The new generation of talk shows, then, shared the therapeutic logic of fusing trauma culture's antagonists of victim and perpetrator into the pathological Other. However, they also revived the tradition of so-called dime museums and carnival side shows and cast the participants as spectacular freaks. While the first-generation shows advocated therapeutic transformations for the dysfunctional, in the universe of the televised freak show guests are largely represented as unredeemable, and to this end their difference from the norm is both embellished and redefined as deviance. Unlike the earlier programs they parody, trash talk shows no longer simulate talking cures. Instead, conflicts are enacted in exaggerated camp theatrics because the new shows seek to be, as Springer put it, "interesting with the sound off."[8]

Pre-1990s shows overtly professed altruism and empathy as their dominant reception mode. However, covertly the programs invited consumers to engage in kitsch sentimentality and condescending pity. While kitsch provides pleasure to spectators as it enables them to relish their own second-tear-jerking emotional arousal, pity flatters them because it establishes the audience as socially and morally superior to the pitied Other. Trash talk shows, on the other hand, parody the absurdity of their predecessors' simulated seriousness and faux empathic altruism. According to Jane Shattuc, "the methods of the earlier programs are so excessively overplayed that they highlight the contradictions of any talk show . . . that unctuously attempts to help disadvantaged people while it simultaneously profits from the act."[9] She furthermore argues that parody was intentionally introduced into the shows by producers and hosts[10] and that "this ironic reading may be the preferred meaning, in that the [talk show] form has become so self-conscious that it overwhelms the pretensions to realism."[11] When victims-cum-survivors gave way to freaks, and the talking cure pretense to blatant spectacle, the sentimental pity of the first-generation shows was replaced by the ethically even more dubious ironically detached, utterly unempathic, and latently voyeuristic *Schadenfreude* of camp parody.[12]

With the rise of the second wave of shows, the older programs saw a significant decline in viewer ratings, due to the increased competition. While at the height of her popularity, in 1990, some nineteen million viewers tuned in to Oprah's talking cure every weekday in sixty-four countries,[13] even the "queen of talk" saw her ratings decline by 7 percent total and 11 percent in her target audience of women aged eighteen to forty-nine by May 1994. By November of that year, the show had lost 11 percent in total ratings, followed by *Geraldo*'s decline of 12 percent, *Sally*'s loss of 13 percent, and *Donahue*'s drop by 21 percent.[14] While most of the about two dozen new shows launched in the early to mid 1990s failed, a few significantly increased their market share: *Jerry Springer* by 25 percent, *Montel Williams* by 27 percent, *Jenny Jones* by an astonishing 88 percent, and *Ricki Lake* even by 108 percent.

Despite her loss of 11 percent in viewer ratings, for the time being, *Oprah* nevertheless remained by far the most watched talk show with a 9.7 rating versus the 5.4 rating of second-placing *Ricki Lake* in fall 1994.[15] In September 1995, that is, immediately before the year's ratings and advertising rates were calculated and just prior to the anti-talk-show media campaign organized by Republican pundit and former Secretary of Education William Bennett, Winfrey publicly pledged that her show would change course and provide spiritual uplift to viewers. Despite this attempt to retain the leading position of her program and regain some of her lost market share by product differentiation, *The Oprah Winfrey Show* would eventually lose its number-one position.

After *Jerry Springer* established its trademark camp parodic theatrics and successfully marketed its freak show spectacles to the new demographic of college students,[16] the show doubled its ratings between November 1996 and 1997, reaching 6.7 million.[17] And after another vast increase in viewer ratings of 183 percent between 1997 and 1998,[18] the show topped even *Oprah* and became the most watched talk show."[19] After *Phil Donahue* and *Ricki Lake* went off the air in 1996 and 2004, respectively, *Oprah* and *Springer* became the paradigmatic shows. While the kitsch-sentimental stories with redemptive endings promoted by Winfrey positioned her program at the higher end of the intra-generic hierarchy, Springer adapted the successful formula of sex and violence to the talk show genre and occupied the lower end of the spectrum. Described by viewers as "a carnival show for weirdoes" and "a circus of idiots,"[20] *Springer* took the desire for spectacle exploited by *Ricki Lake* and "the angst and anger of the poor and uneducated white male of *Morton Downey Jr.*" and transformed them "into a single highly profitable form of television, a carnival of conflict with no pretense of public information or therapeutic 'solutions.'"[21]

The producers and hosts of the new shows sought to differentiate their media products from the competition by counter-programming, particularly against *Oprah*'s and *Donahue*'s core audience of women in their thirties and forties, and thus marketed their shows to women aged eighteen to thirty-four.

Initially the most successful in taking *Sally Jessy Raphael*'s boastful claim to have started the first family feuds[22] and *Geraldo Rivera*'s sleaze element to new heights (or lows) was *Ricki Lake*, which went into national syndication in 1993. Its history "undercuts the industry discourse that the new tabloid shows grew out of audience demand or popular tastes" because the show was deliberately "engineered to capitalize on the youth market and the growth in cable channels."[23] It even tapped into a whole new demographic as 22 percent of its viewers were aged twelve to seventeen and, even more disturbingly, some 600,000 viewers were under the age of twelve.[24] Hosted by the actress who had starred in John Waters' camp cult film *Hairspray* in 1988, the show's no-holds-barred format of spectacle for its own sake was phenomenally successful. In its first season, in the fall of 1993, the show was broadcast on 212 stations.[25] *Ricki Lake* introduced the idea that trash talk shows parodied the first-generation programs and also evoked the old-time carnival freak shows as Lake orchestrated the participants' emotional, and at times physical, combat like a circus ringmaster.[26]

The triumph of *Ricki Lake* changed the daytime talk show industry as its campy freak show format became the new formula. Not only did old shows became more confrontational, but a multitude of new programs, including *Carnie, Tempest, Charles Perez, Gabrielle, Danny!, Richard Bey*, and *Morton Downey, Jr.*, were "trying to out-Ricki Ricki."[27] Their attention-grabbing format reflected two technological developments: the invention of the remote control and the growth of cable channels. The simultaneous availability of two or even three talk shows and the possibility of easily switching channels dramatically changed the basic mode of talk show viewing and TV consumption at large. According to a 1990 *TV Guide*, even when only 70 percent of talk show viewers had a remote control, 30 percent said that they liked to zap between different shows.[28] The new programs adopted the channel surfing "talk soup" consumer as their implied viewer and hence created programs that were both instantly eye-catching and repetitious, because they sought to stop consumers from flipping to the next channel but also had to enable them to easily follow the program from any point of entry.

As the new shows' trademark speed increased to break-neck levels, the number of guests per show multiplied from the traditional three or four to six and even nine during some forty-eight minutes of show time (twelve minutes are taken up by advertising breaks). The expert was largely eliminated, host, guests, and studio audience became younger, and the over-arching themes were replaced with brief, sound-bite conflicts usually unrelated but for their evocation of sex. As the new shows replaced the rhetoric of popular psychology with "street English," profanities, and shouting matches, all pretense of social consciousness gave way to camp spectacle, and conflict rather than resolution became the focus. However, since most swear words are censored on American television, guests were increasingly encouraged to act out their conflicts and engage in exaggerated displays of emotion and the genre-defining "money shot" of people swinging at each other and breaking chairs. The fact that "break-away prop chairs were used because they splintered more easily"[29] constitutes an apt metaphor for the staged theatricality of the shows' nonfictional conflicts. While studio and TV audiences continued to be predominantly women, the share of male consumers increased, and audiences at large tended to be under thirty.[30] The widely held notion that the new shows are aimed at edgy, streetwise and aggressive spectators who enjoy precisely "the obscenity-laced yelling matches and the bar brawls"[31] as they watch the "televised coliseum where the screaming battles of the lower class are carried out as a voyeuristic spectacle"[32] was confirmed by comments of actual studio audience members. As a farmer from Oregon put it, "It's white trailer trash! I love it!" And an eighty-one-year-old grandmother, who attended a taping with her granddaughter, said "I hope they fight. They better fight."[33]

With the ever-increasing popularity of trash talk, criticism from both the political right and left gained momentum. The right was most prominently represented by William Bennett's campaign seeking to convey to advertisers that talk shows were reinforcing deviance and moral decay among its lower-class consumers and hence an unsuitable vehicle for promoting their products. Liberal media outlets like *Ms.*, *Nation*, and *The New Yorker*, as well as *Time*, *Newsweek*, and the *Washington Post* extended the Frankfurt School critique of mass culture as a core constituent of capitalist ideology. They criticized the total lack of social consciousness and the exploitation of the oppressed in the patronizing and stereotyped portrayals of the predominantly lower-class guests.[34] Nevertheless, "the nation's appetite for talk, or rather emotional wrestling which it increasingly became,"[35] seemed endless. At the height of their popularity, between 1989 and 1997, viewers in most American markets could chose between fifteen and nineteen talk shows on any weekday.[36] And by 1995, they had ended the nearly fifteen-year reign of soap operas as the most popular genre of daytime television.[37] It signaled an audience preference for real-life rather than fictional psychomelodramas that would also be reflected in the exceedingly popular genre of reality shows that would come to dominate American and European television in the new millennium, after the trendsetting launch of *Big Brother* in 2000.

This chapter explores, then, how the victim talk rhetoric and popular psychology tropes of first-generation shows were both parodied by vast exaggeration and merged with the reinvention of the carnival freak show for the television age. I also argue that the trash talk spectacles invited consuming the pain of others via the unethical and politically anaesthetizing camp gaze.

## The Camp Gaze

The concept of camp helps to illuminate the audience reception invited by the post-1990 daytime talk shows.[38] In her classic essay, Susan Sontag locates camp primarily in the artifact itself.[39] However, she does acknowledge the significance of reception when she characterizes camp as "a way of looking at things" and hence "a way of seeing the world" and speaks of camp as "a quality discoverable in objects" and the transformative power of "the Camp eye."[40] And Moe Meyer argues that recent analyses of the subject indicate a "shift of focus away from the conventional fixation with the object surface to the process with which the object is handled."[41] Camp, then, does not designate the object itself but rather a particular gaze or mode of reception. Andrew Ross termed this the "camp effect" and argued that it is created when objects "of a much earlier mode of production, which has lost its power to dominate cultural meanings, becomes available in the present, for redefinition according to contemporary codes of taste."[42] Camp, according to Ross, "involves a celebration, on the part of cognoscenti, of the alienation, distance, and incongruity reflected in the very process by which unexpected values can be located in some obscure or exorbitant object."[43] Meyer critiqued Ross's notion of discovering a meaning apparently hidden all along in an object and argued that audiences attribute rather than discover the new camp meaning.[44] And despite Sontag's preemptive assertion that "not everything can be seen as Camp" as "it's not *all* in the eye of the beholder,"[45] Meyer seems to reverse her priority in locating camp predominantly in the object itself and instead considers it to be solely a mode of reception that is potentially applicable to all acts of signification. However, the features of an artifact do restrict the range of possible interpretations. Meaning is constructed in complex, historically and culturally varying interactions between what artifact makers sought to encode and how audiences—in either the same or a different culture—decode the artifact, that is to say, what meanings they attribute to it.

Camp, then, constitutes an aesthetic convention that invites audiences to look at objects, including media products, in a particular way. Artifacts that invite such a decoding are characterized by excess and exaggeration, ostentation and flamboyance, affectedness and overt theatricality. They self-consciously celebrate bad taste. As Sontag put it, "it's good because it's awful" constitutes "the ultimate Camp statement."[46] Camp objects thus intentionally offend dominant aesthetic and moral conventions. Ross argued that camp emerged as a mode of reception when, after becoming obsolete and obscure and thus lingering in a sort of archival limbo, artifacts reentered the cycle of cultural production as meaning that had not been intended by their makers was attributed to them. However, once camp was established as a sophisticated private code for insiders, or as Sontag termed them, *cognoscenti*, it was then increasingly also inscribed into particular artifacts as a potential or even the primary mode of reception. In her analysis of the audience reception of the TV soap opera *Dynasty*, Jane Feuer, for example, argued that "very early on its producers were aware of camp decodings and intended to encode them in the text by devising outrageous plots."[47] Similarly, the fact that ratings for *Jerry Springer* "only rose dramatically when, together with his producer, Richard Dominick, a former *National Enquirer* editor, he decided to aim at the college crowd"[48] implicitly suggests that Springer and Dominick successfully incorporated camp interpretations into the show. Sontag distinguishes between these two types of camp objects, considering only the unencoded or naïve one to constitute true camp.

Like all ironic interpretations, the camp gaze constitutes a more complex cognitive operation than the straight reception encoded into therapeutic shows as the dominant and into trash talk shows as a secondary mode. It may have been this cognitively sophisticated operation that led Sontag to characterize camp as indicative of "snob taste."[49] Moreover, her favoring of naïve camp may signify that she understood that a gaze not encoded into the artifact by its makers or distributors constitutes an even more creative and erudite cognitive operation on the part of the audience than does the decoding of an intended meaning. The notion of the camp gaze has elevated the consumption of artifacts on the lower end of the popular culture scale—such as the made-for-TV *Batman* series and television shows like *CHiPs*, *Gilligan's Island*, and *Fantasy Island*—to signify intellectually and aesthetically sophisticated connoisseurship.

The connoisseurs of camp seek to define their own "aristocratic" taste as not only superior to that of popular culture's implied lower-class spectator but especially as surpassing the bourgeois' savoring of the canon's aesthetic finesse. And they displayed ingeniousness coupled with the utmost arrogance when they invented an exclusive, private code accessible only to the initiated. Sontag wrote that she was "strongly drawn to Camp, and almost as strongly offended by it."[50] One is indeed rather torn between repulsion for the condescending and discriminatory Othering of the *ignoranti* and fascination with the audacity that the *cognoscenti* employed to ascribe themselves the status of those in the know, based simply on their capacity to decipher a secret code that they had invented in the first place.

## The Populist Politics of Camp

The camp gaze encoded into trash talk shows as their primary reception mode does not only define a subset of viewers, but also and especially the participants as *ignoranti*, in order to authorize the consumption of their conflicts as a freak show spectacle for the *cognoscenti's* callous entertainment. While guests are not necessarily dupes and their participation is based on a "complex dialectic in which both consent and exploitation feed into each other,"[51] they are cast in the role of *ignoranti* on the show and required to act accordingly. Two young women who participated as guests on *Ricki Lake* reported that show staff wanted "to get you to say things you would never, ever say"[52] and "they kept telling you that you had to get real mean and vicious when you came on the show, and if you couldn't do that, then you couldn't go on.'"[53] Their comments also indicate that the relationship between participants and the talk show industry is marked by vastly unequal degrees of power. The women felt threatened and coerced when they were told in a stream of phone calls prior to the show that they could no longer back out, as these phone conversations constituted a binding agreement to participate, and when they had to sign legal documents mandating "that they could not talk badly about the show to anyone."[54]

While Sontag conceptualized camp as "disengaged, depoliticized—or at least apolitical" because "it neutralizes moral indignation,"[55] Meyer argued that in queer contexts camp does function politically, specifically as a liberating discourse, precisely because of its disregard of and challenge to bourgeois morals and norms. However, he concedes that because of its "piggy-backing upon the dominant order's monopoly on the authority of signification," camp appears "on the one hand, to offer a transgressive vehicle yet, on the other, simultaneously invokes the specter of dominant ideology within its practice, appearing, in many instances, to actually reinforce the dominant order."[56] Contrary to Sontag's notion that camp is not only apolitical but also amoral, due to its disregard for dominant bourgeois morality and its focus on style over content, camping the pain of others on trash talk shows is anything but an apolitical and amoral endeavor.

Camp is encoded as a possible mode of reception, or even the dominant one, into many mass media products, because it extends the function of popular culture as today's opium for the masses to the cultural elite as it imbues the politically anaesthetizing consumption of mass media products with the appearance of intellectual sophistication. Despite their counter-cultural pretenses, trash talk shows reinforce the sexist, racist, classist, and homophobic status quo as the desirable norm as they transform the pain of others into campy entertainment spectacles and suppress critical thought about socio-economic injustice and oppression. Chuck Kleinhans analogously argued that such canonical embodiments of camp aesthetics as John Waters's movies *Hairspray*, *Cry Baby*, *Serial Mom*, and *Polyester*, for instance, or the solo club performances of drag queen Divine, which frequently included heavy anti-woman humor, "can be easily recuperated into the existing system of sexist oppression."[57] Other popular culture staples like the World Wrestling Federation and gangsta rap also define themselves in opposition to dominant aesthetics and evoke camp in their celebration of spectacle and the hyperbolic embodiment of masculine stereotypes or "exaggerated he-man-ness."[58] Like trash talk shows, these mass media products reflect an interest in reinforcing the socio-economic status quo as they depict the transgression of the norm solely as spectacles of madness and mayhem perpetrated by devious Others. Similarly, the only character on second-generation talk shows to ever challenge the existing order is a deviant and dangerous villain—whether rapist, child abuser, wife batterer, misogynist, cheating spouse, bad mother, out-of-control teen, bulimic/anorexic or obese woman. Not only are there no revolutionaries, but there are not even any reformers in the talk show universe, precisely because challenging the existing order is inherently defined as a deviant transgression, if not as an outright criminal act. The inevitable happy ending consists in disciplining the indocile elements and reestablishing the status quo.

The ideology generated when dominant knowledge-power undermines the public sphere through the Trojan horse of popular culture was termed "authoritarian populism" by Stuart Hall. He argued that, in the *Sun*, Britain's leading tabloid, for instance, "populist interests in individuals, personalities, sex, scandal, violence, sport and amusement are presented in a lively, identifiable language and format which ideologically layers a heterosexual, male, white, conservative, capitalist world view."[59] For all their in-your-face affronting of bourgeois aesthetics, then, such popular culture embodiments as tabloids, gangsta rap, the World Wrestling Federation, and trash talk shows actually promote social conformity, because they encourage the disenfranchised to embrace the very order that subjugates them. Claiming counter-cultural status, they parasitically infiltrate and weaken anti-hegemonic discourse by co-opting its egalitarian rhetoric to undermine and diffuse its politically liberatory potential.

However, the anti-establishment rhetoric of trash talk shows has been taken at face value not only by conservative critics, who loathe popular culture because they consider it indicative of aesthetically and morally inferior "cultural rot," but also by liberal intellectuals. In particular, postmodern feminists, who also hailed Madonna as their new icon in the 1990s, embraced talk shows as an expression of authentic women's culture.[60] The liberal advocates neglected the conformity-inducing and politically acquiescing nature of talk shows as well as their commodity status when they celebrated the genre, and popular culture at large, as counter-hegemonic. But neither the fact that some postmodern ironists have celebrated mass media commodities nor the fact that the political right has so persistently demonized them can hide their inherent counter-oppositional status.

## A Carnival of Freaks

Since trash talk shows market the breaking of taboos as a radical, no-holds-barred anti-establishment act, they not only invite the camp gaze but also invoke the carnival's simulation of anarchic equality. Obliquely analogous to the appropriation of the Holocaust in American culture to minimize the crimes in U.S. history, trash talk shows disseminate traditional American values by showing their negation as a spectacle of freak Otherness. According to Mikhail Bakhtin, historically, carnival embodied a utopian urge for an egalitarian social order.[61] However, Umberto Eco has cautioned against Bakhtin's notion because the rule breaking during carnival does not signify the elimination of hierarchies and oppression, but only their temporary suspension.[62] Authorized by the dominant powers, the pseudo-egalitarian carnival reinforced existing hegemonies by co-opting resistance and cathartically diffusing the revolutionary potential inherent in systems of oppression. Like trash talk shows and other popular culture products today, it thus functioned as an essential part of the bread-and-circuses formula of domination.

Before the exhibition of human abnormalities began to be considered inhumane in the early twentieth century,[63] freak shows were common. Freaks were defined by and reduced to their difference from the norm in appearance or behavior, because the attraction of freak shows lay precisely in the sensationalist display of spectacular Otherness. Exhibitors therefore sought to emphasize the freaks' difference, not only through extravagant costumes and the commentary of dime museum "professors" or circus barkers, but also by casting their difference as deviance when they questioned the freaks' status as fellow human beings and hence their qualification for moral and ethical behavior.[64] To audiences of both the old-time freak shows and their modern-day reinvention as trash talk shows, the fear of the unknown provides an exhilarating spectacle when experienced from a safe distance. And the inferiority they ascribe to the extraordinary and unfamiliar allows spectators to unempathically consume as entertainment the display of difference as titillating Otherness. Freak shows employed not only this exotic mode of representation, but also an aggrandized mode that overtly deemphasized abnormality and focused on how the differently bodied would cope with the difficulties of everyday life.[65] However, the spectators' gaze at others displayed as freaks is always voyeuristic and exploitative. Even in the pseudo-scientific discourse of the faux-elegant dime museum, the overtly aggrandizing mode largely provided a superficial cover for the exotic mode. When the display of Otherness was transposed to the seedy carnival sideshow,[66] the pseudo-scientific rhetoric of educating the public and representations that alternated between the aggrandized and exotic mode gave way to pure exploitation of the freak as spectacle. This transformation was echoed when the representation of Otherness through the pseudo-scientific rhetoric of popular psychology on first-generation talk shows was replaced by the purely exotic mode on trash talk shows. Like their carnival sideshow predecessors, these shows have the ill repute of sleaze and seediness because they discarded the veneer of respectability and overtly employed the exotic mode to represent difference as freakish deviance.

According to Andrea Dennett, there were five types of performers at historical carnival sideshows: Natural freaks like midgets and Siamese twins were born with physical abnormalities. Self-made freaks like excessively tattooed people created and cultivated their freakdom. Snake charmers, mesmerists and hypnotists, sword swallowers and fire-eaters engaged in freakish performances. Non-Western freaks were exhibited as exotic curiosities usually labeled "savages" or "cannibals" and billed as African. Lastly, there were the fake or gaffed freaks who only simulated their freakishness, like Siamese twins who were not attached or the "Armless Wonder" whose arms were hidden beneath the costume.[67] On today's televised freak shows, which likewise revel in sensationalistic hyperbole and superlatives in exhibiting the "tallest, smallest, fattest, ugliest, or hairiest—and of course the most extraordinary or original,"[68] they reappear, with some variation.

Like the carnival sideshow performers of yesteryear, trash talk TV participants are represented as the dominant order's fascinating yet frightening Other largely through markers of physical difference. On talk shows, these markers include obese bodies, missing teeth, excessive makeup, big hair, and clothing which "tends toward the inappropriate—too tight, too skimpy, too polyester."[69] As most shows provide makeup personnel, the often garish, nearly clown-like appearance of participants is at least in part determined by the shows' objective to make them appear as irredeemably Other.[70] Trash talk TV also seeks to heighten the participants' difference by inciting them to engage in performances that are considered freakish because they violate dominant social norms. Production staff seeks to provoke nonconformist behavior on air, most infamously the tirades of profanities and the fights, through heavy pre-show coaching. They also try to get participants to reveal spectacular details about their own or others' lives that likewise transgress the bourgeois norm, particularly with regard to sexual behavior. Carnival freak shows had already titillated the audience's imaginations with hints of deviant sexuality among such incongruous couples as the fat lady and her skeletal husband, the bearded lady (who may not be a lady after all) and her spouse, or Siamese twins and their partners. Talk shows significantly expanded on the voyeuristic appeal of transgressive sexuality by explicitly and extensively discussing subjects such as homosexuality, bisexuality, group sex, swinging couples, interracial sex, overt and covert promiscuity, sex of transsexuals and transvestites, the lack of sex among the obese, and sex between partners with a significant age difference or very dissimilar sex drives. Like their carnival sideshow predecessors, trash talk shows seek to heighten the guests' tabooed difference and turn it into a frightening yet fascinating deviance to create sensationalist spectacles. The potent blend of fear and fascination guarantees high viewer ratings, not least since casting participants as freaks allows and invites audiences to engage in the camp gaze and enjoy the display of Otherness as entertainment from a position marked by a sense of their own moral superiority.

*Ricki Lake* and *Jerry Springer* in particular have frequently been accused of hiring actors as participants or coaching guests to the extent of having them enact scripts verbatim.[71] While producers sought to reinforce the nonfiction status of their programs by asserting that guests and their stories are subject to verification, according to Jane Shattuc, the shows "have a voracious appetite for anyone willing [to] go 'onstage'" and "if a show needs a certain kind of guest, the bookers will look the other way if they have the sense that a potential guest is a poseur."[72] However, rather than generating outrage at this violation of the autobiographical pact and revival of the carnival tradition of the fake freak, the debate over fake guests may even have increased the popularity of trash talk shows. It seems to have added a kind of game element, as home and studio audience are trying to tell fake guests apart from real ones. Some viewers even apply to be guests themselves, in order to see whether they could get away with telling tall tales on air or would be found out as fakes.[73]

Like their carnival predecessors, talk shows furthermore exhibit self-made freaks like "George Reiger, Jr., whose body is covered with tattoos of 311 Disney characters."[74] More dubious is casting anorexic and bulimic women as self-made freaks, or someone like "Cindy Hess, whose multiple breast augmentation surgeries have left her with a bra size of 115-DDD and saline breasts that weigh fifteen pounds each"[75] since both cosmetic surgery and eating disorders are encouraged by the patriarchal notion of female beauty. A *Maury Povich* show, for instance, not only displayed several anorexic women, each weighing between seventy and eighty-seven pounds, but had all of them appear in spaghetti-strapped tank dresses to heighten the freakishness of their bodies.[76] Even worse, rather than admonishing the mutilation predominantly of women's bodies by plastic surgery or the lack of universal health care, both *Maury Povich* and *Sally Jessy Raphael* cast as a self-made freak a woman who had tried to remove her infected silicone implants by cutting her breasts open with a razor blade because she could not afford an operation.[77]

Last but not least, talk shows also obliquely revived the tradition of the exotic freak. Although both race and class are suppressed by framing topics "as if all races and classes might be affected by them in the same degree and with the same frequency,"[78] racist and classist stereotypes covertly permeate the shows. In casting class and race solely as individual experiences through the dubious I-see-no-color/class notion of political correctness, talk shows repress the history of racial oppression, capitalism's inherent division into classes, the material and lived experiences of race and class, and the ethical imperative that any society should seek to establish equality. Furthermore, not only are bodies signifying race or class ubiquitous on trash talk shows, but the programs also increasingly merge the categories. While not all poor and minimally educated guests are ethnic minorities, virtually all ethnic minority guests are lower class to amplify their status as exotic Others. The guests' differences in body shape, hairstyle, makeup, clothing, language use, or behavior is further exaggerated and transformed into deviance by its juxtaposition to the middle-class norm embodied by the host and, if present, the expert.[79]

The ostentatious camp theatricality of trash talk shows could hardly differ more from the simulation of popular psychology's pseudo-scientific rhetoric and the kitsch-sentimental pity masquerading as empathy that dominated the first-generation programs they parodied. Nevertheless, both versions of talk TV generated and disseminated knowledge that is inherently conformist and reinforces existing relations of power. Moreover, on both pseudo-therapeutic and trash talk shows, guests are economically exploited, because they are ascribed a use value and therefore treated as commodities. "Trash," then, is not only the bigoted designation of marginalized groups on the lowest end of the socioeconomic spectrum, but also aptly, if inadvertently, signifies the status of guests on both kinds of shows after their short-term use value has been expended and they are discarded like useless objects.

The genre of daytime talk shows constitutes the core embodiment of popular trauma culture on television. First-generation shows employed the rhetoric of victim talk and demonstrated that claims of victimhood and suffering multiplied and became ever more spectacular as they were ascribed the status of ultimate moral capital. They pathologized the pain of others and, suppressing the notion of political change, proposed transforming individuals by therapeutic intervention as the cure-all solution to the injustices inherent in the capitalist, hetero-normative, patriarchal and bourgeois status quo. The programs also relied on the melodramatic good-versus-evil plot structure embodied by the core characters of the victim-cum-survivor and the (largely absent) perpetrator. As their overt *raison d'être* was to initiate the transformation of helpless victims into strong survivors who would overcome their suffering, first-generation shows also reflected the transition from the victim to the survivor as the core character of popular trauma culture. They encoded kitsch sentiment as their primary mode of reception and reinforced the pervasive notion that ordinary life is dominated by the constant but ineffable threat of extreme danger.

Second-generation shows further merged the trauma culture figures of victim and victimizer from the pathological Other into the deviant freak. They reflected the increasing competition for preeminent victim status paradigmatic of contemporary culture by depicting participants who enacted victim talk as shouting matches and exploited them further by transforming them into a commodity when they cast the conflicts as freak show spectacles. Last but not least, trash talk programs unethically invited the ironically distanced and therefore unempathic camp gaze as the appropriate audience reaction and echoed the appropriation of the Holocaust in American politics as they likewise reinforced traditional American values by showing their negation.

# PART THREE

# Popular Literature

## Reading the Pain of Others
## in Misery Memoirs

"The age of the memoir and the age of trauma have coincided and stimulated the aesthetic forms and cultural practices of self-representation that mark the turn of the millennium."

–Leigh Gilmore, *The Limits of Autobiography*[1]

Since literary and cultural studies scholars predominantly analyze canonical texts and films, their discussions of victimization and suffering are largely restricted to representations they consider to be aesthetically superior. Virtually no mention has been made of the fact that autobiographical narratives of extremity that are emplotted as redemptive tales of trauma and recovery and thematically focussed on child abuse, addiction, or terminal illness have become ubiquitous in popular culture. Since mass media representations reach far greater audiences and consequently have a vastly greater impact on the generation of cultural trends than the literary and filmic canon, they also gave rise to the contemporary trauma culture zeitgeist. Instead of analyzing extremity in the artifacts of highbrow culture, I will therefore explore its representation in the currently most widely read genre of popular literature.

Like popular Holocaust depictions and daytime TV talk shows, misery memoirs are politically anaesthetizing and do not seek to end the suffering they represent as spectacle, but rather serve to reinforce the status quo by casting its negation as dystopia. The discussion of misery memoirs as the preeminent literary embodiment of popular trauma culture will expand the focus of this study beyond the American realm. This accounts for the fact that, while the genre and the larger trend of privileging experiences of victimization and suffering emerged in the United States, both have since come to dominate the Western public sphere at large, like so many other exports of American popular culture.

Contemporary cultural artifacts ranging from canonical literature like Philip Roth's auto-fiction to mass media products like the reality TV series *Survivor* challenge the traditional fiction/nonfiction binary. Nevertheless, "of all the categories in our lives," Susan Rubin Suleiman writes, "those of fact and fiction, with their various literary equivalences such as memoir or novel, remain very strong."[2] The rise of the memoir genre to cultural dominance since the 1990s seems in part to be a reaction to the postmodern affinity for generic ambiguity. Another core factor contributing to the contemporary popularity of memoirs is the significance ascribed to experiences of extremity. As Michael Bernstein put it, a currently pervasive notion, "partially arising out of our collective response to the horrors of the concentration camps, is the absolute authority given to first-person testimony."[3] Contemporary culture thus privileges not only autobiographical over fictional narratives, but particularly representations that allow audiences to consume the pain of others.

However, memoirs "by camp survivors or by those who have endured rape, child abuse, or any devastating trauma,"[4] have been endowed with the "misplaced aura of wisdom"[5] based on a fallacious presupposition. According to Bernstein, they are "regarded as though they were completely unmediated, as though language, gesture, and imagery could become transparent if the experience being expressed is sufficiently horrific."[6] It was precisely this "utterly naïve faith" in nonfictional narratives of atrocity and extremity, as if they "were 'really true' and untouched by figuration and by the shaping of both conscious and unconscious designs on the speaker's part," that catapulted such texts onto the bestseller lists.[7] In other words, autobiographical accounts of victimization and suffering are privileged over both other nonfictional and fictional narratives because they are considered unmediated and therefore authentic forms of representations. Susan Sontag analogously argued that atrocity photographs, which have become ubiquitous in contemporary print journalism, seem more authentic and truthful to Western audiences when they minimize stylization and display documentary immediacy.[8] In popular trauma culture, the newly generated dichotomy of mediatedness and (supposed) unmediatedness is thus both merged with the notions of inauthenticity and authenticity and super-imposed onto the categories of fiction and autobiographic nonfiction. However, trans-posing the traditional distinction between fictional and autobiographical narratives onto the idea that mediation implies inauthenticity and a supposed lack of mediation signifies authenticity is nonsensical. Like all representations, autobiographical texts only provide a mediated, partial, and interpreted reflection of reality, "not a direct, immediate apprehension of the 'thing itself.'"[9] And, as Bernstein put it, "surely there is no reason to assume that first-person testimony about the horrific is more unmedi-ated and complete" than any other mode of signification of this or any other subject.[10]

Rather than based on a dichotomy between mediatedness and a supposed but inherently impossible unmediatedness of the representation, fiction and nonfiction can be distinguished by their respective relation to reality. Although fictional narra-tives often reflect some aspects of past or present reality, their truth claims are not indexical because they do not establish referential relations between reality and its representation. Nonfiction, on the other hand, is "bound by rules of evidence that link the world of the narrative with a historical world,"[11] in other words, the texts are indexical because they establish referential relations to real people and events. However, unlike in all other nonfiction, the author of autobiographical texts is simultaneously "the observing subject and the object of investigation, remem-brance, and contemplation."[12] Consequently, autobiographical accounts create a referential relation to the author's life and it is conventionally understood that their truth claims are not based on an indexical relation to reality itself but to the author's memories of his or her experiences. As readers have no access to the author's mind, they must rely on the explicit or implicit assertion of reliable representation to the best of the author's memory.

While the distinction between fiction and autobiographical nonfiction is vital, textual features alone do not provide sufficient information to determine whether a text fulfils the conditions of what Philippe Lejeune termed the autobiographical pact.[13] For instance, after several publishers had rejected James Frey's *A Million Little Pieces*, he submitted it to Doubleday, not as a novel but as a memoir. Unable to tell based on the text itself that the experiences of recovery from alcohol and drug addiction it depicted were almost entirely invented and thus did not reflect the author's own life, Doubleday did publish it as a memoir. (Despite the rather improbable story line, Doubleday relied solely on Frey's signature under the contract to confirm that the author had reliably represented his own experiences, rather than making independent inquiries to verify his claim.) To cite another famous example, Elie Wiesel had assumed that Jerzy Kosinski's 1965 book *The Painted Bird* was a novel, but when the author told Wiesel that it was an autobiographical account of his childhood experiences of persecution in Nazi-occupied Poland, Wiesel not only believed him but also "tore up [his] review and wrote one a thousand times better."[14] Although the depicted events in both Frey's and Kosinski's books are not only largely invented but also decidedly implausible, common-sense notions of probability can no longer determine whether a literary text adheres to the autobiographical pact in this era of victim talk, when claims to indexical representation of horrific victimization experiences have become ubiquitous. The distinction between fictional and autobiographical narratives is, then, largely determined not by the text itself but by what Gérard Genette called its "paratexts" and distinguished into "peritexts" and "epitexts." The former include such features of a book as its cover, title page, preface, and afterword, which usually state directly or indirectly whether the book contains a fictional narrative or whether its truth claims adhere to the autobiographical pact. Likewise, the epitexts, which include book reviews and bestseller lists as well as the author's own interpretations of the text in diaries and letters, provide indications of its status as fiction or autobiographical nonfiction. The fact that this distinction is vital not only to a few narratologists, was demonstrated by the fact that Wiesel changed his review of Kosinski's book and Doubleday published Frey's based on the authors' claim that the narrated events were autobiographical rather than largely fictional. Both examples furthermore indicate that, if authors of texts depicting victimization and suffering claim indexicality of representation, the valuation of their narratives by publishers, critics, and audiences at large—both Kosinski's and Frey's book were bestsellers—radically changes. This dramatic increase in value accounts for the double trend that increasing numbers of fictional and therefore fake misery memoirs enter the market and that, when exposed as forgeries, they generate large-scale media scandals and lose all value.

# 7

# Selling Misery

"Fiction doesn't cut it anymore because no one really and truly suffers."

–Julia Glass, *New York Times*[1]

According to Nancy Miller, the Clinton era of the 1990s "will go down in history, not just for the halcyon days of endlessly touted national prosperity and the explosion of the dot-com culture, but also for a paroxysm of personal exposure: making the private public to a degree startling even in a climate of over-the-top self-revelation,"[2] not least by the president himself, whose personal indiscretion created an unprecedented political scandal. The relentless exposure of celebrities' personal lives dominated TV entertainment news programs and both pseudo-therapeutic talk shows like *Oprah* and *Donahue* and the freak show spectacles of *Ricki Lake* and *Jerry Springer* revealed the secrets of so-called middle America. It was in this context that memoirs became the literary genre *du jour*. "It used to be said everyone has a novel in him. . . . Just now, though, in 1999, you would probably be obliged to doubt the basic proposition: what everyone has in them, these days, is not a novel, but a memoir,"[3] Martin Amis wrote, naturally in a memoir of his own. Since the cultural dominance of the memoir was in part generated by superimposing the authenticity/inauthenticity onto the nonfiction/fiction dichotomy, it required ascribing the status of memoir's inauthentic Other to fiction, and more specifically the novel. Although the rise of the memoir genre thus eroded the cultural authority of the novel,"[4] paradoxically it also reinforced its significance precisely because the novel was imbued with the new function of memoir's identity- and value-determining inauthentic Other.

The triumph of the memoir was largely a result of its reorganization around trauma.[5] According to Steve Almond, publishers responded to declining readership by cultivating an insatiable appetite for books "that come with 'author survivors' attached" because to sell a book today, requires not only "a pitch dramatic enough to resonate with the frantic metabolism of our perpetual news cycle."[6] It also requires "an inspirational figure the marketing people can dangle as interview bait" because then books "are about 100 times more likely to get reviewed and featured on National Public Radio and anointed by Oprah."[7]

This new literary subgenre has been variously dubbed "misery memoirs," "misery literature," or, reflecting the American affinity for acronyms, "mis lit" in the vast international journalistic coverage of the phenomenon. The texts could also be termed trauma kitsch memoirs because they represent horrific real-life experiences, particularly child abuse, illness, and addiction, according to the plot paradigm dominant in popular trauma culture: They construct a melodrama of suffering and redemption around ethically simplified conflicts of good versus evil embodied in the characters of villain and victim, and they rely on kitsch's clichés and tropes to arouse teary-eyed sentiment in readers. Like daytime TV talk shows and mass media representations of the Holocaust, they reinforce traditional American values by representing their negation as dystopia. They furthermore reinforce existing power structures, because the only character they include who challenges the status quo is the villain. Misery memoirs thus suppress the idea that political action can change contemporary society where victimization is not only ubiquitous but where its representation is also sold as entertainment. In fact, misery memoirs represent a universe in which there is no society beyond dysfunctional and abusive families. And since they also cast victimhood and suffering as common experiences, they "reinforce the idea that the world is a fantastically scary place, and that no one is out of harm's way."[8]

Despite the proliferation of personal narratives in the mass media, the spectrum of represented experience greatly diminished and contemporary self-representations are dominated by accounts of extremity. In fact, the success of mis lit indicates that the lives deemed most meaningful and significant are lives, particularly childhoods, of exceptional pain and suffering, rather than of remarkable achievements. Or rather, surviving and overcoming abuse, dysfunction, addiction, and illness signify the ultimate accomplishment in contemporary American culture. Benjamin Kunkel summarized the epistemologically and ethically dubious trauma culture zeitgeist embodied in mis lit like this: "Suffering produces meaning. Life is what happens to you, not what you do. Victim and hero are one. Hence the preponderance of memoirs having to do with mental illness, sexual or other violence, drug and alcohol addiction, bad parents and/or mad or missing loved ones."[9] Citing Augusteen Burroughs's best-selling *Running with Scissors*, whose plot Kunkel aptly summarized as "a stew of just about all the above ingredients,"[10] he suggested that Burroughs "supplies what might be the motto of the typical contemporary memoirist: 'I survived that. Unwittingly, I had earned a Ph.D. in survival.'"[11] James Bradley's characterization of Frey's fake misery memoir *A Million Little Pieces* as containing the macho version of the Oprahesque message that "life is mean, and hard and shitty, but that hope and love spring eternal" makes an equally fitting motto for the mis lit universe.[12] Michael Bernstein likewise emphatically rejected the notion that overcoming victimization and suffering constitutes the most meaningful experience or is somehow ennobling. According to Bernstein, such an assumption endows the causes of the suffering, including genocidal persecution, child abuse, rape, or illness "or any of the numerous brutalities and inequalities that continue to flourish in our society . . . with the capacity to bring out a previously hidden worthiness."[13]

Christopher Lasch had already critiqued the increasing revelation of the personal and intimate in the 1970s—the decade when identity politics metamorphosed into quests for self-discovery—in texts like Philip Roth's *Portnoy's Complaint*, Norman Mailer's *Advertisements for Myself*, and Norman Podhoertz's *Making It*. Lasch argued that "many writers now rely on self-disclosure to keep the reader interested, appealing not to his understanding but to his salacious curiosity about the private lives of famous people."[14] Richard Sennett likewise admonished "those autobiographies or biographies which compulsively bare every detail of the sexual tastes, money habits, and character weaknesses of their subjects, as though we are supposed to understand the person's life, writings, or actions in the world better by the exposure of his or her secrets."[15] The largely male-authored revelatory memoirs and auto-fictions of the 1970s were cast in the discursive tradition of confession—revealing the narrator's transgressions with a kind of coy exhibitionism to an implied reader modeled on the (likewise male) therapist.

Misery memoirs, on the other hand, extend the exposure of the private and intimate to the lives of ordinary people, predominantly represent the experiences of victimization and suffering by women and children, and employ the tradition of testimony. The bearing-all is justified as an invaluable service to society because, according to the gospel of trauma culture, knowing a victim's story in every horrific detail will protect others from a similar experience, not because it contributes to legal convictions of perpetrators but because it teaches core life, or rather survival, lessons. Despite these significant differences, Lasch's and Sennett's criticism pertains equally if not more so to misery memoirs.

Mis lit is ubiquitous not only in American culture, but in Western culture at large, and received extensive coverage in the English-language press, both national and regional, from the United States to the United Kingdom, Canada to Ireland, and Australia to South Africa, because the questions that misery memoirs provoke "are at the heart of contemporary literary culture and current media ethics."[16] Nevertheless, scholarship, not only in literary and cultural studies, but even in popular culture studies, ignored this phenomenon. My analysis will draw extensively on the international journalistic discourse, not only because there are no scholarly analyses, but also because, given its vast readership, print journalism itself either reinforces or curtails cultural trends.

The journalistic discussion of mis lit differs significantly from the scholarly analyses of canonical literature in trauma studies because it explores different primary texts, is written for a much broader readership, and cannot engage in the analytical depth and breadth of scholarship. And most important, unlike trauma studies scholars, who still advocate representations of extremity as the liberatory testimony of the disenfranchised, journalists largely condemn what Sam Leith aptly described as the "competitive pornographization of suffering" in misery memoirs.[17]

## Pornographic Suffering

According to the annual Bowker Industry Report, sales in the auto/biography category have risen from $170 to $270 million since 1999, largely because of misery memoirs.[18] While the genre was once the province of minor American publishers,[19] it became literature's largest growth industry and thus a significant constituent of the international book market.[20] HarperCollins, for example, reported a 31 percent increase in annual profit thanks to mis lit alone.[21] And between January and April 2008, the top ten mis lit titles sold some 600,000 copies.[22] In Britain, the genre accounts for 9 percent of the book market, selling some 1.9 million copies per year and generating £24 million of revenue.[23] In fact, misery memoirs have become such major sales items that the two largest British book store chains, Waterstones and W. H. Smith, have each created a special shelf marker in addition to the traditional "fiction" and "biography" with Waterstones opting for "Painful Lives"[24] and W. H. Smith for "Tragic Life Stories."[25] However, British book stores only sell between 10 and 15 percent of misery memoirs. The vast majority of them are sold in supermarkets, where they are predominantly bought by women "who would not visit a bookshop but buy 'true life' magazines such as *Pick Me Up* or *Chat*, which feature stories about abusive fathers, cheating husbands, and distasteful diseases."[26] Offering "in truncated form all the manifold pleasure of the misery memoir, along with puzzles and cash prizes,"[27] they are the fastest growing market in women's magazines and are expected to outsell traditional British tabloid magazines like *Heat* and *Hello*.[28]

Dave Pelzer's 1995 memoir *A Child Called* has been widely cited as introducing mis lit into the mass market. Promoted by Oprah Winfrey,[29] *A Child Called* and its sequels "spent a combined total of 448 weeks on the *New York Times* bestseller list, despite the chorus of doubts about its veracity."[30] Characterized as a "mix of abasement and aggrandizement," the books depict the abuse he suffered as a child at the hands of his alcoholic mother, who not only beat, starved, and stabbed him, but also rubbed his face in filthy diapers, force-fed him bleach and his own vomit, and burnt his penis with cigarettes.[31] Frank McCourt's 1996 Pulitzer Prize–winning *Angela's Ashes*, the best-selling Irish nonfiction text of all time, depicting his impoverished childhood with an alcoholic father in Ireland

and New York, is also frequently cited as setting the misery lit trend.[32] It indicates that the genre does include a few texts deemed by some critics to represent misery in aesthetically superior form.[33] The aesthetic quality, or rather lack thereof, of most mis lit, however, reflects its popular literature status, since "the idea that you're close to real suffering is the selling point, not the writing."[34]

Although misery memoirs also depict both addiction and potentially terminal illness, their primary subject matter is physical and sexual child abuse. Torey Hayden's *Ghost Girl*, which sold some twenty-five million copies worldwide, for instance, tells the story of a child so chronically abused that she seemed half-dead.[35] Equally gruesome is Jenny Tomlin's *Behind Closed Doors*, which depicts her childhood dominated by her father's violent beatings and sexual assaults.[36] Jennifer Lauck's *Blackbird* recounts her childhood misery suffered at the hands of her step-mother, and Cathy Glass's *Damaged* tells the story of a horrifically abused seven-year-old foster child.[37] Stuart Howarth's *Please, Daddy, No*, which sold 13,000 copies in its first week, describes "how his father repeatedly raped him and forced him to eat pigswill, among other things too hideous to mention," how the author was furthermore "abused by pedophiles, becomes a homeless, cocaine-addicted arsonist, and ends up killing his father and going to prison."[38]

Although the mis lit trend originated in the United States, when Pelzer's and other misery memoirs were published abroad, the genre was quickly embraced and its popularity reinforced by "homegrown" versions. In Britain, they include Kevin Lewis's *The Kid*, Richard McCann's *Just a Boy*, and Constance Briscoe's *Ugly*.[39] Both *Angela's Ashes* and the fact that it was followed by Kathy O'Beirne's *Don't Ever Tell*, called in the United States *Kathy's Story: A Childhood Hell Inside the Magdalene Laundries*, as the second best-selling Irish nonfiction text with more than 400,000 sold copies, indicate that misery memoirs are also popular in Ireland. And both Frey's *A Million Little Pieces* and Briscoe's *Ugly* were bestsellers in Australia.[40] However, after the Frey scandal a growing number of other authors, including Briscoe and O'Beirne, have been accused of fabricating their memoirs.[41]

Childhood misery has also become a dominant subject in children's literature. In May 2009, four of the *New York Times* top ten bestsellers in the paperback category of children's literature depicted suffering children. At number three was John Boyne's novel *The Boy in the Striped Pajamas* about the friendship between a Jewish boy in a concentration camp and the young son of the camp's commander.[42] Ellen Hopkins's *Glas*, an addiction-and-recovery novel in verse, was in sixth place, followed by another addiction-and-recovery story, *Tweak*, by Nic Sheff, whose story had already been told by his father in the bestselling *Beautiful Boy*, which was now narrated from the boy's own perspective. Kelley Armstrong's *The Summoning*, which depicts a girl who sees ghosts and is locked up in a psychiatric institution, occupied ninth place.[43]

The mis lit trend is not limited to the English-language book market. The December 2007 German *Weltbild* book and media catalogue, for example, included a double-page spread that sought to entice potential consumers with the following instances of mis lit: a memoir of an African child slave, a memoir of an abused Turkish woman, two collections of autobiographical accounts by post-Second-World-War German refugees, two biographical accounts of children with terminal diseases written by parents, a memoir of a child Holocaust survivor, a memoir of sexual child abuse, and another of an emotionally neglected child.[44] Despite the thematic diversity, the texts are nonfictional accounts depicting experiences of extreme victimization and suffering, and the main characters are suffering women or children. Even their cover designs are rather similar, as each includes a photographic image of a woman and/or child, presumably the protagonist.

The resemblances among paratextual features of the subset of child abuse memoirs are even closer. Marketed by the soft-sell approach, the back cover blurbs proclaim that "the stories are human stories, 'deeply moving' and full of the stuff pathos is made of: fear, anger, pain, love, struggle," they are "'penetrating and powerful,' 'personal,' 'terrifying,' 'shocking' and 'unforgettable.'"[45] Moreover, the genre and subject matter are "invariably signaled by a photograph of a mournful little face against a pale cover, under a handwritten title."[46] And the category of "customers who bought this item also bought" on amazon.com creates an endless ribbon of essentially identical covers with formulaic titles that include: *Punished, Hidden, Unloved, Abandoned, Damaged, Sickened, Shattered, Scarred, The Little Prisoner, The Step-Child, Friday's Child, Child C, No Way Home, Someone to Watch Over Me, Tears at Bedtime, Rock Me Gently, No-One Wants You, Don't Tell Mummy, Don't Ever Tell, Dance for Your Daddy, Please Let It Stop, He Sold Me for a Few Cigarettes.* And there were even three memoirs, published in as many years, called *Our Little Secret.*[47] The seemingly endless chain of misery memoirs thus generated indicates not only the generic nature of their titles, but also that the strategy of marketing mis lit as identikit books to the same audience is confirmed by actual consumer behavior.

Due to their formulaic nature, if a misery memoir is to stand out, the depicted horror must be "the vilest imaginable, relentless, related in obscene detail and, ideally, accompanied by some uniquely nasty twist," as James Bone sarcastically put it.[48] For instance, *Not Without My Sister* tells the story of three sisters who were "raped by the Children of God's pious pedophiles" and thus gives the consumer "three victims for the price of one."[49] And Joe Peters's *Cry Silent Tears* narrates the abuse experienced by the author as a child at the hands of his schizophrenic mother and two of his older brothers, who beat and raped him, locked him in the cellar and "one hardly needs to add that he survived on scraps and almost froze, both are now routine in this market."[50] Advertised by HarperCollins as "a truly inspirational account of how one small boy found the strength to overcome almost impossible odds and become a remarkable man," it comes with the twist that the author is mute and was thus unable to ask for help or scream in pain.[51] Quite a challenge, then, for the competition, "who must now come up with something just as humanizingly inspirational, yet more freakishly harrowing."[52] It seems that to outsell the competition, mis lit authors employ the victim talk logic of seeking to outsuffer each other and thus the plot lines escalate: "Beaten by nuns? Ten a penny. Addicted to crack? A bit last year, sorry. Given AIDS by your Dad? Now we're talking,"[53] Sam Leith wrote with scathing sarcasm.

Needless to say, the violence depicted in mis lit is deeply unethical. However, it is also questionable for authors to sell their experiences of extremity—presuming the accounts are autobiographical as claimed, rather than invented—in a manner that makes pornography out of personal pain.[54] While Louise Armstrong published *Kiss Daddy Goodnight*, the first American memoir about father-daughter incest, in 1979 as part of her feminist activism, seeking political change that would put an end to the violence inflicted on children and women, the aim of mis lit is not to make the personal political but to sell the pain of others as entertainment. It is clearly unethical for publishers to mass market such accounts and reinforce the readers' seemingly insatiable quasi-pornographic appetite for other people's misery in the interest of profit margins.[55] Or, as Sam Leith put it, "there is an unappealing disjunction . . . between the vulnerable, damaged people whose stories the books tell, and the pound signs flashing up . . . in the eyes of their publishers (or, indeed, those of the writers who produce sequels)."[56] And it is likewise ethically untenable "to get your kicks from devouring pages of grim detail about someone else's stomach-churning misery—[full of] details that offer no insight, that shine no light, but that merely confirm what you already knew: that some people are monstrous and that some people's lives are desperate."[57]

What, then, "is the attraction of reading endlessly about child torture"[58] and other mis lit horrors? A *Boston Globe* article suggests that "readers crave more gore, humiliation, betrayal, and raw pain" and "the worse it gets for some readers, the better, because then the inevitable plot turn comes, recovery starts, and the supposedly true story delivers the yearned-for promise that people can get over the blackest events."[59] The following section will take recourse to media studies research on the reception of screen violence to explore the reception of misery memoirs.

## Consuming Violence

Martha Woodmansee's description of readers "devouring greedily one after another of these new titles, forgetting the last one the moment they turned to its replacement"[60] could well describe the reception of misery memoirs. It was, however, intended to characterize another popular literature craze some two hundred years earlier—which gave rise to the so-called German reading debates of the 1790s—when the likewise predominantly female readers "were reading too many of the wrong books for the wrong reasons."[61] Misery memoirs especially bear resemblances to the gothic novel because both titillate the reader's imagination by depicting the suffering of victims whose innocence is absolute. Child abuse memoirs in particular invoke the gothic figure of the maiden-in-distress that merged the Romantic innocence of childhood with the Christian virtue of the virgin. Prominently prefigured in Fritz Lang's 1931 film *M*, misery memoirs furthermore evoke the dark and evil gothic villain in the figure of the ever-lurking child abuser. However, while gothic novels restricted the fear of the unknown to haunted castles, in the mis lit universe every overtly happy home is cast as nothing but the respectable cover of a childhood hell. Moreover, both gothic novels and child abuse memoirs share the preoccupation with the incest taboo. However, while the former employed inadvertent brother-sister incest, the latter invoke the trope of the maiden-in-distress relentlessly pursued by the villainous father figure. And while Romantic readers were content with titillating fiction, today's readers require that the pain and suffering not only be depicted in gory detail but also that it really happened.

And like the gothic romances, which were panned by critics at the time, misery memoirs, and their enthusiastic reception have been unanimously criticized in the print media, which exposed the vast and lucrative trauma culture industry behind the fig leaf of mis lit's purportedly altruistic status as victim testimony. While journalists rightly condemned the genre, they did not explore why misery memoirs are so widely consumed. However, since there are no empirical reception studies of misery memoirs, any explanation remains tentative, as it can only propose hypotheses based on related fields of scholarship.

Susan Sontag argued that voyeuristic fascination pertains not only to displays of nudity but also of pain, and that for many centuries Christian art offered both these elemental satisfactions in depictions of hell.[62] In contemporary culture, atrocity photographs—which often echo the aesthetics of images depicting liberated concentration camps—and popular screen representations of the Holocaust often dubiously employ the titillating potential inherent in displaying bodies that are both naked and in pain. And although the representation in misery memoirs is verbal rather than visual, one can make an analogous argument for those that narrate physical and sexual abuse. Sontag suggested that the voyeuristic lure of seeing the pain of others is partly based on the spectator's "satisfaction of knowing, this is not happening to *me*, I'm not ill, I'm not dying, I'm not trapped in a war."[63] While being safe and observing violence in mediated form constitutes a necessary condition for spectators to experience voyeuristic titillation, it is not a sufficient explanation for the attraction of media violence.

Michael Bernstein wrote that "the fascination with the brutal and the dangerous holds a compelling place in our culture's imagination"[64] and particularly deplored the unethical fascination with Holocaust horror. He considered the consumption of Holocaust representations characterized by a "feverish excitement that arises when abandoning oneself to the contemplation of horror" as "an extraordinarily misplaced and even pernicious response" but one that is "nonetheless sufficiently seductive and widespread to require conscious resistance."[65] The current fascination with depictions of extremity, which Bernstein dubbed "a kind of lumpen Rashkolnikovism,"[66] recycles the Christian notion of spiritual purification though physical mortification as a kind of post-Holocaust existentialism. He rejected the quasi-religious quest for "a revelatory moment that will disclose the *one* truth that matters"[67] and the notion that it can only be found in representations of extremity because it casts the ordinary as "an endless repetition of identically meaningless units suddenly punctuated and redeemed by the thunderclap of the cataclysmically significant crisis."[68] The trauma culture doctrine that only representations of extremity reveal some ultimate truth about human nature is thus both nonsensical and unethical.

Misery memoirs may be read widely because of a voyeuristic fascination with representations of bodies that are both naked and in pain coupled with the exculpatory belief that extremity reveals some absolute and profound truths. One might also invoke the two most common explanations for the appeal of screen violence—the notion that there is a certain, if ethically dubious, beauty in depictions of violence and that they serve to cathartically purge audiences of negative emotions—to understand the mass appeal of mis lit. However, media studies scholar Dolf Zillmann discounts both lines of argument. He maintained that justifying screen violence based on aesthetic merit merely restates what is to be explained, that is, if the appeal lies in its beauty, the question becomes why audiences perceive representations of violence as beautiful (if indeed they do).[69] Zillmann likewise rejected catharsis theory, which is widely evoked in "an exceedingly liberal extension of the doctrine"[70] in literary and film studies to explain the popularity of representations of violence. However, empirical media studies research of audience reactions to screen violence established that spectators do not cathartically purge negative emotions like fear[71] and anger[72] through these consumption experiences. On the contrary, exposure to mass media violence—including thrillers; disaster, horror, and slasher movies; athletic contests like boxing and auto racing; disturbing news reports; and trash talk shows—does not reduce the level of the spectator's hedonically negative arousal state, but instead perpetuates and even increases it.[73] While Zillmann discounted the two dominant explanations for the appeal of screen violence, based on empirical audience research, he proposed three alternative explanations—excitation transfer, mood management, and disposition theory—which can be extended to account for the popularity of misery memoirs.

Zillman argued that anticipating or witnessing violence gratuitously inflicted on likable characters, either fictional or non-fictional, elevates the arousal level in the viewer's autonomous nervous system and generates a hedonically negative or dysphoric state. The elevated state of excitation, which is physiologically indicated by increased heart rate and sweat excretion, decays only slowly. The remaining residues of the heightened arousal are no longer dysphoric, but value-neutral, and combine with the subsequent positive or euphoric neuronal excitation at the happy ending and thereby intensify those reactions. Zillman termed this process "excitation transfer."[74] The positive arousal at seeing good characters rewarded (or at least unharmed) and evil ones punished is thus the more intense the greater the prior distress, because the latter generates maximum value-neutral arousal residue in the nervous system that will in turn maximally elevate the euphoric excitation at the happy ending.[75] Zillmann developed excitation transfer theory based on empirical analyses of audience reactions to screen violence. Given the simplistic good-versus-evil conflicts and their formulaic resolution of rewarding the innocently wronged victim and punishing the evil perpetrator in misery memoirs, it seems likely that readers likewise experience elevated euphoric arousal levels at the happy endings based on excitation transfer.

Zillmann furthermore argued that the mass media provide a wealth of divisionary stimuli and thus have a capacity to involve the mind and enable consumers to temporarily escape from their own lives. Given their intervention potential, audiences can use television, commercial cinema, or popular literature to regulate their mood states. Audiences predominantly employ the media, particularly television, which has been widely recognized as "the nation's favorite unwinder," to "calm down after the stressful activities of daily life."[76] The divisionary stimuli provided by television interrupt stress-maintaining mental rehearsal processes "that would perpetuate states of elevated arousal associated with negative affective experiences."[77] Audiences of course also watch television when bored, and it is when they are in a low arousal state that they seek to elevate it by consuming screen violence (not, as catharsis theory suggests, when angry or fearful, that is, when their level of nervous arousal is high).[78] Given the prevalence of horrific violence in misery memoirs, they most likely share television's capacity to elevate levels of emotional arousal and can thus likewise be employed as a means of mood regulation.

In addition to catharsis theory and aesthetic pleasure, scholarship in literary and film studies still tends to evoke "with untiring fascination and conviction," as Zillman put it, the Freudian notion of vicarious identification to explain the reception of cultural artifacts in general and the appeal of media violence in particular.[79] According to Freud, the spectator is a "poor soul to whom nothing of importance seems to happen, who some time ago had to moderate or abandon his ambition to take center stage in matters of significance" and who can fulfill his thwarted wishes only though identification with a hero in the world of make-believe.[80] It is through such ego-confusion, which is cognitively effortless and deliberate only with respect to the unrestricted choice of identification targets, that experiential sharing of the character's pleasures and sorrows is enabled. Audiences, then, are said to identify with media characters in order to transcend their own limited personal experience and vicariously attain the characters' gratifications.[81] Zillmann developed what he termed "disposition theory" as a viable and, in media studies, widely accepted alternative to the notion of vicarious identification to explain core aspects of media reception, including the appeal of screen violence.

Empirical studies on empathy and emotional response in social psychology and media studies established that spectators develop particular dispositions toward media characters similar (but not identical) to those they create toward real people.[82] Person perception and character perception differ because different information is available in interpersonal and mass media communication, as the former allows social interaction while audiences cannot interact with media characters. Although in social interaction feedback provides significant information not available to media consumers, the latter nevertheless often have more information about the motivations and constraints of a character's behavior, based on the observation of prior critical events. Furthermore, the information spectators receive is scripted and enhanced though features like sound track, camera angles, close-ups, and editing techniques designed to influence their selection and interpretation of character-relevant information, while the exposure to others' behaviors in interpersonal settings is much less planned, systematic, concise, and unambiguous.[83]

Despite the differences in the available information about them, "the cognitive processes involved in forming impressions of characters and real people" are quite similar, as they are based on what cognitive psychologists term "stimulus generalization."[84] According to Joanne Cantor, "if a stimulus evokes either an unconditioned or conditioned emotional response," similar stimuli will evoke similar responses.[85] Reactions to media representations thus resemble, but also differ from, responses to unmediated stimuli, because the former contain evidence that they were elicited by representations rather than the immediate perception of reality. Hence, no matter how gripping the action, we are neither personally in danger nor morally obliged to intervene as we would be if we observed an identical scene of violence and victimization at first hand.

Spectators thus do not react to media characters via Freudian identification based on ego-confusion, but rather like they react to nonmediatized others, namely as third parties. We judge media characters analogously to the moral assessment we continually, if largely without conscious awareness, apply to real people, predominantly by evaluating their actions.[86] Audiences develop a favorable or positive disposition and react empathically toward characters whose actions are deemed good and right, and an unfavorable or negative disposition toward those whose behavior they consider, wrong, selfish, or contemptible. They furthermore develop a neutral or indifferent disposition toward characters whose actions are deemed neither good and right nor evil and wrong and an ambivalent disposition toward those whose actions they value as equally good and bad, right and wrong.[87] Based on these dispositions, audiences decide in moral terms what fate media characters deserve analogously to their judgment of real people.[88] They consider characters toward whom they developed positive dispositions as deserving of good fortunes and undeserving of bad ones. Similarly, characters toward whom audiences developed negative dispositions because they exhibit antisocial behavior like dishonesty, betrayal, and especially gratuitous violence, are considered undeserving of good fortunes and deserving of bad ones. Dislike of a character thus not only disbands empathic concerns but inverts affective reactions, a tendency termed "counter-empathy" in media studies. As the infliction of gratuitous violence that dominates not only television programming and commercial cinema, but also misery memoirs, is unanimously considered unjust, it creates strong desires among audiences for punitive-retaliatory violence.[89] Media violence is thus morally sanctioned as just when it is inflicted on disliked villains as punishment because it restores the moral equilibrium.[90]

Displays of violence in television programs, commercial cinema, and popular literature genres like misery memoirs are widely consumed neither because of their supposed aesthetic appeal nor because they enable audiences to engage in vicarious identification and/or cathartically purge negative arousal states. In fact, the appeal is not primarily the represented violence itself, but rather the melodramatic plot structure and particularly the redemptive-happy ending, which ensures consumers that, despite all apparent evidence to the contrary, the good forces will always triumph over the evil ones and we thus live in a just world.[91] Merged with the notion that punitive media violence provides a morally sanctioned space for the counter-empathic sensation of *Schadenfreude* directed against the villain, the promise of a just world is powerful enough to overwrite the intrinsic human aversion to the dysphoric arousal states elicited by the consumption of media violence.[92] However, popular culture depictions of violence are politically acquiescing, because they not only suggest that the world need not be changed but, as they depict only villains as violating social norms, they also widely disseminate the notion that challenging the status quo inevitably leads to disaster and severe punishment.

# 8

# Fake Suffering

"It seemed universally taken for granted that a writer should want to pretend to a history of extraordinary suffering, that fantasies passed off as true should be fantasies of crime and pain rather than of achievement or happiness."

–Benjamin Kunkel, *New York Times*[1]

The immense commercial successes of misery memoirs also gave rise to counterfeits, supposedly autobiographical texts that depict partly, largely, or entirely invented tales of victimization and suffering. Literary forgeries "are like those old black-and-white films where a bolt of lightning illuminates for a split second the murderer in the upstairs bedroom with the knife raised above his head," Michael Heyward wrote, because "the weird light they cast allows us to glimpse the cultural weather that let them happen."[2] For centuries, only the most important texts were forged. Put differently, literary forgeries signify which objects are aesthetically or commercially most valuable in a given culture. Hence, they should not be regarded solely, or even primarily, as individual transgressions, but as artifacts that are indicative of the zeitgeist they embody in concentrated form. Forgeries thus constitute ideal objects of analysis for examining such ephemeral phenomena as cultural trends.

For instance, the famous faux-medieval manuscripts of James Macpherson's Ossianic ballads and Thomas Chatterton's Rowley poems indicate the nostalgic longing for the past that dominated the Romantic age.[3] Analogously, the forgery of misery memoirs further substantiates my argument that narratives of surviving abusive childhoods, dysfunctional families, addictive behavior, and life-threatening illnesses have come to dominate the American and, more generally, the Western public sphere. Contextualized in a discussion of the literary traditions that likewise established false claims of autobiographical status, this chapter explores mis lit fakes as core embodiments of popular trauma culture.

## Faking Autobiographical Indexicality

While "nothing human is created *ex nihilo*" as "everything is made of something else, and in that respect a *bricolage*,"[4] some texts have been intentionally created to be mistaken. According to K. K. Ruthven, like literature itself, its forgery is not "a transhistorically stable essence, but a culturally variable construct" and encompasses a vast range of diverse phenomena.[5] Ruthven conceptualizes literary forgeries "as the repressed text of literary studies" and "an indispensable critique of those cultural practices that foster the so-called genuine article" because they reveal the processes involved in "the creation and destruction of value."[6] Some forgeries are indeed created to ridicule dominant literary values. For instance, in 1944 two conservative Australian poets created avant-garde poetry under the pseudonym Ern Malley, only to reveal it as a hoax after publication in Australia's preeminent poetry journal *Angry Penguins*, because they sought to mock precisely the kind of poetry they had fabricated.[7] However, contrary to Ruthven's notion that literary forgery is at least a potentially counter-hegemonic practice, most forgers are not intent on exposing the dubiousness of aesthetic values by revealing their forgeries as hoaxes, but rather in passing them off as an original in the interest of fame and fortune. Moreover, although forgery requires great technical skills and an exceptional understanding of cultural trends, it is not only an unethical practice, but also an aesthetically conservative one, because forgers simulate dominant artistic styles and thus reinforce rather than challenge the literary canon. Most forgers, then, produce fakes rather than hoaxes, that is, texts whose deceptive claim to original status is intended to remain unexposed. Macpherson and Chatterton did not want their forgeries of medieval manuscripts to be revealed as such, nor did Frey or any of the contemporary mis lit forgers, because their texts' value and the authors' fame and fortune depended precisely on maintaining the pretense of originality.

The contemporary simulation of misery memoirs was prefigured by five diverse traditions of fraudulent writing practices. False slave narratives constitute the literary tradition that can probably be most immediately related to mis lit fakes. American slave narratives share with misery memoirs the depiction of a protagonist who overcame horrific victimization and suffering and a plot structured around a clear-cut a conflict of good versus evil, personified in the dichotomous flat characters of the innocent victim and the evil perpetrator. They enjoyed great popularity with nineteenth-century audiences and hence gave rise to forgeries, which were written by both white authors, such as Richard Hildreth and Mattie Griffith, and free blacks like James Williams. Although the false claim to the subject position of former slave and of autobiographical status for fictional texts is unethical, unlike mis lit fakes, false slave narratives were often written with the altruistic intention of furthering the ethical cause of abolishing slavery.

The second tradition of violating the autobiographical pact dates back even further, to the eighteenth century, when it was common for novelists to incorporate mock-provenances in a preface or a note on the title page, in which authors, speaking in their own person, gave a misleading account of the story's origin. Claiming, for instance, to have found and edited a manuscript, as Daniel Defoe did in *Journal of the Plague Year* and *Robinson Crusoe*,[8] allowed writers to "distance themselves from their own narratives by presenting them ironically as someone else's."[9] Although the novels were not considered forgeries at the time nor have literary critics classified them as such subsequently, H. M. Paull convincingly argued in his 1928 study on *Literary Ethics* that misleading readers to take one's novel for another's autobiographical account was deceptive and thus unethical.[10] The literary convention of false provenances thus foreshadows the fraudulent practice of mis lit authors, who likewise disingenuously claim autobiographical status for their fictional texts.

Fake misery memoirs also reflect the so-called new journalism of the mid-1960s, favored particularly by *The New Yorker*,[11] because the writers likewise claimed nonfiction status for largely, or even entirely, fictional stories. Its most famous example is Truman Capote's *In Cold Blood*, the supposed nonfictional narrative depicting the gruesome slaughter of a Kansas family in 1959. As Martin Arnold commented in the *New York Times*, "well, the murders did take place, but the conversations, thoughts, and events leading up to them in the book were recreated, were in fact fiction."[12] And Nik Cohn's *New Yorker* article "Tribal Rites of the New Saturday Night"—the source of the era-defining movie *Saturday Night Fever*—though claiming to be based on journalistic research, was entirely invented. The new-journalist tradition can in turn be related to the more recent, and equally dubious, practices of so-called wow journalism, which prefigures mis lit with regard to the subject matter and rhetoric as it relates the pain of others in an overly emotional manner. The difficulty in verifying the reliability of representation in wow journalism has led writers to invent stories. For instance, *USA Today* foreign correspondent Jack Kelley wrote largely imaginary reports from Iraq, Bosnia, Chechnya, Israel, and Cuba that earned him five Pulitzer Prize nominations.[13] It was the entirely fabricated misery tale by *Washington Post* journalist Janet Cooke about a "precocious little boy with sandy hair, velvety brown eyes and needle marks freckling the baby-smooth skin of his thin brown arms,"[14] who was forcefully addicted to heroin by his ex-prostitute mother's drug-dealing boyfriend, that particularly anticipated mis lit fakes. Awarded a Pulitzer Prize for her piece in 1981, Cooke admitted when pressured that she had heard rumors of the boy's existence, but, unable to find him, had made up the story to please her editors.[15]

The fraudulent claims to nonfiction status in fake misery memoirs also echo the simulation of ethnic minority literature by authors whose pseudonyms served to falsely signify that their novels are autobiographical to the extent that they shared their characters' experience of being a member of a minority group. Largely rejected in literary studies as appropriating the subject position of the disenfranchised, in a 1991 *New York Times* article, Henry Louis Gates critiqued these gate-keeping practices and argued that such texts have a place in the cultural history of minority literature even if the authors are not members of the depicted group. For instance, Danny Santiago's novel *Famous All Over Town* could be considered part of Chicano literature and Shane Stevens's *Way Uptown in Another World* could be read as a black protest novel.[16] However, Forrest Carter's novel *The Education of Little Tree*, which was authenticated as a Native American text by many critics and sold more than 600,000 copies, was subsequently revealed to have been written by white supremacist Asa Earl Carter, the infamous author of Governor George Wallace's 1963 speech notorious for the line "segregation now, segregation tomorrow, segregation forever."[17] As such, novel and author will probably remain suspect as performing a kind of ventriloquism that silences authentic minority voices and as engaging in ethnic drag "equivalent of whites donning 'blackface' when performing in minstrel shows."[18]

Like the fabrication of misery memoirs, the simulation of ethnic minority status by authors via pseudonyms and the false claim that their fiction was autobiographically inspired extends beyond American culture. Britain, for instance, has likewise has had its scandals of exposed fraudulent inter-ethnic literary cross-dressing. As early as the 1930s, a supposed Native American published a sequence of books in Britain, including *Indian Legends and Lore* and *The Perils of Woods Travel*, under the pen name of Grey Owl, only to be exposed as an Englishman named Archibald Belaney.[19] And Rahila Khan's 1987 short-story collection *Down the Road, Worlds Away* about the acculturation problems of Pakistani immigrants was revealed to have been written by a white Englishman, Toby Forward.[20] Furthermore, Australian literature has had a history of fake Aboriginal narratives. In fact, the supposedly first Aboriginal text to be published, Colin Johnson's autobiographically inspired novel *Wild Cat Falling*, was exposed in 1996 as a fabrication. The novel had been published in 1965 and in 1988, coinciding with Aboriginal protests against the bicentennial celebrations, Johnson had even changed his name to Mudrooroo ('Paperback') Nyoongah. However, when the Nyoongah community challenged his ethnicity, Johnson's sister came forward and revealed that the author had no Aboriginal ancestors but had inherited his dark skin from an African American grandfather.[21]

Last but not least, fictional, and therefore fake, misery memoirs were prefigured in such problematic Holocaust narratives as Jerzy Kosinski's *The Painted Bird* and Ka-Tzetnik's *House of Dolls*. Kosinski survived the Holocaust as a hidden child in Nazi-occupied Poland. Ka-Tzetnik was a camp survivor and even employed as his pseudonym the German acronym "KZ" (pronounced "kah tset"), for concentration camp. And although both authors relied on their witness status for claim that their novels are partially autobiographical, the depicted events are largely, if not entirely, fictional. Both texts thus share not only the subject matter of horrific and quasi-pornographic violence with fake misery memoirs, but also their status as fiction simulating autobiographical nonfiction.

## Fake Misery Memoirs

Mis lit fakes echo the violation of the autobiographical pact through fake provenances in early novels, as well as both the false assertion of nonfiction status and the subject matter of victimization and suffering in false slave narratives, fabricated Holocaust accounts, and fake reports in wow journalism. False misery memoirs also reflect the tradition of impersonating ethnic minority writers, but took this ethically dubious practice from simulating autobiographically influenced novels to faking memoirs, while also extending the subject matter by stressing that minority lives are dominated by victimization and suffering. For instance, a supposed half Native American author called Nasdijj published three memoirs that described how he was hungry, beaten, raped, and forced to work in the fields as a child by his white father[22] and as an adult adopted a Navajo child who suffered from fetal alcohol syndrome and fostered another with AIDS.[23] However, in 2006 it was revealed that Nasdijj was actually a white middle-class man named Timothy Barrus who had previously written gay pornography.[24] While Barrus had merged interethnic imposture with the core mis lit subjects of child abuse and terminal illness, Kent Johnson incorporated the subject of historical catastrophe into his version of interethnic impersonation when he fabricated a memoir about surviving the American atomic attack on Hiroshima under the pseudonym of Araki Yasusada.[25] K. K. Ruthven interprets Johnson's literary forgery as analogous to the *japonaiserie* of Kenneth Rexoth, who in 1978 published a collection of faux translations of poetry by a Japanese woman named Marichiko.[26] In other words, Ruthven takes Johnson's false memoir solely as another instance of simulating the voice of an ethnic Other in Orientalist fashion. However, as he not only engaged in interethnic impersonation but claimed the subject position of someone who had survived the nuclear attack, in addition to practicing *japonaiserie*, Johnson also appropriated the status of victim, witness, and survivor. Furthermore, ethnic minority writers themselves have also engaged in deceiving audiences by claiming autobiographical status for fictional stories. For example, in 2004 Norma Khouri's bestselling *Forbidden Love*, a supposedly autobiographical account of the author's narrow escape from Jordan after the honor killing of her best friend, was exposed as entirely fabricated. Khouri was revealed as a pseudonym of Norma Bagain Toliopulous who had left Jordan as a small child and had not lived there since, apart from a three-week stay during which she gathered material for her fake memoir.[27]

Moreover, in two widely publicized cases, actual victims of historical crimes committed in the so-called developing world have been exposed as having partly fabricated the accounts of their victimization. An international scandal erupted on December 15, 1998, when Larry Rohter published an article in the *New York Times* based on David Stoll's study *Rigoberta Menchú and the Story of All Poor Guatemalans*. Rohter argued that key events in Rigoberta Menchú's *I, Rigoberta Menchú: An Indian Woman in Guatemala*, for which she had been awarded the Nobel Peace Prize in 1992, had not happened as described.[28] While Stoll asserted that the overall portrayal of the hardships of poor Guatemalan Mayas under the military dictatorship was reliably represented, Menchú's *testimonio* contained several false details. For instance, she claimed not to have attended school, not to have known Spanish, and to have been illiterate until shortly before she dictated her life story. However, according to Stoll, she was neither monolingual nor illiterate since she had learned Spanish as a child and received a tenth-grade education at a Catholic girl's school. Furthermore, a younger brother, whom Menchú wrote she saw die of starvation, never existed, and another brother "whose suffering she says she and her parents were forced to watch as he was being burned alive by army troops, was killed in entirely different circumstances when the family was not present."[29] In addition to falsifying details of her own life, Stoll argued, Menchú also represented events known to her only second-hand as her own experiences and condensed several events into one. Last but certainly not least, Menchú had concealed not only her family's active involvement with the guerillas but also her own instruction in Marxist political theory.[30] The predominantly Latin American genre of *testimonio* differs from autobiography and memoir because the individual life narrative functions primarily as a metonymic representation of subaltern lives. Menchú had thus incorporated into her life story experiences she considered exemplary of the oppression of the Mayas in Guatemala. Moreover, *testimonios* tend to be narrated orally to a Western interlocutor, in Menchú's case, anthropologist Elisabeth Burgos-Debray, who imposed her own interpretation on the story as she turned it into a written text. Nevertheless, as autobiographical narratives, *testimonios* too are bound by Lejeune's autobiographical pact, and the inaccuracies damaged the impact of Menchú's account.[31]

Most recently, Ishmael Beah was accused of distorting his experiences in the bestselling 2007 memoir *A Long Way Gone*, which chronicles his time as a child soldier who lost his family in Sierra Leone's civil war.[32] Prior to the allegations, some 650,000 copies of the book had been sold, which catapulted it to the second and third positions on the bestseller lists for nonfiction books of the *New York Times* and the London *Times* respectively, and made the author "the most famous orphan on earth."[33] It was excerpted in the *New York Times* and chosen for Starbucks' book club, which donated $2 from the sale of every copy to UNICEF. Beah dates the key event in the memoir, the destruction of his home village Mogbwemo and the nearby titanium mine, as January 1993. However, historical documents and surviving eyewitnesses indicate that the attack in fact occurred in January 1995. Hence, Beah was fourteen rather than twelve years old at the time, and since he writes that following the attack on his village, he spent ten to eleven months wandering war-torn Sierra Leone he was not thirteen, but fifteen years old when he was forced to become a child soldier. Furthermore, as he was chosen by UNICEF for rehabilitation in January 1996, he cannot have spent some two years as a soldier but only two or three months.[34]

There is no doubt that Menchú and Beah are victims and witnesses to the horrific brutalities they and countless others like them suffered, or that the accounts of their respective group's recent history of oppression are historically reliable in most respects. Nevertheless, the inaccuracies about key details in their lives significantly damaged the status of their narratives as political testimony. It also provided American neo-conservatives with arguments against including minority literature in college curriculums. The political right had already attacked the teaching of subaltern writing in general and Menchú's text in particular prior to the scandal in what have come to be known as the "culture wars" of the 1990s and readily seized the opportunity to further denounce the discussion of testimonial narratives at American universities.[35] Despite the partial violation of the autobiographical pact and its self-serving appropriation by neo-conservative critics, Menchú's and Beah's texts, then, differ significantly from fake misery memoirs, as they neither fabricated their experience of horrific violence nor engaged in inter-ethnic impersonation as, for instance, Margaret B. Jones most recently did in *Love and Consequences*.

In late March 2008, Jones's memoir was exposed as a complete fabrication and the most meticulously planned mis lit forgery to date. The author, whose real name is Margaret Seltzer, falsely claimed to be half Native American, to have been abused at home and at age five been taken from her family, and gone through many foster homes for three years before being taken in by an African American foster mother in East Los Angeles. The text furthermore depicts how her two foster brothers became gang members at the ages of eleven and thirteen and how Jones, too, became a gang member and drug runner in her early teens.[36] Before its exposure, the chief book review editor of the *New York Times*, Michiko Kakutani, praised it as capturing "both the brutal realities of a place where children learn to sleep on the floor to avoid the random bullets that might come smashing through the windows and walls at night and the succor offered by family and friends."[37] The *New York Times* also published a portrait of the author by Mimi Reed, who called the book "a heart-wrenching memoir" and "an intimate, visceral portrait of the gangland drug trade of Los Angeles."[38] The book was also positively reviewed in the *L.A. Times*, featured on NPR, and praised in Oprah Winfrey's *O Magazine* as "startlingly tender."[39] The scandal broke when the author's actual sister, who had seen Reed's *New York Times* article, called the publisher, Riverhead Books, a unit of Penguin Group USA, to inform them that the story told in the memoir was entirely made up. Seltzer later confirmed this but stressed that many of the details "were based on the experiences of close friends she had met over the years while working to reduce gang violence in Los Angeles."[40] Mimi Reed, who had interviewed the author in her home; Geoffrey Kloske, who publishes Riverhead Books; and Sarah McGrath, Seltzer's editor at Riverhead, all stressed the extraordinary lengths to which the author had gone in her deception. Seltzer signed a contract in which she legally stipulated that her book truthfully recounted her own experiences. She had also displayed photographs of gang members around her house when Reed visited her and provided photographs of her supposed foster siblings as well as a letter from a gang leader corroborating her story. A professor of creative writing and writer, Inga Muscio, also vouched for the story, and Selzer had even introduced her agent, Faye Bender, to a person who claimed to be a foster sister.[41] William Shaw, whose acclaimed 2001 book *Westsiders* is based on journalistic research of life in South Central Los Angeles, commented on *Love and Consequences* that "to Americans, the ghetto is largely an imaginary place. . . . Ghetto hip-hop—the cultural genre that created South Central's mystique—has profited by pandering to a middle class that wants to imagine the landscape only as one of race, immorality and excess."[42] While drug dealers and gangs do feature in Shaw's own book, it "was also about young, hardworking men who never swore—a species curiously absent from Seltzer's book" because "her South Central is an imagined hellhole, in which young black men are little more than killers, robbers, sadists, misogynists and addicts."[43]

As Seltzer had essentially generated a *bricolage* of racist stereotypes about life in the American inner city, James Frey's *A Million Little Pieces*, the misery fake most widely discussed in the media to date, recycled tropes of the recovery movement in his macho version of addiction and recovery. Steve Almond aptly wrote that Frey's sentimental tale of "the ex-addict with the heart of gold, the bad seed who survived his trip to hell and returned with self-help platitudes dipped in gangster dialect" did not ask readers "to regard addiction in a new light, merely to confirm their stereotypes, as seen in a thousand made-for-TV movies."[44] Worse even, a number of addiction counselors and former addicts argued that the horror scenario Frey created of the recovery process may in fact make addicts less likely to seek help.[45] Before its exposure as largely invented, Frey's text was catapulted to bestseller status in September 2005, after it had been featured on her book club by Oprah Winfrey, who revels in trauma kitsch and promotes books whose plots predominantly resemble the countless recovery tales of victimhood and suffering, surviving and surpassing told on her show. After being anointed by Winfrey, *A Million Little Pieces* sold 600,000 copies in the following week, shot to number one on the *New York Times* bestseller list, and became the second highest selling book in 2006, after *Harry Potter and the Half-Blood Prince*.[46] By March 2006 it had sold some 3.8 million copies.[47]

When the investigative web site thesmokinggun.com revealed on January 8, 2006, that all but the fact that Frey had been addicted to alcohol and drugs was fabricated, it generated an international media scandal. It was more widely reported than the exposure of other fake misery memoirs, not only because the book was a bestseller, or even because it had been endorsed by Winfrey, but especially because "Court TV, the network that owns the Smoking Gun, undertook a publicity blitz" and sent out paperback copies of the book "to more than 400 journalists, along with copies of the site's reportage."[48] As a result, the site had nearly sixty-nine million page views, the second-highest number in its history, surpassed only by the seventy-seven million hits when they reported in October 2004 on the sexual harassment suit brought against Fox News host Bill O'Riley.[49] Despite the accusations, Frey maintained on *Larry King Live* on January 11, 2006, that only some 5 percent of the plot was "embellished."[50] However, former staff of the clinic, which is unnamed in the book but identifiable as the Hazeldon drug and alcohol detox center in Minnesota, where the plot is largely set, have contested Frey's account and argued that 98 percent of that book is false.[51]

Rejected by seventeen publishers as a novel before Doubleday published it as a memoir,[52] Frey's publisher Nan Talese said that she also "would not have published it as a novel."[53] And although both author and publisher have publicly acknowledged that Frey's supposed memoir contains numerous fabrications, it is kept in circulation and continues to be marketed as nonfiction.[54] While sales numbers initially dropped by about half,[55] especially after Winfrey invited Frey back to her show on January 26, 2006, and forced him to admit to lying, the book kept selling at record numbers. Even after the scandal broke, it remained on the *New York Times* bestseller list. In early February 2006, it was still number two on the paperback list,[56] sandwiched between a new and the old translation of Elie Wiesel's *Night* in the first and third positions. The versions of *Night* were catapulted there because, unaware that the veracity of Wiesel's memoir has been questioned in literary studies,[57] Winfrey followed her disastrous book club choice of *A Million Little Pieces* with *Night*. As Frey's book continued to sell well even after it was exposed as almost entirely invented, rather than remove *A Million Little Pieces* from publication as other presses did when misery memoirs were exposed as fake, Doubleday published a new edition of 100,000 paperback and 3,500 hardcover copies.[58] The post-scandal edition eliminated the *Oprah's Book Club* label and included a "watery disclaimer,"[59] in with Frey states that he "altered events and details" and that the "memoir is a combination of facts about my life and certain embellishments."[60] While any alterations violate the autobiographical pact and would thus require that the book be designated as fiction, Frey's disclaimer also vastly understates the magnitude of his so-called embellishments, namely that virtually the entire text is made up, which he elsewhere confirmed by admitting that the report by thesmokinggun.com was essentially accurate.[61]

In the aftermath of the Frey scandal, other bestselling misery memoirs, including those of Augusteen Burroughs, Jennifer Lauck, and Dave Pelzer, have come under attack for being partly fabricated.[62] As Maureen Dowd put it, the "Frey effect chilled publishers and agents."[63] In Burroughs's case, the "Frey effect" is compounded by the $2 million libel suit over his *Running with Scissors*, which was a *New York Times* bestseller for seventy weeks[64] and adapted into a Hollywood movie that premiered in early 2007.[65] *Running with Scissors* tells the allegedly true story that Burroughs's alcoholic father left his mentally unstable mother who in turn gave their son up for adoption to her rather unconventional psychiatrist. The doctor lived in a house with a room designated as a "masturbatorium" and assisted in Burroughs's fake suicide attempt to get him out of attending school. He also had patients live with the family, one of whom raped his fourteen-year-old daughter, for which the psychiatrist's medical license was revoked. Another live-in patient, a pedophile, raped the thirteen-year-old Burroughs, but the boy maintained a sexual relationship with him for several years because he was the only person who paid any attention to him. Several of the psychiatrist's children brought the libel suit against Burroughs arguing that, while their childhood was not conventional, the memoir is nevertheless fabricated.[66] And in the wake of the Frey scandal, St. Martin's Press hurriedly put a rather Freyesque disclaimer on Burroughs's latest memoir, *Possible Side Effects*. It states that "some of the events described here happened as related; others started with memories and were expanded or changed by my imagination. Some of the individuals portrayed are composites of more than one person and many names and identifying characteristics have been changed as well."[67] Such texts used to be known as novels.

Child abuse is thus not only the core subject of misery memoirs, but is also simulated in partly, largely, or entirely fake memoirs. Prior to the post-Frey scramblings of mis lit authors and publishers, another child abuse memoir, Lorenzo Carcaterra's bestseller *Sleepers*, which depicts the systematic beatings and multiple rapes the author supposedly experienced as a thirteen-year-old in a juvenile detention center, was revealed as fake in 1995.[68] Furthermore, Anthony Godby Johnson's memoir *A Rock and a Hard Place* and JT LeRoy's autobiographically inspired novels *Sarah*, *The Heart Is Deceitful Above All Things*, and *Harold's End* were exposed as fabricated by Vicki Fraginals and Laura Albert respectively. Albert and Fraginals also performed inter-gender and cross-generational impersonation of the chronically abused, and in Johnson's case terminally ill, authors in extensive phone, e-mail, and internet chat conversations with hosts of fans and celebrities over the course of several years.

But not only American authors have been exposed as having fabricated childhood misery. Kathy O'Beirne's memoir *Don't Ever Tell*, called in the United

States, *Kathy's Story: A Childhood Hell Inside the Magdalene Laundries,* was challenged in 2006 as entirely made up by several of her siblings and journalist Hermann Kelly.[69] The book's initial success was aided by a contemporary fascination with the Magdalene laundries, which were established in Ireland as homes for "fallen women" in the nineteenth century and only closed in 1996. They were depicted as the epitome of Dickensian cruelty in the 2002 film *The Magdalene Sisters.*[70] O'Beirne furthermore employed the trope of clerical sex abuse, when she accused, among others that include her own father, Fr. Fergal O'Connor of raping her. A year-long legal investigation exonerated the priest,[71] and Herman Kelly's research found no evidence for any of O'Beirne's claims of abuse. For instance, although the Sisters of Charity in Hyde Park were most meticulous record keepers, they have no record of O'Beirne, and the Magdalene Laundries admitted neither pregnant women nor girls as young as thirteen. And seven of her siblings argued that O'Beirne had been neither adopted nor abused, and said that during the years 1968–1970, when O'Beirne claims she was in a Magdalene laundry, she was at home. According to her siblings, she had been in a children's home for a brief period, in a psychiatric hospital, and in prison, which may well be enough for a misery memoir, but not the one she wrote.[72] Based on O'Beirne's birth certificate and school documents, Kelley confirmed that she had lied about her age, education, and alleged adoption. When he confronted her with these documents and his accusations on television, a spectacular altercation occurred as a furious O'Beirne reacted *Jerry Springer*–style and slapped him.[73]

Fake misery stories have not only transcended the national borders of America, but even the genre of memoirs, and entered internet blogs and local newspapers. The virtual space of the internet is the sphere where violations of the autobiographical pact are most likely and it is not surprising that fake tales of misery have also been generated through the new genre of blogs. In one such fake online diary, terminally ill nineteen-year-old Kaycee Nicole captivated thousands of internet users for nearly two years with almost daily entries about her heroic battle with leukemia and a host of other illnesses, only to be exposed as the figment of the imagination of Debbie Swenson, who had also written another fake blog in the voice of Kaycee's mother.[74] Fraudulent misery stories have furthermore been circulated by local newspapers, such as the *Messenger-Inquirer* of Owensboro, Kentucky, which published five columns in which a woman named Kim Stacey recounted an invented diagnosis and treatment of terminal cancer.[75]

Fabricated misery stories are not even restricted to the mass media. They also circulate orally in legal testimony, despite the fact that the witness is required to uphold the autobiographical pact by a legally binding oath. For instance, when Australian Dianne Lesley Burgess was accused in 2000 of stabbing a man in the neck while drunk, her defense during the trial was constructed around her claim of physical and sexual child abuse. In her own testimony, she furthermore stated that she had lost four children, twin sons in infancy, a daughter at age thirteen, and a son who died only a month before the trial. Invoking another core mis lit trope of potentially terminal illnesses, Burgess also said that she had survived both a brain tumor and liver cancer, and that the stabbing had occurred on the anniversary of her daughter's death. While the rather improbable tale convinced the judge to suspend her jail sentence, when Burgess's actual son came forward after seeing some of the media coverage of the case and revealed that none of his mother's story was true, the suspended sentence was reinstated.[76] However, judges are not only gullible listeners to tales of woe; well-known American judge James Ware even told his own misery yarn. Ware shared both the name and African American ethnicity of Virgil Ware's older brother, who had seen the shooting of thirteen-year-old Virgil by a white teen in Birmingham, Alabama, while he was perched on the handlebars of the bike James was riding. For years, the judge had not only falsely claimed to be this James Ware, but in many a speech had spoken passionately about how the experience of his brother's murder had led him to seek justice. Until it was exposed, the unethical usurpation of another man's boyhood experience of interracial violence benefited the judge's formidable career, which culminated in a 1997 nomination for a seat in a San Francisco–based appeals court, essentially one step below the U.S. Supreme Court.[77]

The most recent development in the universe of fake misery is that the exposure of fraudulent tales has itself become an increasingly common plot line. For instance, in an episode of *Law & Order: Criminal Intent*, a wealthy Pulitzer Prize–winning reporter is murdered after he discovered that the mysterious girl, who suffered from a terminal neuro-muscular disease and had become the author of an inspirational best-seller, did not actually exist.[78] Furthermore, the recent German film *Die Anruferin* (*The Calling Game*) tells the story of Irm Krishka, a solitary woman who works in a laundry and takes care of her mute, bed-ridden mother. Her life is joyless and dreary, apart from her nightly phone calls to strangers, when she pretends to be a young girl with leukemia. A master at improvisation, she builds up relationships with people at the other end of the line. Rather inexplicably, she suddenly kills off the child, gives out funeral information, and secretly watches the mourners who turn up at the cemetery for a nonexistent funeral. When Irm actually goes to visit one of her telephone interlocutors, a young woman who recently lost her husband, she pretends to be the dead girl's mother, and the two women form a friendship around their supposedly shared experience of loss and grief. While the friendship briefly improves Irm's life, this is not a Hollywood movie, and there is no redemptive-happy ending; rather, the friendship quickly deteriorates and her life now seems even more dreary.[79]

The plot line of uncovering fabricated stories of victimization and suffering has been disseminated most widely via Armistead Maupin's recent bestselling novel *The Night Listener* and its 2006 movie adaptation. The story recounts in fictionalized form Maupin's five-year friendship, maintained solely over telephone and e-mail, with the child abuse victim turned misery author Anthony Godby Johnson and Maupin's gradual realization that the boy probably never existed but was impersonated by Vicki Fraginals, who also claimed to be the boy's adopted mother.

## Reading Fake Misery

Mis lit confabulators clearly act unethically because, unlike fiction writers, they do tell lies, and because their forgeries will eventually cast suspicion on actual victim testimony. It is no less disconcerting that, despite the extensive critique of both book and author, of the over 1800 reviews on amazon.com, the majority of readers still recommend Frey's *A Million Little Pieces.* And of the over 20,000 messages posted about the book on the message boards of oprah.com, the majority do not resent Frey, but rather Winfrey for criticizing him.[80] New readers are still buying the book despite the fact that most of them must be aware of its status as a fake memoir. Daniel Mendelsohn argued in the *New York Times* that the notion of truth has "become dangerously slippery" because "the feeling on the part of many readers that, true or false, [Frey's] book had given them the feel-good, 'redemptive' experience they'd hoped for when they bought his novel—er, memoir."[81] As the events depicted in misery memoirs—child abuse, terminal illness, and addiction—are radically different from ordinary life experiences, the probability standards that readers use to evaluate what to believe are thus determined only second hand, by other media products. In a culture dominated by narratives of gruesome violence and victimization, readers are willing to suspend disbelief and trust the author as honoring the autobiographical pact, even if the depicted events vastly differ from their own life experiences and seem unimaginably horrific. However, upon exposure as forgeries, misery memoirs seem to lose their spell upon the audience. They no longer have the power to provide access to some mystical ultimate truth, to imbue the lives of late-modern individuals with authenticity, to reassure their sense of ontological security, or to teach core life lessons, especially the ultimate lesson of how to survive. The continued publication and consumption of Frey's macho recovery fantasy are, then, the exception rather than the rule, since the other exposed misery fakes are no longer in print. The decision to let them go out of print may indicate the publishers' realization that fake memoirs would eventually destroy the mis lit market, as the appeal of the genre lies precisely in the claim that the suffering was real. It may also reflect minimal sales of the exposed texts and thus the readers' demonstrated uninterest in fake accounts of pain and suffering.

Moreover, the fact that misery memoirs exposed as fraudulent generated scandals, especially "if the experiences recounted are traumatic, whether in the framework of an individual life, as in memoirs of sexual abuse, or in the framework of collective experience, as in memoirs about war and genocide,"[82] indicates that readers do not tolerate such literary lies.

When mis lit is revealed as forgery, the texts lose their attraction because this change in status from memoir, not to novel, but to the new genre of fake memoir fundamentally alters their reception. This idea of an intrinsic relation between a text's genre and its reception is not only central to Lejeune's concept of the autobiographical pact but was also implicit in Wiesel's comment that he significantly changed his review of *The Painted Bird* when Kosinski (falsely) claimed autobiographical status for his book. Ruth Klüger's comment on Wilkomirski's *Fragments* thus pertains to all misery memoirs exposed as fabricated: "A passage is shocking perhaps precisely because of its naive directness when read as the expression of endured suffering; but when it is revealed as a lie, as a presentation of invented suffering, it deteriorates to kitsch."[83] However, she also asserted that "the original readers have nothing to be embarrassed about" because "a few weeks ago they had a very different book in their hands from the one they have now, even though the text has remained the same."[84] Stefan Maechler, who conducted the most thorough investigation into the genre status of *Fragments*, likewise argued that "once the relationships between the first-person narrator, the death-camp story he narrates, and historical reality are proved palpably false, what was a masterpiece becomes kitsch."[85] The notion that a moving Holocaust memoir is transformed into kitsch when exposed as fabricated was echoed in a different false memoir scandal.

In 2001, Tad Friend revealed that Anthony Godby Johnson's *Between a Rock and a Hard Place* was entirely fabricated, because it had not been written by a sexually abused and HIV-infected teenage boy, but by a physically healthy, middle-aged woman called Vicki Fraginals. Friend also exposed that Fraginals had impersonated the boy for several years in telephone and e-mail conversations with vast numbers of people, including Pulitzer Prize–winning AIDS memoirist Paul Monette and *Tales of the City* author Armistead Maupin.[86] The latter had been so moved by the text when he believed it to be a memoir that he had contacted the boy and maintained a five-year friendship solely by telephone and e-mail, despite growing doubts about his existence. When Maupin was asked whether he had re-read the book after the exposure, he replied: "I've skimmed it—to my huge embarrassment, because once you know it's a fake, it reads like the most godawful kitsch!'"[87]

According to Jean Baudrillard, simulation jeopardizes value by neutralizing polarities.[88] When fictional narratives simulate non-fiction status, they not only constitute instances of deceit but they also threaten to annul the difference between nonfiction and fiction and hence obliterate the commodity value of life narratives. It seems that the violation of the autobiographical pact in a number of misery memoirs has not yet affected the popularity of the genre as a whole. Readers continue to believe that even the most horrific tales of depravity constitute reliable accounts of real-life events for the dubious pleasure of relishing their own kitsch-sentimental emotional arousal. However, unlike the use of fake guests on trash talk shows, the forgery of misery memoirs has not increased the popularity of the genre. While the impostors introduced another playful duplicity to talk shows that reinforced the spectator's ironic camp gaze, false victimhood claims in mis lit counteract its teary-eyed reception, because audiences need to believe that the suffering was real rather than fictional. Since misery memoirs thus rely to a larger extent on their nonfiction status, forgeries constitute a greater threat to their commodity value than the inclusion of fake guests on talk shows. However, since trash talk shows claim that, despite their outlandish performances, guests are real and their stories fulfill the conditions of the autobiographical pact, they too rely on the fiction/nonfiction binary. If the trend of forging autobiographical narratives continues in either genre, both mis lit and talk shows will lose their appeal, since it rests precisely on the claim that the incredible stories did really happen.

# 9

## Forging Child Abuse

"The greed with which publishers devour childhood-abuse memoirs has
led to the genre becoming a natural home for liars and fantasists."
–Cathrine Bennett, *The Observer*[1]

Holocaust kitsch continues to be a popular commodity, as the commercial
success of the novels *The Boy in the Striped Pajamas* and *The Reader* as well as their
successful 2008 movie adaptations indicate. However, its preeminent position
particularly in American culture has been taken over by other narratives of
victimhood and suffering, survival and recovery, for which it generated the paradigm. Tropes like the melodramatic good-versus-evil plot structure, its culmination in the kitsch-sentimental redemptive-happy ending, and its embodiment in
the lead characters of innocent victim and evil villain have been widely employed
for representing terminal illness, recovery from addictions, and especially child
abuse. Such popular culture narratives are furthermore constructed analogously
to the dominant plot paradigm of before-during-after of Holocaust memoirs and
movies. And they likewise focus almost entirely on the during-phase of victimization and suffering, while only briefly touching on the before-phase of supposed
innocent bliss for melodramatic contrast, and often entirely excluding the after-
phase of recovery. Moreover, the artifacts that embody and disseminate popular
trauma culture reflect and reinforce the dominant notion that past victimization
in general and child abuse in particular explain any and all present dysfunctions.
Daniel Ganzfried's ironic critique that, represented as a tale of trauma and recovery, "the Holocaust explains everything," including "why your girlfriend left you,
why you have headaches, [and] why you have school problems,"[2] can thus be
expanded to the currently dominant understanding of victimhood at large. For
instance, comedienne and TV star Roseanne claimed in her 1994 memoir *My Lives*
that her eating disorder, alcohol addiction, self-mutilation, teenage pregnancy,
and stints of delinquency and prostitution can all be explained (and excused) in
a conveniently mono-causal swoop by her abusive childhood.[3]

After the nineteenth-century moral notion of cruelty to children had been
recast in the early 1960s as the medico-therapeutic category of Battered Child

Syndrome, in the 1970s it was merged with incest into the new and vastly expanded concept of child abuse.[4] In a further paradigm shift, it was aligned with the notion of trauma in the mid-1980s, when claims of therapeutically "recovered" memories of child abuse became ubiquitous, first in American and subsequently other Western media. According to therapeutic discourse, the infliction of child abuse is a psycho-social dysfunction. However, recently the earlier notion that cruelty to children is immoral resurged and child abuse currently constitutes the embodiment of ultimate evil, particularly in American culture. Oprah Winfrey's spectacular exposure of her sexual abuse as a child, the extensive discussion of abuse and supposedly related subjects like Post-Traumatic Stress Disorder and Multiple Personality Disorder on daytime talk shows, and the representation of sexual abuse in the new popular literature genres of incest novels and misery memoirs saturated the public sphere with abuse stories in the 1990s. They increasingly replaced Holocaust survival as the dominant subject for depicting the victimization of the innocent by the equally one-dimensional character of the evil perpetrator.

Perhaps the most prominent indication that the Holocaust is being replaced by child abuse as the prime subject for representing both the individual suffering of victims and the ultimate embodiment of evil in American culture was provided on *The Oprah Winfrey Show*. As her book club selection of *Night* and her televised visit with Wiesel to Auschwitz indicate, Winfrey has embraced and reinforced the questionable incorporation of the Holocaust into American cultural memory and one might take her prior selection of Bernhard Schlink's *The Reader* for the show's book club to signify her proclivity for Holocaust kitsch. The reviews of the novel in German and French newspapers explored the author's attempt to exculpate Hanna, a former concentration camp guard, not only from guilt, but from any responsibility for her actions. The author's apologetic stance is based on the insubstantial and unethical argument that Hanna's illiteracy made her morally illiterate and that therefore her actions were amoral rather than immoral. However, Winfrey led the discussion on her show, which aired in February 1999, in a direction that not only largely ignored the question of Hanna's guilt as a former camp guard but also noticeably surprised Schlink. It focused on another plot line about the relationship between fifteen-year-old Michael, who narrates the novel in the first-person, and thirty-year-old Hanna. Winfrey and her guests recast into an act of child abuse the age-old convention of an adolescent's sexual initiation by an older woman of lower socio-economic standing, typically a maid. While Schlink's novel dubiously represents Hanna as a victim rather than a perpetrator, the *Oprah Winfrey Show* transformed her from a Nazi into a child abuser, in other words, from the previous to the current preeminent embodiment of ultimate evil in American culture.

Child abuse also became the dominant subject in misery memoirs and their fakes. Libbi Brooks, for instance, inadvertently reflected this development in her comment that "scanning the supermarket shelves that heave with misery memoirs, each detailing abuses and degradations more hideously imaginative than the last, I can only marvel at so many terrible childhoods."[5] And Simon Caterson's sarcastic comment that "the credibility of so-called misery lit, memoirs of childhood abuse and suffering, is taking a battering, so to speak"[6] indicates, it seems likewise inadvertently, the conflation of mis lit forgeries with depictions of physical and/or sexual child abuse. Literary forgers, like art or currency forgers, only seek to simulate those entities to which a particular culture ascribes its highest value, whether monetary, aesthetic, or moral. Hence, the fact that forged memoirs primarily depict childhood misery, even when they focus on Holocaust survival, as in the false memoirs of Misha Defonseca and Binjamin Wilkomirski, reinforces my argument that child abuse replaced the Holocaust as the preeminent embodiment of victimization and suffering in contemporary American culture. Contextualized in a brief genealogy of child abuse discourse, this chapter therefore explores the recent trend of supposedly autobiographical but actually fictional and therefore fake narratives of abusive childhoods as core embodiments of popular trauma culture.

## Representing Child Abuse

Violence toward children entered the public sphere in the late nineteenth century via the concept of "cruelty to children" almost simultaneously with the provocative early writings of Sigmund Freud about sexual acts involving children. Nevertheless, both discourses remained distinct at the time and disappeared largely from the public sphere around the turn of the twentieth century. It was only in 1962, when a group of American pediatricians under the direction of C. H. Kempe provocatively claimed that the healed fractures in the arms and legs of young children, perceivable in x-rays, were the result of child battering, that the moral concept of cruelty toward children was revived and transformed into the concept of Battered Child Syndrome.[7] The subject generated a vast professional discourse: The journal *Child Abuse and Neglect* was founded in 1976 and between 1975 and 1980 over 1,700 research articles were published on Battered Child Syndrome. Books on the subject written in English rose from zero in 1965 to 9 by 1975, 105 by 1980, and over 600 by 1991.[8] The radically new ideas generated by Kempe et al. in 1962 were also disseminated widely through reports in major American newspapers and journals, for instance, *Newsweek*, *Time*, and *The Saturday Evening Post* featured articles on the subject in the same year.[9]

Although Kempe et al. were pediatricians and their primary concern was children's physical health, their paper contained ideas that would come to permeate the growing fields of psychiatry and clinical psychology. They hypothesized that child battery, that is, the infliction of pain that far exceeded accepted notions of corporal punishment, was considerably widespread and damaged not only children's bodies but also had detrimental long-term effects on their psyches that needed medical attention just like their physical injuries. The physicians furthermore cast the battering parent not as immoral, but as mentally ill and hence likewise in need of therapeutic treatment by experts. In other words, they claimed not only the children's bodies but also both their and the batterer's psyches as new objects of medical knowledge-power. Since therapeutic discourse defines physical and sexual child abuse as forms of abnormal behavior, it transformed the infliction of incest and violence on children from a socio-political subject into an individual pathology. As Louise Armstrong criticized, "incest, medicalized, was neutralized; stripped of its character as a deliberate act of aggression."[10] Consequently, the therapeutic master narrative is politically acquiescing, because it advocates that individuals rather than society be changed.

Feminist discourse had sought to use the momentum generated not only to make the physical and sexual violence inflicted on women and children in the privacy of the home public, but also to establish it as an eminently political concern, because it constituted an expression of patriarchal oppression. However, when the zeitgeist of political activism that dominated the late 1960s gave way to the so-called me-decade of the 1970s and identity politics was increasingly transformed into quests of personal self-discovery, the rise of therapeutic knowledge-power quickly absorbed interpersonal violence into its inherently de-politicized sphere. Although feminists initially rejected the de-politicization of interpersonal violence engendered by therapeutic discourse, they adopted its notion that battery and incest are instances in the same category. In other words, despite the fact that therapeutics suppressed feminism's central goal of making the personal at large and interpersonal violence in particular political, feminists reinforced the radical paradigm shift initiated though therapeutic discourse of fusing the previously distinct categories of battery and incest as child abuse.

The newly generated concept of child abuse exceeds the sum of its two constitutive parts. The sub-category of sexual abuse, for instance, defines much more behavior than incest as illicit. It vastly extended the notion of what constituted sexual acts, because it encompasses not only very rare intra-familial child rape, but also an array of other sexualized behavior euphemistically designated as "touching" or "fondling"[11] and, in America, even virtually all parental and/or child nudity. Moreover, it expanded the group of potential perpetrators beyond family members to all adults.

In the 1980s, the understanding of child abuse underwent two further interrelated changes. The first is evident in the writings of Ellen Bass, a poet and creative writing teacher, who also worked as a child abuse counselor since 1970. In 1983, she published a collection of child abuse narratives called *I Never Told Anyone*. While the authors of these autobiographical accounts told their stories for the first time, they had never forgotten the abuse. However, in the 1988 bestseller *The Courage to*

*Heal,* which Bass co-authored with Laura Davis, the justified claim that sexual child abuse had been suppressed in the public sphere was extended to the individual mind and generated the nonsensical idea that children can repress memories of sexual abuse for years, and even decades, to the extent of complete amnesia.[12] The notion of "recovery" simultaneously underwent a change in signification. While it used to designate the physical and, especially, the psychological recovery from abuse, it came to denote the recovery of repressed memories of abuse suffered long ago. According to the new paradigm constructed in recovered memory therapeutics, sexual abuse inflicted severe psychological trauma on the child and since it had not been therapeutically treated, it was repressed, often by way of generating multiple, split-off personalities called alters. The repressed trauma was said to be obliquely expressed in a host of dysfunctional behaviors and beliefs, even decades after the abuse. *The Courage to Heal* provides a checklist of some seventy-eight phenomena, including the need to be perfect, a lack of a sense of one's interests, trouble expressing feelings, feeling alienated or lonely, the inability to say "no," and the over-protectiveness of one's children.[13] As recovered memory gospel defines these characteristics, which are pervasive among American women, as symptoms of child abuse rather than as consequences of socio-economic inequality in inter-gender power relations, it is politically anesthetizing and reinforces the oppressions inherent in the current status quo.

Between the mid-1980s and the mid-1990s, "recovered memories" of sexual child abuse went from virtual nonexistence to ubiquity in the "American middle-class culture's symptom pool."[14] For example, Harvard psychiatrist and feminist Judith Herman claims in her influential 1992 study *Trauma and Recovery* that "50–60 percent of psychiatric inpatients and 40–60 percent of outpatients report childhood histories of physical or sexual abuse or both," despite the fact that the patients have few, if any, memories of the abuse.[15] And according to Bass and Davis's *The Courage to Heal,* as many as one in three girls and one in seven boys in the United States have been sexually abused. The supposedly vast numbers of abuse victims, and thus the significant pool of potential patients claimed, can be explained by the fact that "recovered memory is big business in the United States, with self-help tapes, T-shirts, recovery groups, and even a mass-market best-seller [*The Courage to Heal*],"[16] not to mention countless hours of therapy. Women, in particular, may have eagerly embraced recovery doctrine, not only because it allowed them to abdicate responsibility for their present unhappiness and dissatisfaction, but also because it constituted the dominant narrative among the few culturally available paradigms to express female suffering. However, the estimates made by the American Professional Society on the Abuse of Children are significantly lower, at 1.3 percent of American women who have experienced sexual child abuse.[17]

While "recovered" memories tend to be subjectively experienced as reliable because they share their predominantly visual nature with actual autobiographical memories, after large-scale legal investigations and extensive scholarly analysis, no empirical evidence that they reflect actual experiences was found.[18] Rather, they constitute therapeutically co-created confabulations or fantasies, that is, narratives dialogically constructed by patient and therapist that were facilitated by a shared belief in the omnipresence of abuse, the omnipotent explanatory power of past trauma for present dysfunction, and familiarity with formulas and tropes of recovered memory narratives. Essentially, patient and therapist mistake the patient's memories of recovery narratives, which are ubiquitous in the vast popular psychology literature and the mass media, for autobiographical memories of the patient's own experiences.

Incest has a long tradition as a literary motif that reaches at least as far back as the famous Oedipus myth of Aeschylus and Sophocles in the fifth century B.C. and became a favorite taboo to break for British and German Romantics, but it only recently returned as a literary subject after a virtual absence of some two centuries. However, it reemerged with a vengeance and, transformed into child abuse, became ubiquitous, not only in canonical literature and film,[19] but also in children's literature,[20] popular fiction,[21] and of course misery memoirs. However, contemporary representations of child abuse replaced Romantic fatalism of inadvertent brother-sister incest with spectacularly violent abusive relations between father-figures and daughters and, in the case of physical abuse, mothers and both sons and daughters. Incestuous father-daughter abuse may once have been a daring subject in the novels of Toni Morrison, Alice Walker, and Maya Angelou, and early memoirs like Louise Armstrong's *Kiss Daddy Goodnight* because they were written with the decidedly feminist political agenda of exposing the crime in order to end it. These texts also represented abuse as anything but forgotten. However, as the subject became omnipresent in the 1990s, misery memoirs transformed child abuse into trite tropes and eliminated the political agenda in order to generate titillating horror kitsch spectacles by narrating sexualized violence in pornographic detail.[22]

Before abusive childhoods became *de rigueur* in mis lit, the subject had already generated another new literary subgenre of so-called incest novels which includes, among others, the following: Donna Tartt, *The Secret History*, Dorothy Allison, *Bastard Out of Carolina*, Mary Gaitskill, *Two Girls, Fat and Thin*, Marilyn French, *Our Father*, Russell Banks, *The Sweet Hereafter*, E. Annie Proulx, *The Shipping News*, Amy Bloom, *Come to Me*, Joyce Carol Oates, *You Must Remember This*, Heather Lewis, *House Rules*, Geoffrey Wolf, *The Age of Consent*, Anne Ice, *The Witching Hour*, Josephine Hart, *Damage*, Stephen King, *Gerald's Game*, and the first novel by an unknown poet named Sapphire, called *Push*, which, after a spectacular bidding war over the manuscript, sold for an astonishing half a million dollars.[23] Published in 1996, *Push* narrates the physical and sexual abuse of an obese and illiterate black girl by her parents. Her father repeatedly rapes her, has impregnated her twice, and infected her with HIV. While the narrator stipulates that "We is [sic] a nation of raped children," Katie Roiphe acerbically commented on this compilation of mis lit tropes that "whatever the truth of that, we are certainly a nation that wants to read about them."[24] In 2009, the novel was adapted into a movie called *Precious*, which by February 2010 had already grossed more than $50.8 million and was nominated for six Academy Awards. Roiphe's remark thus still holds some fifteen years later and can even be extended, since it seems that the nation not only wants to read about child rape and battery but even to watch it on screen in Technicolor.

Incest novels even entered the literary canon. Jane Smiley's Pulitzer Prize–winning *A Thousand Acres* transposes the plot of *King Lear* to a farm in Iowa, and transforms it in accordance with the recovered memory paradigm, so that the two oldest daughters recover memories of incestuous child rape by their father.[25] And the fact that the most prominent canonical incest narrative, Sylvia Fraser's *My Father's House*, is subtitled *A Memoir of Incest and Healing* indicates the transition from the novel to the memoir as the preeminent mode of representing incest and child abuse generally. Despite the fact that Fraser has no memories of the abuse, she is convinced it happened, and creates a kind of multiple first-person plot, narrated by her MPD alters who she believes emerged as a consequence of the repressed abuse. Judith Herman discussed the text as a paradigmatic tale of recovered memory and Multiple Personality Disorder, that is, she took it as established that the abuse had indeed occurred, despite Fraser's total amnesia.[26] However, Elaine Showalter convincingly argued that Fraser entirely imagined the abuse because it allowed her to abdicate responsibility for her present behavior and thus to exculpate herself for destroying her marriage by having an affair.[27]

While families may have been unhappy in their own unique fashions in the days of *Anna Karenina*, the families in incest novels and misery memoirs are dysfunctional in rather formulaic ways.[28] Claiming to reveal the dark secrets ubiquitous among the overtly happy middle-class families portrayed on TV sitcoms, their plots, conflicts, and characters are equally lacking in complexity, ambiguity, and development.[29] Reflecting the two paradigm shifts in therapeutic discourse, incest novels and misery memoirs emplot sexual child abuse as kitsch-sentimental melodrama in two core plot types. In the first, employed, for instance, in Cynthia Grant's novel *Uncle Vampire* and Constance Briscoe's memoir *Ugly*, the abuse is represented as occurring in the narrated present and depicted in horrific detail by an uncomprehending naïve child's voice. Some texts are narrated in the present tense, which is always inherently nonsensical, because it conflates the experiencing and the narrating self and claims the simultaneity of the depicted action and its narration. Others are retroactively told from an unspecified place and time in the future after the abuse ended by a narrator who is no longer a naïve child. Either way, sexual abuse stories related through the voice of an uncomprehending young child employ a logically impossible narrative perspective to heighten the absolute innocence ascribed to childhood by juxtaposing it to the ultimate evil embodied by the abusive villain.

The second stock plot employed in incest novels and the subset of misery memoirs that depict sexual child abuse reflects the recovered memory paradigm, that is, the abuse is unknown to the adult narrator-protagonist, and usually also to the reader, until the memories are recovered at the end. Beyond mis lit and incest novels, the recovery of abuse memories also constitutes a standard plot twist in other lowbrow genres. Gory paperback thrillers depict serial killers with multiple personalities who were sexually abused as children.[30] And in so-called black lace novels, which narrate pornography for women readers, incest functions in the tradition of gothic melodrama, as the spellbinding dark secret in the heroine's harrowing past. In fact, according to Maureen Freely, in the latter "the deep, dark secret that you have to plow through hundreds of pages to discover is always—but *always*—what the blurb writers like to call 'society's last taboo.' So it's not much of a surprise anymore."[31] Novels and memoirs that employ the recovered memory plot formula depict an adult woman who experiences any number and combination of the dozens of common problems listed in *The Courage to Heal* and a host of other self-help books and, couched in the melodramatic rhetoric of the family secret, eventually remembers the abuse. After the reader has been kept in suspense, the revealed abuse explains everything with the simplicity of a solved riddle to which the abuse is the monocausal, teleological answer. As recovered memory rhetoric borrowed much of its imagery from gothic melodrama and it's interpretation by Freud, gothic tropes abound in these texts. For instance, the architecture of the gothic castle, with its dungeons, attics, trap doors, and grave yards provides the core metaphor for the structure of the unconscious.

Child abuse has also become increasingly common fare on television. Kitsch-sentimental redemption stories of abuse and recovery became a staple on first-generation talk shows. Oprah Winfrey disclosed her own sexual abuse in an interview with Barbara Walters and narrated the television documentary *Scared Silent*, which aired simultaneously on PBS, CBS, ABC, and NBC on September 4, 1992.[32] Moreover, victims of sexual child abuse have been featured on the cover of *People* magazine, among them several former Miss Americas, comedienne Roseanne, and actresses Rita Hayworth, Marilyn Monroe, and Lana Turner.[33] Sexual child abuse has also been the focus of highly publicized celebrity news stories, including LaToya Jackson's allegations that her father sexually abused several of the Jackson children, accusations against Michael Jackson for sexual molestation of boys, and Mia Farrow's allegation in her divorce from Woody Allen that he had molested her adopted daughter.[34] And the subject was even taken up in the comics, according to Ian Hacking, "*Spiderman*, *Rex Morgan*, and *Gasoline Alley* had run stories on the topic and *Mary Worth* was flirting with it."[35]

Empirical media studies established that, while depictions of gratuitous violence tend to generate strong arousal reactions,[36] "the stimulus category or genre that . . . consistently produc[es] the strongest excitatory reaction in both adult men and women is pornography."[37] Furthermore, "harm inflicting actions believed to have actually happened tend to be more arousing (or tend to perpetuate initially elevated levels of arousal for longer periods of time) than the same actions believed to be fictional."[38] As misery memoirs of child abuse merge the three elements that generate the highest levels of excitation—(deviant) sexuality, gratuitous violence, and autobiographical status—in all probability they generate the highest level of autonomous arousal in consumers. Moreover, since child abuse constitutes the ultimate embodiment of absolute evil in contemporary American culture, audiences develop the most negative dispositions toward the abusive father-figure villain and the most positive dispositions towards the innocent child victim. The highest dysphoric arousal levels are experienced when consuming the gratuitous physical and sexual violence inflicted on the child leads to the most value-neutral excitatory residues, which in turn maximally enhance the euphoric arousal via excitation transfer at the inevitable redemptive-happy ending. It was most likely for these reasons that non-fictional accounts of physical and sexual child abuse have become ubiquitous and more popular than fictional and nonfictional Holocaust representations, incest novels, or misery memoirs of terminal illness or recovery from addiction.[39]

Given the apparently insatiable appetite of readers, and hence publishers, for narratives of horrific child abuse, writers began to exaggerate or even entirely fabricate their tales of childhood misery. This chapter thus analyzes the recent cultural trend of child abuse narratives that falsely claim autobiographical status as core embodiments of popular trauma culture. It explores Anthony Godby Johnson's false misery memoir *A Rock and a Hard Place*, published in 1993, and JT LeRoy's likewise fraudulent autobiographical texts *Sarah* and *The Heart Is Deceitful Above All Things*, which appeared in 2000 and 2001, as exemplary instances of child abuse narratives that fraudulently pretend to be nonfiction. Although the texts and extensive literary scandals upon their revelation as forgeries have been discussed widely in the international English-language press, this constitutes their first scholarly analysis.

## Inventing Anthony Godby Johnson's Childhood Misery

In the postscript to his bestselling *The Night Listener*, Armistead Maupin recounts the experience that inspired the novel. Maupin had been sent the galley proofs of *A Rock and a Hard Place* by David Groff, an editor at Crown Publishing, on the recommendation of Maupin's friend, fellow writer Paul Monette, with a request for a brief quotation to be used on the book's back cover. Since Maupin believed, like Monette and Groff, that the manuscript was a memoir by an adolescent who had been severely physically and sexually abused and in the course been infected with syphilis and HIV, he was so moved by what he read that he contacted the author, "Anthony Godby Johnson."[40] Thus began a friendship maintained entirely through telephone and e-mail conversations. Although Maupin began to have doubts of "Tony's" existence when his partner pointed out how similar the voices of "Tony" and his adoptive mother "Vicki" were and because "Vicki" continuously refused to let Maupin visit "Tony," he nevertheless maintained the friendship for five years.[41] "There would be weeks when I was utterly convinced that he was real," he explained, "then weeks when I suspected that Vicki was creating him."[42] Eventually he came to believe that the abused and terminally ill boy was indeed nothing but a figment of Vicki Fraginals's imagination and that she had not only written the supposed memoir but also impersonated "Tony" in their phone and e-mail conversations.[43]

Maupin explained that he "was easy to dupe because, in all honesty, there's something very flattering about someone who's about to die that wants to talk to you, casting you in the role of savior."[44] He also admitted that, although he is convinced that "Tony" never existed beyond Fraginals's mind, he is "still more real to me than many people who demonstrably do exist" and that he has "great trouble killing that child in my head."[45] While Maupin's comment reflects Vicki Fraginals' talent for impersonation and testifies to the power of virtual reality, it also indicates that, paradoxically, "Tony" was such a convincing figure precisely because he was not real, but rather a compilation of trauma culture tropes. Or as Tad Friend put it, he was "a symbol of modern victimhood, his body torn apart by the most appalling end-of-the-millennium traumas—child abuse and AIDS."[46]

According to Friend's thorough journalistic investigation, published both in *The New Yorker* and in slightly abridged form in the British *Independent on Sunday*, "the first public record of Tony Johnson is a beguiling letter he wrote in August 1991 to Paul Monette, a U.S. National Book Award–winning writer and gay activist, who himself had AIDS. In it, the thirteen-year-old Tony . . . said that he too was very sick, and that in the hospital he had bartered sports magazines for Monette's books *Love Alone* and *Borrowed Time: An AIDS Memoir*."[47] Monette thought the letter peculiar and did not intend to reply but his partner, a psychotherapist, convinced him otherwise, because the boy was dying. And "the more Monette heard of Tony's story, the more convinced he became that Tony should write it down."[48] Monette, who published sixteen books before he died of AIDS in 1995, became his mentor and acted in the capacity that Ken Plummer dubbed coaxer and described as a sympathetic, accepting listener who largely elicits and thus co-creates the story but whose role is obscured in the manuscript.[49] Monette himself described their interaction and his role when he was defending himself against the double accusation, raised by Michelle Ingrassia in

*Newsweek*,[50] that "Tony" did not exist and that Monette, who wrote the foreword to *A Rock and a Hard Place*, was in fact the author: "I never touched a word of Tony's manuscript. I talked to this kid every night for an hour and a half for a year, and he would read a piece and I'd say, 'Very good. Keep going.'"[51] And when "Tony" hit an impasse and "worried that no one wanted to hear an obscure boy's tale of woe, Monette urged him to remember that 'the greatest human testament we have from the Second World War was written by a fourteen-year-old girl,'"[52] a comparison to Anne Frank made explicit (without reference to Monette) on the book's back cover: "Like *The Diary of Anne Frank*, this moving testament by a young teenager touches our hearts and our consciences." Monette also referred "Tony" to his agent, Wendy Weil, and his editor at Crown Publishing, David Groff.[53]

In addition to Monette and Maupin, "Tony" had a third telephone confidant, Jack Godby, an AIDS activist and counselor, whose last name he adopted as his own middle name. While Vicki Fraginals had contacted Monette impersonating "Tony" via a letter, she first called Godby pretending to be "Tony's" adoptive mother. In his introduction to *A Rock and a Hard Place*, Godby writes that "Tony" essentially decided to adopt him as a father figure. However, the preface is misleading, since it creates the impression that Godby regularly interacted with "Tony" in person. For instance, he describes picking up the sweets "Tony" liked for their weekly ritual of watching TV together and wrote that he tucked him into bed at night. He neglects to mention that their relationship existed only in the virtual reality of telephone conversations, that he only metaphorically tucked "Tony" into bed over the phone, and that they watched TV each in his own home while talking on the phone as "Tony' was eating the sweets Godby had sent him. While Maupin acknowledged that he became convinced that "Tony" never existed and Monette voiced some concern when no one came forward to vouch for his existence after Michelle Ingrassia's *Newsweek* accusations, Jack Godby never publicly rescinded his belief that "Tony" is real.

Ingrassia had noticed that the book cover did not bear an author photograph and that *A Rock and a Hard Place* was also short on verifiable facts. When she began to investigate, she was struck by the fact that no one had ever met "Tony."[54] In addition to Monette, Godby, and Maupin, neither his agent Wendy Weil nor his editor David Groff, TV personality Fred Rogers (who wrote the afterword to the book), ESPN sportscaster Keith Olberman (who was writing a novel with Tony over the phone), Norma Godin—the executive director of the New Jersey Make A Wish Foundation, which gave "Tony" a computer on which to write his memoir—nor her son Scott, who installed it in "Tony's" apartment, had ever seen him.[55] She concluded that "there is no evidence that Tony exists beyond a telephone voice" and suggested that the soprano could belong to a woman as easily as to a fifteen-year-old boy.[56] The *Newsweek* article caused a stir both in the United States and abroad. HBO rescinded the contract for the planned film adaptation of *A Rock and a Hard Place* when "Vicki" refused to let the scriptwriter meet "Tony"[57] and the British *Times* cancelled plans to excerpt the memoir.[58]

Since Vicki Fraginals had created a figure whom she could only impersonate in virtual reality, "Anthony Godby Johnson" could not appear in public. However, to counter the suspicions raised by Ingrassia's article, "Vicki" permitted one journalist to visit "Tony" to confirm his existence. She chose Associated Press reporter Leslie Dreyfous, who had written a favorable review of the book.[59] Dreyfous visited "Tony" on May 25, 1993. However, "Vicki" imposed strict guidelines upon the visit, such that Dreyfous was permitted to say neither for how long she had seen and talked to "Tony" nor how close she had been to him physically. Dreyfous was not even permitted to write about the visit herself. Another AP reporter, Mitchell Landsberg, wrote the story.[60] He cites Dreyfous, who confirmed that she met "Tony," stated that "his face was swollen and that he was wearing dark glasses and a baseball cap but that the voice was the same she had spoken to on the phone."[61] However, after Maupin published *The Night Listener*, Dreyfous told him that, though she kept in touch with "Tony" until 1999 and had had no doubts about having met him in 1993, she was no longer sure whether he existed or not.[62] Whoever impersonated "Tony" for Lesley Dreyfous's visit has never come forward.

Misery memoirs typically depict abuse in minute detail. However, in *A Rock and a Hard Place* the frequent parental beatings, utmost neglect—"Tony" has no bed, no winter coat, not even a toothbrush, and lives on scraps of food—and repeated rapes by a ring of pedophiles with his parents' approval occur offstage, are mentioned in passing only, and are largely limited to the first chapter. The fake memoir instead focuses on "Tony's" life outside the abusive home, including chapters chronicling his caring relationships with the mentally handicapped janitor of his building, with a stray cat and her kittens, and with his best friend, with whom he spends many nights on the New York subway to avoid home. Furthermore, unlike most protagonists of misery memoirs, "Tony" is not saved at the end of the story, but at the end of the first chapter, which summarizes his abusive childhood and depicts the rather improbable story of his rescue. At age eleven, after a particularly brutal beating, "Tony" is on the verge of killing himself and calls a national suicide hotline. He talks to "Earnist Johnson,"[63] a black man from the South, who gives him the number of a child welfare center in New York. At this point, Vicki Fraginals writes herself into the story. When "Tony" calls the center, he speaks to a social worker named "Vicki." Furthermore, not only did "Earnist Johnson" travel all the way to New York to visit "Tony" in the hospital into which "Vicki" had checked him, but "Earnist" and "Vicki" fall in love, marry, and adopt "Tony." And since fairy tales tend not only to end happily for the good characters but meet out punishment for the bad ones, "Tony's" abusive parents have magically been prosecuted for child abuse and imprisoned. The first chapter, which constitutes a condensed compilation of misery memoir tropes, also introduces the paradigmatic mis lit subject of terminal illness, which dominates the latter part of the text. Evocative of Battered Child Syndrome, when "Vicki" checks "Tony" into the hospital, he is found to have fifty-four bone fractures that have poorly healed as none of them had been treated. He also suffers a stroke and is diagnosed with an advanced case of syphilis and subsequently with HIV.

While the lives of authors naturally continue after the publication of an autobiographical text and some publish further accounts, "Anthony Godby Johnson's" story developed significantly beyond the fake memoir into the quasi-virtual realm of phone conversations in which it had begun and expanded into the emerging sphere of cyberspace via e-mail and internet chat rooms. He became the co-leader of a chat room called Teen Talk, and in 1997 he set up his own web site, Tony's World, where he regularly posted updates on his life, particularly his constant health crises.[64] With the transition from the telephone to cyberspace, "Tony's" story became even more extreme and improbable. His father was murdered in prison by other members of the pedophile sex ring, who also sought to kill "Tony." Reflecting the rise to prominence of terminal illness narratives in both misery memoirs and online diaries, "Tony" also vastly expanded the detailed reports on his many severe health problems. He is constantly bedridden as he not only continues to suffer from early-onset AIDS, but from a burgeoning number of other illnesses, caused by his weakened immune system, including tuberculosis, recurrent pneumonia, a near-constant fever of 102°, shingles, and neuropathy. He needs an oxygen tank to breathe, has lost his spleen, a testicle, sight in one eye, and even had a leg amputated.[65]

Like Bruno Dössekker and Monique DeWael, who fabricated the not only fake but also rather unlikely memoirs of "Binjamin Wilkomirski" and "Misha Defonseca," Vicky Fraginals created a story that had serious probability flaws and has been reliably established as a confabulation. Tad Friend's journalistic investigation found no records of a social worker named "Vicki Johnson" registered in New York or New Jersey, a former U.S. Air Force sergeant and suicide hotline volunteer called "Earnist Johnson" or a Vietnam veteran and former Vietcong POW by the name of "Jerry DiNicola" (a character introduced in a later chapter and continued into cyberspace). There are no records either of "Tony's" parents being sentenced for child abuse or of his father's murder in prison. Friend also made inquiries in the apartment building at Union City, New Jersey, which "Tony" had given to various friends and supporters as his mailing address after moving there from New York with "Vicki" and "Earnist" upon their marriage and his adoption. While neighbors did remember Vicki Fraginals, who had grown up in the neighborhood and lived in the particular building as an adult, no one had seen or knew of her supposed husband or adopted son. Furthermore, the vast number of serious illnesses "Tony" suffered but from which he never died—rather like "Binjamin" in *Fragments,* who likewise continued to survive the impossible—make the story highly improbable even for people with limited medical expertise. Armistead Maupin, for example, "couldn't help wondering how Tony kept on living, even as he kept on almost dying."[66] Furthermore, the frequent and extensive phone conversations belied the claim that "Tony's" lungs had been ravaged by both tuberculosis and chronic pneumonia and that he used an oxygen tank, as his voice showed no evidence of chronic illness.[67] For instance, "in a lengthy phone interview with *Newsweek* and in a syndicated radio chat, Tony never once wheezed, coughed, or struggled for breath."[68] Last but not least, Vicki Fraginals invented a persona whom she could only impersonate in virtual reality and therefore—apart from the performance put on for journalist Lesley Dreyfous—"Tony" could never interact with anyone in unmediated reality. All of these vast improbabilities and serious flaws in logic and factual veracity suggest that Vicki Fraginals generated her confabulation in the same gradual and impromptu manner in which Bruno Dössekker created "Binjamin Wilkomirski" rather than the way Margaret Seltzer carefully planned the imper-sonation of "Margaret B. Jones" to publish her fake misery memoir *Love and Consequences.*

However, unlike other false memoirists, Vicki Fraginals included what, with hindsight, appear as clues to the confabulated nature of both "Tony" and *A Rock and a Hard Place,* in both the memoir itself and in related texts. For instance, "Tony's" first letter to Armistead Maupin was a 1992 Christmas card that displayed both Virginia O'Hanlon's famous question of whether there is a Santa Claus, sent to the *New York Sun,* and the editor's answer: "Yes; Virginia, there is a Santa Claus. He exists as certainly as love and generosity exist. You might get your papa to hire men to watch all the chimneys on Christmas Eve to catch Santa Claus, but even if they did not see Santa Claus coming down, what would that prove? The most real things in the world are those that neither children nor men can see."[69] In addition to a personal note, "Tony" had written "my favorite" with an arrow next to the editor's answer. Re-read with hindsight, Fraginals seems to be saying, whether wittingly or unwittingly, that "Tony" is as real as Santa Claus or, as his editor David Groff stated, "Tony's like God. . . . He's someone you just have to believe in."[70] The memoir itself contains a similarly revealing allusion to "Tony's" dubious notion of what is real. In one of several intertexual references, he refers to "Earnist Johnson's" favorite book, Margery Williams's *The Velveteen Rabbit.* In this children's novel, a toy rabbit comes alive because a boy truly loves him and, puzzled by this transformation, the rabbit is told that "real isn't how you are made. . . . It's a thing that happens to you."[71] Furthermore, as a character in *A Rock and a Hard Place* "Tony" ironically remarks that he is an accomplished fiction writer, since all his school essays about sub-jects like family, Christmas presents, and vacations were fictitious, and, in another intertexual reference, he cites Charlotte, the spider of E. B. White's *Charlotte's*

*Web*, who considered humans gullible because they believed everything they saw in print.[72]

Despite the stir caused by Ingrassia's *Newsweek* article, the mystery of whether "Tony" ever existed beyond Vicki Fraginals's imagination "may have faded into the media badlands of chat rooms and remaindered bookshops"[73] had it not been for Maupin's fascination with this question and his increasingly dire need to write a new novel. The publicity generated in 2000 by his best-selling *The Night Listener* and its 2006 movie adaptation revived public interest in the story and led to Tad Friend's investigation. Friend convincingly argued that "Tony" existed only as a figment of Vicki Fraginals's imagination and also revealed further—and even more bizarre—developments in the story. After reading *A Rock and a Hard Place*, TV documentary producer Lesley Karsten had approached "Vicky" and "Tony" in 1995 to ask if "Tony" would participate in a documentary about abused children. *About Us: The Dignity of Children*, which aired in March 1997 on ABC, presented a series of vignettes about children with difficult childhoods, including one about host Oprah Winfrey, but "Tony" was undeniably its star.[74] However, his voice-over narration had been taped over the phone and, as was only revealed in the credits, he had been represented on camera by an actor. The documentary thus further contributed to the creation of "Tony" as a hyper-real simulation by expanding the group of co-creators from Vicki Fraginals and her many interlocutors, including Armistead Maupin, Paul Monette, and Jack Godby, to the actor who portrayed "Tony" and especially to producer Lesley Karsten, who appeared to grow unusually protective of "Tony" as the project developed.[75]

The cyberstory "Tony" constructed after 1997 undid the fairy tale ending of the fake memoir's first chapter—"Earnist Johnson" disappeared when he was called to a secret mission in the Gulf War, "Vicki" miscarried their baby after a car accident, and subsequently they divorced—only to repeated it with different figures as "Tony" now lived with Lesley Karsten and her new husband "Jerry DiNicola." Perhaps even more astonishing than the claim made by both Karsten and "Tony" that she married "Jerry" and adopted "Tony"—who are after all fictional characters invented by Vicki Fraginals—is that Fraginals's alter ego "Vicki" also disappeared from "Tony's" story. Fraginals, who invented "Tony," "Vicki," and "Jerry DiNicola" along with the other characters of *A Rock and a Hard Place,* and impersonated "Tony" and "Vicki" in countless phone conversations and interactions in cyberspace, apparently wrote herself out of her elaborate fantasy. This happened at about the time when she married child psychiatrist Marc Zackheim, who had written a fan letter to "Tony," and subsequently they adopted four boys.[76] Maybe once Vicki Fraginals had four actual sons and a real husband, she no longer needed the virtual social life of her imaginary family. However, she has never publicly admitted to having written the false memoir and impersonated "Tony" and "Vicki." When Tad Friend tried to interview her, Marc Zackheim called the police.[77]

However, "Tony" did not cease to exist in virtual reality when Vicki Fraginals abandoned the story she had created and lived for at least seven years, from 1991 when "Tony" first wrote to Paul Monette, through 1997, when Fraginals found an actual family and let go of the imaginary one. It seems that Lesley Karsten began to impersonate him. According to Tad Friend, the transition seems to have occurred without coordination between the women and may not have been amicable. There seems to have been a temporary overlap, when both women impersonated "Tony" for some time after "Vicki" had left the story and "Tony" began living with—or rather in the mind of—Karsten, in mid-1997.[78] Apparently, like Vicki Fraginals, Lesley Karsten had both the need and the capacity to imagine a husband and a sick son—except that she did not create the characters herself but rather appropriated the figments of Fraginals's imagination as her own. Hence, "Tony" and "Jerry DiNicola" lived on for some time in cyberspace, even after the mind that had generated them no longer participated in the fantasy it had created.

It rather stretches credibility that Vicki Fraginals generated an imaginary family and life for herself in her fake memoir and countless phone conversations, e-mails, and internet chats over the course of at least seven years and that, furthermore, Lesley Karsten adopted two of the characters as her own imaginary son and husband. However, some children develop imaginary friends, and all fiction writers create imaginary characters, who often take on lives of their own in the writer's mind. And "Tony's" transition from one mind to another actually reflects a trend in postmodern literature. A number of contemporary writers have taken up literary characters created by other writers, often decades or even centuries ago. They re-narrated canonical texts from the perspective of a minor character, as Nobel laureate J. M. Coetzee did in his retelling of Defoe's *Robinson Crusoe* from the perspective of Man Friday in *Foe*. Or they invented a life for a minor character that took place before the one depicted in a canonical text, as Jean Rhys did in *Wide Sargasso Sea*, when she told the story of Mr. Rochester's first wife, the gothic madwoman in the attic in Charlotte Bronte's *Jane Eyre*.

*A Rock and a Hard Place* reverberates the platitudinous tropes of 1990s trauma-and-recovery discourse, for instance, the notion that subjective feeling-truth supersedes representational veracity and the idea that the root of all individual and interpersonal dysfunction is a lack of self-esteem. Furthermore, the fact that "to the faithful friends who continue to communicate with him, Tony is nothing less than a magical boy," who "brimmed with the passionate moral authority of doomed youth,"[79] reflects the nonsensical and unethical trauma culture gospel that exceptional suffering bequeaths extraordinary wisdom. However, "Tony" is too wise and too good to be true, not because child rape and battery or any other form of extreme violence imbues victims with quasi-mystical powers, but because he was co-generated by Fraginals, Karsten, and their many interlocutors as a pastiche that merged all of the ubiquitous tropes of popular trauma culture. In fact, "Anthony Godby Johnson's" fake misery memoir itself and especially the peculiar story behind it of one women imagining an abused and terminally ill child as her son, another taking over this fantasy as her own, both impersonating him and his respective maternal caretaker in virtual reality, and countless spectators believing the confabulations are paradigmatic for the trauma culture zeitgeist.

## Faking JT LeRoy's Auto-Fiction

After the exposure of James Frey's *A Million Little Pieces* as a fabrication, the revelation that "JT LeRoy," the abused cross-dressing boy prostitute-turned-wunderkind author and celebrity, was a figment of Laura Albert's imagination and had been impersonated in public by Savannah Knoop generated the second literary scandal of 2006. The JT LeRoy affair bears some striking parallels to the story of "Anthony Godby Johnson."[80] Both boys were invented by a middle-aged woman who claimed to have met the particular physically and sexually abused boy as a social worker and taken him in. Posing as the boy, both women had contacted mis lit writers, Paul Monette and Dennis Cooper respectively, which eventually led to the publication of their fake autobiographical texts, for which Monette and Cooper functioned as the primary coaxers. Both Albert and Fraginals also communicated with numerous writers, celebrities, and a growing number of fans, via telephone, e-mail, and internet chat in the guise of the abused boys as well as their maternal caretakers. Their stories developed significantly after the publication of their respective books through these virtual interactions with countless interlocutors: "Tony" changed parental figures from "Vicki" and "Earnist" to "Lesley" and "Jerry" and developed ever more illnesses, while "JT" had a sex-change operation and became a transgender woman. Last but not least, in both cases the impersonation eventually included another woman, Lesley Karsten and Savannah Knoop respectively.

However, unlike the transition of "Tony" from Fraginals to Karsten, the impersonation by Albert and Knoop was largely simultaneous as well as coordinated and cooperative. Both Vicki Fraginals and Laura Albert had created alter egos that differed from them in both gender and age, and thus they could not impersonate them outside of virtual reality. While "Anthony Godby Johnson" therefore never appeared in public, when rumors emerged that "JT LeRoy" did not exist, Laura Albert asked her partner's young and petite half-sister to impersonate him in public, clad in a Warholesque drag of blond wig, large sunglasses, and large dark hat. In a sort of female take on Frankenstein or Pinocchio, Albert interpreted Knoop's impersonation as bringing the boy figure she had invented to life by comparing it to giving birth to her actual son: "He wanted his own body. He so wanted to be out of me. I wanted this other child I had to be out in the world."[81] She furthermore explained that Knoop "became JT. It's like a trinity. We experienced it. It was as if he would leave me and enter her—I know how it sounds."[82] While the transition of "Tony" between Vicki Fraginals and Lesley Karsten seems to have been less cooperative and coordinated, Albert's notion may also describe how Fraginals and Karsten experienced the passing of "Tony" from the former to the latter. However, unlike "Tony," "JT" was not only co-constructed by Albert and Knoop as well as their numerous interlocutors in virtual reality via telephone, e-mail, and chat rooms, but also by the private and public interaction between Albert and Knoop over some five years. After Knoop began to impersonate him in public, Albert variously posed as "JT's" chaperone or roommate in both unmediated and virtual communication with a growing number of celebrities and fans while continuing to impersonate him on the telephone and in cyberspace.[83]

"JT LeRoy" had burst onto the American literary scene in October 1997 when his short story "Baby Doll," published under the pseudonym Terminator, appeared in an anthology of autobiographical texts entitled *Close to the Bone* and was singled out in the enthusiastic review of the collection in the *New York Times Magazine*.[84] Subsequently included in his collection of inter-locking stories, *The Heart Is Deceitful Above All Things*, which takes its title from Jeremiah 17:9,[85] "Baby Doll" already contained the core elements of the other stories and of the likewise supposedly semi-autobiographical novel *Sarah*: transvestite prostitution of young boys, physical and sexual child abuse, drug addiction, and the insular setting at Appalachian highway diners. Published a year after *Sarah* in 2001, the stories collected in *The Heart Is Deceitful Above All Things* were supposedly written prior to the novel. Set in the dystopian universe of truck stop prostitution, both books depict the childhood misery of an androgynous, cross-dressing twelve-year-old boy, variously named Jeremy or Jeremiah, who is regularly beaten and abandoned by his drug-addicted prostitute mother and at least once raped by one of her men. Whenever his mother abandons him, he has to live with her father, a fire-and-brimstone preacher who likewise beats him frequently and makes him recite scripture during the abuse. However, rather than reject his mother, he idolizes her to the extent that he transforms himself into her miniature drag doppelganger, when at age twelve he begins to work as a cross-dressing truck stop prostitute and even adopts her name, Sarah.

Although officially both books are designated as fiction, they became art house cult favorites and sales, particularly of *Sarah*, significantly increased when it was leaked that they were based on the author's real life story.[86] *Sarah* was said to be 60 percent true,[87] and publicity materials for *The Heart Is Deceitful Above All Things* describe the stories as journal entries, most of which had been written when "LeRoy" was in his mid-teens.[88] He also claimed autobiographical status for his oeuvre in interviews[89] and personal communications with admirers. For instance, he wrote in an e-mail: "I guess I agree with my publisher that my stories are autobiographical fiction. *Sarah* is considered fiction, but it tells you everything there is to know about me really, so the labels are confusing to me mostly . . . sigh."[90] Furthermore, he wrote on his web site, jtLeRoy.com, that "JT" stands for Jeremy Terminator, so the author shares the first name of his protagonist. (He also explained on his web site that Terminator is an ironic nickname from his time as a street hustler, that he adopted as his middle name, initially used as a pseudonym, and still employs as his handle in the e-mail address provided at the end of his books asking readers to get in touch.) While the texts were officially sold as fiction, "LeRoy" falsely claimed that they fulfill the core condition of autobiographical writing, namely the identity of author, narrator, and protagonist. And as Gregory Curtner, the lead lawyer for Antidote Films, the company that had bought the film rights to *Sarah* and then sued Albert for fraud after the imposture was revealed, put it, it was precisely "the whole autobiographical back story aura that made this so attractive."[91]

After the exposure, Albert claimed that "she was merely partaking in the revered literary tradition of using a pseudonym, plus a little Andy Warhol–inspired performance art"[92] and that, because the texts were designated as fiction, their truth value was independent of whether "LeRoy" existed or not.[93] However, the function of a pseudonym is "to take attention away from a real person, so that the work may be judged without the filter of the personality" rather than "to create a three-dimensional false author,"[94] and as such it is inherently antithetical to celebrity. Albert's argument was further contradicted by the fact that she had signed the contract with Antidote Films for the screen adaptation of *Sarah* as "JT LeRoy." Last but certainly not least, Albert had asked Knoop to impersonate "LeRoy" in public appearances and readings to quench the damaging rumors that "LeRoy" did not exist. All of this indicates that Albert actively generated the notion that the texts were autobiographical because true stories sell better. After all, to sell books today, publishers "have to get media attention, and to get media attention you need a real, live author who can be interviewed on TV and radio and profiled in magazines" especially when "that author has a fascinating life story" which "will be the subject of interviews."[95]

While "Baby Doll" had revealed "JT LeRoy" as a literary wunderkind in 1997, the publication of *Sarah* in 2000 "thrust the writer into stardom"[96] and "earned him underground cult figuredom and celebrity endorsements, not to mention raves from serious publications."[97] The *New York Times* praised *Sarah* as "an Alice in Wonderland on Acid."[98] And the South African *Sunday Times* gushed that *Sarah* "spins a comical coming-of-age adventure laced with folk magic" that juxtaposes "coarse, profane, some would say pornographic, passages" of "drug addiction, pedophilia, prostitution, and murder" with others that are "haunting, poignant, and exquisitely lyrical."[99] The only two scholarly articles about "LeRoy," written by Alan Hickman and Woody Wilson before the exposure, read the texts as autobiographical and are similarly laudatory.[100] According to Wilson,

*Sarah* is "a postmodern *Bildungsroman*"[101] and he particularly praises "the weirdly rich texture of LeRoy's writing" which "masterfully blends hilarity with horror."[102] Hickman considered "LeRoy" "a genius-in-the-making" and deemed *Sarah*, "a heartbreaking, brutally honest portrait of childhood that may be the most gut-wrenching of its type since Jean Genet first took up his pen or Arthur Rimbaud spent his season in hell."[103]

Reflecting "LeRoy's" widely noted capacity to instantly bond with strangers via telephone and e-mail,[104] Hickman also ascribed him a "nearly messianic hold"[105] on his interlocutors, and was himself "beginning to think of [']JT'] as a kind of stepchild"[106] after only a few e-mail exchanges. As David Segal put it in the *Washington Post*, "who could resist helping a charming reformed junkie with such a tragic biography, and with such laudable ambitions for a drug-and-psychosis-free life?"[107] As countless celebrities, to whom he had written fan letters, likewise found him irresistible, "LeRoy" "became the damaged darling of the art house set."[108] According to Warren St. John's *New York Times* article, "Tom Waits, Bono, and Liv Tyler have singled out his writing in interviews and he has been embraced by established writers including Tobias Wolff, Michael Chabon, and Mary Gaitskill, and by a cadre of celebrities with, as it happens, their own troubled pasts, like Courtney Love, Winona Rider, Tatum O'Neal, and Billy Corgan."[109] He corresponded with Bob Geldoff's daughter[110] and authors like Sharon Olds, Mary Karr, and Dennis Cooper, all of whom also offered him feedback on his writing.[111] Impersonated by Knoop, he graced the cover of *Vanity Fair*, which also published an interview with him by Tom Waits in 2003.[112] He hung out with Carrie Fisher and Harper Simon, her son with Paul Simon, and with John Lennon's son Sean Lennon.[113] Madonna sent him a book on Kabbalah[114] and REM singer Michael Stipe regularly attended his readings[115] at which "LeRoy" rarely read himself but instead had celebrities like Lou Reed, Nancy Sinatra, and Tatum O'Neal read from his books.[116] He was also reported to have either "collaborated on early drafts of"[117] or even written "the original draft of *Elephant*, Gus Van Sant's film that won the Palme D'Or at Cannes in 2003."[118] Last but not least, he has "had a song written about him—'Cherry Lips,' by Shirley Manson."[119] In short, as Alberto Mobilio wrote in the *New York Times* before the impersonation scandal broke, "LeRoy's brief career has generated the kind of magazine-feature publicity usually reserved for movie stars."[120]

The spectacular claim that Laura Albert was impersonating "LeRoy" in virtual reality, first made in Steven Beachy's 2005 *New York Magazine* article,[121] was confirmed in early February 2006, when Warren St. John, who in 2004 had written a laudatory portrait of "LeRoy" in the *New York Times*,[122] published an article in the same paper. It was based on his phone interview with Geoffrey Knoop, Laura Albert's by now ex-partner and half-brother of Savannah Knoop, in which he not only exposed the deception but also implicated himself, claiming a significant role in creating "LeRoy" and running the business side of the operation.

He wanted to sell a movie idea about his own experience and, since he was not married to Albert, if he was "to share in any of the monies generated by JT LeRoy's books and films, he might need to demonstrate that he was an integral part of the deception."[123]

More light was shed on the "LeRoy" affair in the course of the 2007 trial when Antidote Films sued Albert for fraud. According to Alan Feuer's *New York Times* article, Albert claimed that "she had been sexually abused by a family friend, starting at the age of three," and by her mother's former boyfriend. She had run away from home as a teen, and had been hospitalized for depression, an eating disorder, and suicidal feelings.[124] She began "calling suicide hotlines from a payphone on the street and, incapable of speaking as herself, she adopted the personas of various teenage boys."[125] She entered phone therapy, and in her conversations with Dr. Terrence Owens over some thirteen years, she posed as an abused boy variously named Jeremy or Jeremiah, an embryonic version of "JT LeRoy." When Owens wanted to meet her, "Albert paid a street waif to appear as Jeremiah, and then went along as his roommate Speedy—which is to say, a patient standing with her alter ego in the third-degree remove of the alter ego's friend."[126] "Speedy" remained with Albert as a character she would impersonate for years, for example, she accompanied Knoop impersonating "LeRoy" to a dinner as "Speedy" when meeting with Steven Shainberg, the proposed director of the film adaptation of *Sarah*.[127] Albert not only posed as "JT" in phone conversations with her therapist, but also while working as a phone sex operator when she "would talk endlessly in the guise of LeRoy."[128] Seeking to promote her writing, Albert also contacted Dennis Cooper, pretending to be a street hustler with a troubled past nicknamed Terminator and thus rather like a character from Cooper's own novels, in order to awaken his interest. She succeeded in deceiving Cooper, who not only provided valuable editorial advice in many phone conversations but also championed "LeRoy" "to writers like Bruce Benderson as well as several prominent Manhattan editors."[129]

Armistead Maupin suggested that the narrator of *The Night Listener* that he created based on himself, may well be, like the boy modeled on "Tony," an unreliable narrator, which creates a story-within-a-story construct in which both stories are told by unreliable narrators. While Maupin's editor and a number of critics and readers enjoyed this narrative complexity, which is not resolved at the end, "others were simply confused or downright infuriated; they were being swept along by a mystery, hungry for a solution, only to get a handful of fairy dust thrown in their faces," Maupin commented in an interview. He added, "join the club, kids; that's exactly how *I* felt when living in the heart of the real-life conundrum. Sometimes there just *isn't* an ending."[130] However, unlike in Maupin's novel or the story of "Anthony Godby Johnson" that inspired it, the mystery of "JT LeRoy" was solved. Maupin furthermore suggested in the 2006 postscript to *The Night Listener* that, given the similarities between the stories of

"Anthony Godby Johnson" and "JT LeRoy," Laura Albert may have been inspired to create "JT" by Vicki Fraginals's confabulation of "Tony." However, as Albert generated versions of "JT" on the phone with suicide hotline counselors, her therapist, and pedophile phone sex clients years before "Tony" entered the public sphere, Albert had to have confabulated "JT" independently. The striking parallels in the stories can rather be explained by the high commodity value contemporary culture ascribes to formulaic accounts of childhood misery emplotted as kitsch-sentimental melodrama of trauma-and-recovery and the consequent saturation of the public sphere with such tales. In fact, Maupin relates another instance of this trauma culture plot paradigm:

> Rosie O'Donnell called me after my book was published and told me the same thing happened to her. She'd been talking to a fourteen-year-old girl who'd supposedly been raped and was putting her child up for adoption through Rosie's agency. And Rosie took an interest in the kid, wanted her to feel better about life. At the same time Rosie also developed a phone friendship with the kid's adopted mother. And Rosie was totally taken in until Kelly, her partner, pointed out that there was a very strong similarity between the two voices. Rosie and Kelley couldn't believe it when they read my book, because it so closely echoed their own experience.[131]

G. Beato commented in the *Washington Post* that "LeRoy" is Britney Spears's "dark doppelganger, the sexualized child as taboo commodity taken to its lurid, logical conclusion."[132] This comment also pertains to "Anthony Godby Johnson" and the all depictions of horrific childhoods in contemporary popular culture that function not to end abuse, but as titillating entertainment. The books of Fraginals, Albert, and the countless other mis lit authors, whether their texts are reliably autobiographical, partly exaggerated, or even entirely fake, bear such striking resemblances because the formulaic narratives are generated by recycling culturally dominant tropes of victimization and suffering. And since mis lit forgers seek to fake what is most valuable in a given culture, fictional and therefore fake misery memoirs reflect and reinforce the significance of the trauma culture zeitgeist.

# 10

## Simulating Holocaust Survival

"Without an audience, there would be no Wilkomirski."

–Stefan Maechler, *The Wilkomirski Affair*[1]

Although child abuse is increasingly replacing Holocaust survival as the pre-eminent subject for depicting victimization and suffering, it is represented through the suffering-and-redemption plot paradigm generated in American Holocaust discourse. Contemporary media products moreover merged both subjects in the Holocaust victimhood of children. Prefigured by the stage and movie adaptation of Anne Frank's diary in the 1950s, it was particularly Jerzy Kosinski's 1965 novel *The Painted Bird* that fused Holocaust survival and child abuse. The pseudo-autobiographical bestseller represented the Holocaust as a titillating horror spectacle of physical and sexual violence perpetrated on a young boy. It thus echoed the two fundamentally new discourses about victimization and violence that were dominant at the time: the survivor testimony from the 1961 Eichmann trial and the widely publicized accounts of Battered Child Syndrome by pediatricians C. H. Kempe et al. from 1962.

Kosinski's misleading claim that, despite its genre designation as novel, *The Painted Bird* depicted his own experiences,[2] foreshadowed the development that autobiographical accounts of victimhood would be ascribed significant moral and commodity value and that authors would be prepared to lie. Such recent Hollywood fare as *Life Is Beautiful* and *The Boy in the Striped Pajamas* likewise fuse Holocaust survival and child abuse, but they are designated as fiction. And Martin Gray's 1971 bestselling fake Holocaust memoir *Au nom de tous les miens* (*For Those I Loved*) combines the fraudulent claim of autobiographical status with the subject of the Holocaust, though it narrates the survival of an adult. It is thus the false memoirs of Binjamin Wilkomirski and Misha Defonseca, published in 1995 and 1997 respectively, that most immediately echo Kosinski, as they likewise fuse child abuse with Holocaust suffering and falsely claim autobiographical status.

Elie Wiesel radically altered his review of Kosinski's book for the better after learning that it was supposedly autobiographical, which suggests that he holds fictional and nonfictional Holocaust narratives up to different aesthetic standards and thus that he clearly distinguishes between them. However, his own memoir, *Night* also violates the autobiographical pact, if to a much lesser extent. For instance, contrary to Wiesel's claim that his religious crisis occurred in Auschwitz, he subsequently wrote in *All Rivers Run to the Sea* that this core event in his life happened a decade later.[3] Wiesel once explained his notion of truth in a well-known anecdote. When a Hassidic rabbi had asked him, whether the things he writes about happened or not, Wiesel had replied that "some were in fact invented from almost the beginning to almost the end," and the rabbi had commented "that means you are writing lies." However, the Platonic rejection of fiction as lies only pertains to fictional texts that falsely claim to be reliably representing autobiographical events. Yet, in his response Wiesel invoked neither the indexical relation between reality and its representation nor the autobiographical pact—the implicit promise of the author to depict experiences truthfully—that conventionally distinguish literary nonfiction and fiction. Instead, he evoked a mystical notion of truth that supposedly pertains to both, or rather dubiously evades the core distinction between the two modes of representation: "Things are not that simple, Rebbe. Some events do take place but are not true; others are—although they never occurred."[4] Wiesel thus understands truth as a mystical constant absolute rather than a discursively generated and culturally changing convention, which in the case of nonfiction is grounded in the referentiality of representation. Given his status as America's preeminent survivor, Wiesel's mysticism contributed to the rise to cultural dominance of the notion that, where the Holocaust is concerned, truth is not solely established based on an indexical relation between reality and representation. As truth claims in Holocaust narratives were less and less tied to verifiable facts, they were increasingly based on the display of intense affect by the narrator-protagonist or, in the case of filmic representations like *Life is Beautiful* or *The Boy in the Striped Pajamas,* by the actors. Even such inherently improbable narratives as Wilkomirski's and Defonseca's fake memoirs were believed to be truthful accounts precisely because consumers have become unwilling to question the authority of affect,[5] which constitutes another core characteristic of the trauma culture zeitgeist.

The genealogy of truth claims in Holocaust narratives based less and less on a referential relation to reality can thus be traced from Wiesel via Kosinski to Defonseca and Wilkomirski. Wiesel's genre-defining Holocaust memoir is reliable with regard to his imprisonment in Auschwitz, but he altered core events he supposedly experienced in the camp. Kosinski likewise shares the subject position with the narrator-protagonist of his autobiographical novel. As Wiesel survived Auschwitz, Kosinski survived in hiding as a child in Nazi-occupied Poland. However, he was not separated from his parents and did not experience most or any of the horrific violence he depicts. While Kosinski thus shares the personal experience of the Holocaust with Wiesel, he invented far more of the events he narrated, but nevertheless claimed autobiographical status for his novel.

Defonseca's connection to her narrator-protagonist is even more tenuous. She is neither Jewish nor did she wander war-torn Europe. Apart from the fact that she lost her parents as a small child, because they were deported as members of the resistance when Belgium was under Nazi occupation, the events in her supposed memoir are entirely invented. The furthest position in the spectrum of unreliable truth claims in Holocaust narratives is marked by Wilkomirski's likewise entirely confabulated memoir, because he has no connection to the Holocaust, but, like Sylvia Plath and to a large extent also Misha Defonseca, employs Holocaust tropes to express his historically unrelated suffering.

In this concluding chapter, my analysis of popular trauma culture comes full circle as it returns to American Holocaust discourse. However, it also extends the overall argument because it relates the previous discussions of the survivor figure and of fake child abuse victims in the analysis of the public personas of fake Holocaust child survivors Binjamin Wilkomirski, Misha Defonseca, and Laura Grabowski. The fraudulent life stories generated by these Holocaust imposters fuse the cultural trends of false claims to autobiographical status in mis lit fakes with the merging of Holocaust victimhood and child abuse.

## Imagining Holocaust Child Victims

Like Roberto Benigni's fictional son in *Life Is Beautiful*, the Jewish boy in previously little-known Irish children's author and novelist John Boyne's bestselling *The Boy in the Striped Pajamas* and its movie adaptation is a fictional Holocaust child victim. While Benigni, who also directed the film, used slapstick humor, Boyne employed the more common plot paradigm of sentimental melodrama to represent the Holocaust. Indicative of the apparently insatiable appetite for ahistorical Holocaust kitsch, the novel was a bestseller in Britain in the nonfiction paperback category, with more than half a million copies sold by December 2008.[6] It also spent more than six months at the top of the children's bestseller list in Ireland and reached the third place on the *New York Times* children's paperback bestseller list. Adapted for the screen as a Miramax/Disney co-production, *The Boy in the Striped Pajamas* thus literally constitutes a Disney version of the Holocaust. Beyond its tear-jerking sentimentality, it is characterized by the historical impossibility of the plot about the friendship between a Jewish boy imprisoned in a concentration camp and the son of the camp commandant. Unlike such other mainstream Holocaust representations as

*Schindler's List, The Pianist,* and to a lesser extent *Life Is Beautiful,* which end happily-ever-after, both boys are killed, and death dominates the end of the film. However, evocative of the ending in the American stage and movie adaptations of *The Diary of Anne Frank,* death is "spiritualized and rendered aesthetically palpable by an overlay of maudlin sentiment"[7] and "saccharine promises of redemption."[8]

The sentimentality of novel and film likewise characterizes those reviews that hailed both by invoking such trite tropes as that the story is beautiful, moving, and important. James Christopher, for instance, wrote in the British *Times* that "this is a hugely affecting film," a "beautifully balanced chamber piece," and "one of the most moving and remarkable films about childhood I've ever seen" but fails to explain why he praises an ahistorical fantasy of child murder in such terms. He added that this "magical piece of cinema" has "the rhythm of a children's adventure."[9] One probably need not even be familiar with the complex scholarly discussions about the aesthetics and ethics of Holocaust representation[10] to realize the incongruity of representing genocide as a children's adventure story. Christopher's review reflects the trauma culture zeitgeist in its unethical ascription of moral, aesthetic, and educational value to narratives that fuse Holocaust victimhood with child abuse into such horror kitsch as Boyne's novel or Wilkomirski's fake memoir.

Prior to Christopher's laudatory film review, John Boyne had outlined the aesthetics of his novel in the same newspaper. He argued that representing the Holocaust "through the eyes of suffering children" constitutes the sole appropriate perspective because "one can focus directly on specific aspects while ignoring issues that adults perceive as wholly important but which children do not even recognize and which, from a purely technical point of view, are surplus to requirements."[11] He furthermore explained that "the only respectful way to deal with such a subject was through innocence, using the point of view of a rather naïve child who couldn't possibly understand the horrors of what he was caught in" because "that naiveté is as close as someone of my generation can get to the dreadfulness of that time and place."[12]

Boyne thus absurdly stipulates that the only mode of representing the Holocaust that is appropriate or even possible—he seems to conflate these distinct ideas—is one that mimics the naïve perspective of child victims. Replete with trauma culture tropes, his vague and convoluted statements also seem to suggest that understanding the Holocaust in a way that (apparently all) adults seek to do, by which he probably means as a complex historical event, is unnecessary, because the child victims did not comprehend their experiences in this way. Boyne furthermore untenably conflated the genocidal murder of the Jewish boy with the accidental killing of the German one—who functions as a sort of mini-Schindler, an infantilized version of the good-German figure—through the Christian-cum-Holocaust trope of suffering innocents. And likewise in sync with the trauma culture zeitgeist, he invoked the notion of emotional truth, which he juxtaposes to and favors over historical truth, when he argues that to "truly understand the horrors of Auschwitz" one must "uncover as much emotional truth within that desperate landscape" as one can.[13]

Boyne created an absurd argument in his *Times* article and an ahistorical Holocaust fantasy in his novel. Moreover, seeking to convey the dread, terror, and despair of Holocaust child victims to young readers is unethical, because it constitutes an unnecessary and therefore gratuitous infliction of extreme fear and upset on the child readers. After all, India Knight's indictment of misery memoirs—that they offer no insight but "merely confirm what you already knew: that some people are monstrous and that some people's lives are desperate"[14]— also applies to Boyne's Holocaust kitsch. His claim of seeking to communicate the emotions of the youngest Holocaust victims to readers comparable in age, moreover, is nonsensical, because Boyne simply cannot know how children felt in concentration camps and thus, essentially, makes it up. Although inventing the characters' emotions is a necessary and legitimate endeavor for a novelist, it becomes unsound when an indexical relation is implied to the feelings experienced by empirically real individuals.

Another recent story which circulated widely in the media contributed to the further transformation of the pain of others into entertainment kitsch spectacles and the infantilization of Holocaust victimhood. While Herman Rosenblat likewise depicted the suffering of a child victim, and his story even shares the sentimental and historically implausible plot line of two children meeting at a concentration camp fence, unlike Boyne's novel and its film adaptation, Rosenblat's story was said to be autobiographical. Not only was his survival as an eleven-year-old boy in the Buchenwald satellite camp of Schlieben supposedly made possible by a young Jewish girl, who was hiding in a nearby village and would throw bread and apples over the fence, but he met her again many years later on a blind date in New York and they subsequently married. Initially, he only told the story to friends and family, but after he entered and won a newspaper contest for the best Valentine's story in 1995, it was featured on the cover of the *New York Post*. This in turn led to an invitation for the Rosenblats to the *Oprah Winfrey Show* in 1996, when Winfrey commented teary-eyed that this was "the single greatest love story we've ever told on the air."[15] Subsequently, Rosenblat was signed by a literary agent who brokered a book deal, and the memoir was slated for publication in early 2009. Despite the improbability of the tale, Berkely Books did not check its factual accuracy. The Rosenblats appeared again on the *Oprah Winfrey Show* in 2007 to promote the memoir. In 2008, Laurie Friedman's *Angel Girl*, a children's book version of the story, appeared. In December 2008, Jewish studies scholar Ken Waltzer contacted Berkely Books and documented that it was not only historically impossible for either Schlieben prisoners or anyone outside to get near the electric fence surrounding the camp, but also that Rosenblat's future wife lived some two hundred miles away at the time. The news broke that the story of the "angel at the fence," as it had come to be known, was a complete fabrication, apart from the fact that Herman Rosenblat had been imprisoned as an eleven-year-old boy in the Schlieben satellite camp. After that, the publication of the memoir was aborted, the children's book was pulped, and Oprah Winfrey declared herself "very disappointed."[16] Although the largely fake memoir was never published, the story entered the public sphere through the *New York Post* and *The Oprah Winfrey Show* and was widely circulated in newspaper articles, not only in the United States, but also in the United Kingdom,[17] and even in Australia[18] and New Zealand.[19] After the exposure, Rosenblat explained that he wanted to bring happiness to people with his story and to remind them not to hate. While the means were clearly wrong, this is nevertheless an admirable notion, particularly after Rosenblat's exceptionally difficult life. It included not only a Holocaust childhood and a marriage to a wife who suffered from clinical depression, but also the armed robbery of his Brooklyn store, in which both Rosenblat himself and his son were shot, which left the son paralyzed and Rosenblat with a bullet lodged in his body.[20] Stephen McGinty's comment about Kathy O'Beirne's fake memoir of childhood misery in Ireland that while her life certainly contained suffering, the memoir she wrote was false as she did not write about her actual life[21] likewise pertains to Rosenblat's extensively embellished Holocaust story, and to some extent also to Misha Defonseca's false memoir of Holocaust child survival.

Published in 1997 and exposed as a fake in the same week in late March 2008 as Margaret B. Jones's *Love and Consequences*, Misha Defonseca's *Misha: A Memoir of the Holocaust Years* is the most recently discredited Holocaust memoir. Like the other largely (Kosinski, Rosenblat) or entirely (Wilkomirski) fabricated autobiographical accounts, Boyne's Holocaust fantasy, *The Boy in the Striped Pajamas* and its film adaptation, as well as Benigni's equally ahistorical *Life Is Beautiful*, Defonseca's fake memoir narrates a historically impossible tale of how a child survived the Holocaust. Since it is the most obviously fantastic story, it is all the more astonishing that it not only took more than ten years to be revealed as a complete confabulation but also that it was only exposed because of a complex legal battle between the author, the editor Vera Lee, and the publisher Jane Daniel. Prior to its exposure, it had been translated into eighteen languages and adapted into a commercially successful film in France entitled *Survivre avec les loups* (*Surviving with Wolves*). The Disney Corporation had optioned it for a movie and only pulled out because of the endless legal dispute over rights and royalties among author, editor, and publisher.[22] Oprah Winfrey, whose penchant for trauma-and-redemption tales has led her to promote more than a few fake misery yarns, had selected the memoir for her book club and was only spared another blunder because it was exposed before the taped program was scheduled to air, so it could be withdrawn.[23]

Upping the ante of incredibility, Defonseca not only claimed, like Kosinski, that she had wandered the rural parts of one country alone and experienced mostly hostility from the people she encountered, but to have trekked some two thousand miles across war-torn Europe in search of her deported parents. Like both Kosinski and Wilkomirski, Defonseca tells a story about a small child who overcomes the impossible and, like Wilkomirski, encounters, but is not harmed by, major Holocaust events. She slips in and out of the Warsaw ghetto, witnesses the massacre of children at Otwock, and—apparently a favorite trope in fake accounts of Holocaust survival of children—even walks up to a concentration camp fence. Defonseca furthermore claims to have killed a German soldier in self-defense and, most spectacularly, that she was adopted by not one but two packs of wolves. Unlike Wilkomirski, who continued to assert the historical truth of his memoir for some time after its exposure, Defonseca, whose real name is Monique DeWael, invoked the trauma culture trope of emotional truth when she admitted that "the story is mine. It is not actually reality, but my reality, my way of surviving."[24] She explained that her parents were deported by the Nazis when she was four years old, not, however, because they were Jewish, but because they had fought in the Belgian resistance. She was cared for by her grandfather, uncle, and eventually by hostile adoptive parents who considered her the daughter of traitors. Like Wilkomirski, she chose to express her own idiosyncratic story of childhood suffering through the most culturally available story paradigm of Holocaust survival, supplemented by the mythical element of the feral child. And like Sylvia Plath, she unwittingly employed the Jew-as-victim trope when she explained that her childhood exclusion and discrimination led her to feel Jewish.[25]

Defonseca's fabrication is revealing because it indicates the extent to which readers are willing to suspend their disbelief and to accept in a supposed Holocaust memoir that a young girl could walk across Europe in the midst of the Second World War and even that she was adopted by wolves. It is also illuminating because the ensuing legal battle between author, editor, and publisher constitutes the clearest indication to date of the vast commercial potential of representing the Holocaust as an ahistorical, kitsch-sentimental horror fantasy of trauma-and-redemption in contemporary Western culture.

Jane Daniel, a freelance writer and owner of the one-woman enterprise Ivy Press, convinced Defonseca to write a memoir with editorial help from Daniel's neighbor and friend Vera Lee, a former French professor fluent in Defonseca's native language. Supposedly, Defonseca narrated her story orally to Lee, who transcribed and probably also translated and edited it, and that Daniel did further rewriting of the manuscript. After its completion, an argument ensued over who had contributed what and eventually led Defonseca and Lee to each file a lawsuit against Daniel. Lee sued her one-time friend claiming that her rights as co-author had been violated because her name only appeared on the copyright page but not on the cover of the book. Defonseca filed a suit over unpaid royalties from overseas book sales and breach of contract because Daniels had not promoted the book in the United States as contractually stipulated. After some ten years of litigation, Lee was awarded $9.9 million[26] and Defonseca won $22.5 million.[27] Daniel then sought to establish that the memoir was a forgery in order to claim fraud on the author's part, challenge the previous judgment, and not have to pay Defonseca, and possibly not Lee, either.[28]

Daniel told her side of the saga in her blog, which intrigued a genealogical researcher, Sharon Sergant, who eventually uncovered Defonseca's true identity.[29] There had been an article by German-Jewish author Henryk Broder in the German magazine *Der Spiegel* that questioned the reliability of Defonseca's story prior to publication,[30] and both literary scholar Lawrence Langer and historian Deborah Dwork had strongly advised Daniel against publishing it. While Daniel had thus knowingly published a fake Holocaust memoir—which she had convinced Defonseca to write in the first place—she sought to establish a legal claim of fraud on Defonseca's part after being forced to pay millions to her and to Vera Lee, for which she cited Langer's and Dwork's reports as evidence. However the legal battle ultimately plays out, it is not only an indicator that the Holocaust industry has expanded its range of profitable commodities to fake memoirs but it is also an indication of the trauma culture zeitgeist that a publisher has no qualms about printing a fake Holocaust memoir in hopes of stellar riches only to accuse the author of fraud when sued for royalties.

Despite their diversity in other respects, the fictional account in John Boyne's novel *The Boy in the Striped Pajamas* and its movie adaptation, the largely fabricated story by survivor Herman Rosenblat, and the fake memoir by Misha Defonseca share the fact that they do not reliably establish a referential relation to past reality. Moreover, they depict the persecution of children, thus merging the Holocaust with popular trauma culture's other core subject of child abuse. It was, however, the exposure that Binjamin Wilkomirski's memoir, which likewise depicts the Holocaust survival of a young child, was entirely fabricated that caused the most extensive international literary scandal.

## Inventing Binjamin Wilkomirski

Originally published in German as *Bruchstücke: Aus einer Kindheit 1939–1948* by the Jüdischer Verlag imprint of the prestigious Suhrkamp Verlag in 1995, *Fragments: Memories of a Wartime Childhood* is probably the most widely discussed fake memoir in literary studies. However, it was treated as an isolated incident, rather than an integral part of a larger cultural trend.[31]

When contextualized in the growing micro-genre of fake misery memoirs, "Wilkomirski's" simulation of a Holocaust childhood—which merged the preeminent mis lit subject of child abuse with the canonical genre of Holocaust memoirs—no longer appears as an isolated incident but rather as a paradigmatic embodiment of popular trauma culture. Scholarly discussion of *Fragments* not only lacked contextualization in mis lit and its forgery, but also neglected the significant discrepancy between the fact that, before its exposure, the memoir received extensive and unanimously laudatory publicity but sold very poorly. In a market where misery memoirs often sell several hundred thousand copies and Defonseca's fake Holocaust memoir generated millions of dollars in revenue, *Fragments* sold only some 32,800 copies in the United States, 13,000 in Germany, 8,100 in Italy, 6,000 in France, and editions in other languages sold even fewer books.[32] The poor sales figures contradicted the great expectations of the many international publishers clamoring for the manuscript to an extent "Wilkomirski's" renowned Swiss literary agent Eva Koralnik had never experienced in her career of some thirty years.[33] The commercial failure despite the vast international publicity may indicate that readers prefer misery memoirs to be set in the present or that audiences retain a vague sense of the Holocaust aura of pseudo-sacredness and that they have an inclination to associate it with high culture and formal education rather than pleasure reading. It may also reflect that, although *Fragments* does employ the melodramatic structure of an innocent victim who overcomes a seemingly omnipotent evil victimizer, it lacks the necessary happy ending of popular trauma culture's paradigmatic suffering-and-redemption plot.

Prior to its exposure, *Fragments* was an unprecedented critical success. If the poor sales were mentioned at all, they were implicitly taken as an indication of the memoir's aesthetic merit because highbrow texts are only read by an educated elite. Mostly, however, its success was based on the awards it received, the unanimously euphoric scholarly discussion, and the plethora of stellar newspaper reviews. For instance, the *Neue Züricher Zeitung* hailed the memoir as carrying the weight of this century and one of the most essential testimonies of the death camps,[34] and British journalist and daughter of Holocaust survivors, Anne Karpf, praised it in *The Guardian* as "one of the great works about the Holocaust."[35] Germany's preeminent historian of anti-Semitism, Wolfgang Benz, ascribed to *Fragments* not only authenticity, but also literary merit.[36] Excerpts were read at the famous Salzburg Festival, together with poems and passages from Elie Wiesel, Paul Celan, and Elfriede Jelinek.[37] In Britain, "Wilkomirski" was awarded the Jewish Quarterly Literary Prize, and in France the Prix Mémoire de la Shoah.

In the brief three-year period between publication and the first public accusations of fraud by Daniel Ganzfried in 1998, "Wilkomirski's" public profile skyrocketed. Extending beyond dozens of reviews, interviews, newspaper articles, and radio presentations, it also included a European book tour and participation in the 1994 Israeli TV documentary *Wanda's List* and its 1995 sequel about Holocaust child survivors' search for their origins.[38] "Wilkomirski" was furthermore the subject of two documentaries, Ester van Messel's 1997 *Fremd geboren* (Born a Stranger), which documents his life story and particularly his search for origins, and Eric Bergkraut's *Das gute Leben ist nur eine Falle* (The Good Life Is Only a Trap), "a visual essay" on *Fragments*.[39]

However, "Wilkomirski's" memoir was most successful, both commercially and critically, in the United States. It was frequently cited as on par with other texts in the pantheon of Holocaust literature like Anne Frank's diary and Elie Wiesel's *Night* and was awarded the National Jewish Book Award over such other finalists as Wiesel's *All Rivers Run to the Sea*. Wiesel himself had praised *Fragments* in a review. Arnost Lustig even compared its author to Homer, Cervantes, and Shakespeare and predicted that "the book is destined to become one of the five or ten lasting books about the Holocaust."[40] It was read in college courses and "Wilkomirski" was invited to speak at conferences.[41] He furthermore "provided video testimonies for Spielberg's Survivors of the Shoah Visual History Foundation and the U.S. Holocaust Memorial Museum, and went on a six-city fund-raising tour for the museum."[42] Daniel Goldhagen considered *Fragments* "a small masterpiece" and maintained that "even those conversant with the literature of the Holocaust will be educated by this arresting book."[43] And although Lawrence Langer had thought it was a novel before realizing that the text was supposedly a memoir, he did consider it to be a very good novel.[44] Jonathan Kozol even "drops to his knees in reverence before the author,"[45] as Stefan Maechler put it, in his review of *Fragments* in *The Nation*, in which he gushed that "this stunning and austerely written work is so profoundly moving, so morally important, and so free from literary artifice of any kind at all that I wonder if I even have the right to try to offer praise."[46] Last but not least, "Wilkomirski's" memoir even entered the popular culture realm when Rosie O'Donnell held up a copy on her TV show and recommended it to her viewers.[47]

Tova Reich considered the "Wilkomirski" reverence paradigmatic for American Holocaust culture to the extent that she included it in her satire *My Holocaust*. One of the main characters, the ex-kindergarten teacher Bunny, who becomes director of the U.S. Holocaust Memorial Museum when her wealthy mother makes this the condition for her multimillion-dollar donation, considers *Fragments* her "main source for studying the Holocaust." She even describes it as her "bible," reads "a passage . . . every night before bedtime like a prayer," and even hopes that "some day portions from this classic will be included in the official Passover seder service."[48]

Virtually none of the vast publicity acknowledged the discrepancy between the documented identity of the author as the Swiss-born Bruno Grosjean, who became Bruno Dössekker after his adoption, and his claim to be a Holocaust child survivor named "Binjamin Wilkomirski."[49] Because Hanno Helbig, the former feuilleton head of the *Neue Züricher Zeitung*, had warned Suhrkamp publisher Siegfried Unseld in a letter that *Fragments* was fiction some nine months before the publication, "Wilkomirski" was asked to provide an author's note that addressed the difference between his documented and claimed identities. While he acknowledges the discrepancy, not only did the author not satisfactorily explain it, but he used the imposed statement to preempt further critique by invoking "the plight of a victim who finds that his memories are doubted and dismissed,"[50] which he had also recycled throughout *Fragments.* The idea had become widely known in Holocaust discourse through Primo Levi's memoir *Survival in Auschwitz*, in which he describes the nightmare of a survivor that after returning home his story would not be believed. It was likewise adopted as the core doctrine of believe-the-children by the recovered memory movement. In "Wilkomirski's" author's note, the reader is preemptively admonished that questioning the narrative's historical veracity and hence the author's identity and status as a child survivor and witness would be tantamount to re-victimization, even a second Holocaust experience.

Daniel Ganzfried's spectacular accusations that that *Fragments* was a fake and "Wilkomirski" an impostor, published in the Swiss newspaper *Weltwoche* on August 27, 1998, and subsequently widely disseminated, particularly in Swiss, German, French, and American newspapers, thus caused an international media scandal.[51] The responses to the allegations "in both academic circles and the popular press, were vehement, often quite nasty, and to a surprising extent aimed not at . . . Wilkomirski" but rather at Ganzfried."[52] The initially almost unanimous defense of "Wilkomirski" reflected the fact that Ganzfried had not only citicized *Fragments* and Dössekker's public persona as fraudulent but also exposed the false pieties of official Holocaust memory, such as the depiction of extreme violence as enlightening or the belief that testimony must not be questioned with regard to historical veracity. Nevertheless, a number of independently researched articles, such as Jörg Lau's in the German newspaper *Die Zeit*, Philip Gourevitch's in *The New Yorker*, and Elena Lappin's in *Granta*, a *60 Minutes* segment on "Wilkomirski," Blake Eskin's journalistic monograph *A Life in Pieces*, and especially Stefan Maechler's study *The Wilkomirski Affair*, all confirmed and even further extended Ganzfried's accusations.

*Fragments* had resonated so strongly with critics, particularly in the United States, before the exposure because "looking angst-ridden and tearful, Wilkomirski embodied the Holocaust for American audiences as no one had since Wiesel."[53] Put differently, his public persona constituted an exaggerated kitsch derivative of the preeminent American survivor figure. He publicly performed his simulation particularly at readings, when he not only reduced his audience but, unlike actual survivors, also himself to the derivative or second tears that Milan Kundera considered indicative of kitsch sentiment. Moreover, Bruno Dössekker inadvertently enacted what Eric Hebborn described as his core strategy for art forgery. In *Drawn to Trouble*, Hebborn advises forgers not to "imitate what you personally think are characteristic features of an old master's work" but instead to "produce something that complies with what is currently being said about it by experts, who will then mistake your forgery for the genuine article."[54] Literary critics considered *Fragments* a genuine Holocaust memoir precisely because it was a collage of tropes, compiled from many of the same primary sources from which they had generated their expert discourse, and thus proved a better fit with dominant theories of trauma and Holocaust aesthetics than actual memoirs.

*Fragments* extensively employs the rhetorical figure of paradox, which was introduced into Holocaust discourse by Elie Wiesel through such claims as that, although the Holocaust constitutes a unique historical event, it is of universal significance and abounds in trauma theory, particularly in Cathy Caruth's arguments.[55] "Wilkomirski," for example, paradoxically stresses the many gaps in his childhood memories but also asserts the certainty of his testimony based on the "exact snapshots" of his "photographic memory."[56] "Wilkomirski's" references to gaps in his memories moreover echo the notion, central to the Holocaust and trauma studies discourse generated in literary scholarship, that trauma is inherently unknowable and unrepresentable, and therefore encoded, not in the language an author employs to communicate the experience, but rather in the text's silences and absences. The contrary assertion that his memories are of photographic literality likewise echoes a core notion of postmodern trauma theory, because traumatic experiences are said to be cognitively encoded in unintegrated and unmediated form, and traumatic memories therefore supposedly constitute literal copies of the traumatizing event. In fact, *Fragments* fit the trauma theory of Cathy Caruth, Shoshana Felman, and Dori Laub, Marianne Hirsch's postmemory concept, and Lawrence Langer's Holocaust aesthetics so well that, even after its exposure as a fake, Michael Bernard-Donals used these theories to argue that *Fragments* nevertheless constitutes a viable and valuable Holocaust testimony.[57] However, the dominant post-exposure opinion among literary scholars is Susan Rubin Suleiman's apt rejection of rehabilitating "Wilkomirski's" false memoir based on the notion that it reveals the effects of the Holocaust on the contemporary imagination.[58] She furthermore argued that since *Fragments* obfuscated its own fictionality because "Wilkomirski" claimed it was a memoir, it cannot simply be relabeled as a novel, but rather belongs in its own category, that of discredited, deluded, or false memoirs.[59]

"Wilkomirski" inadvertently reflects the status of his fake memoir as a collage generated from fragments of culturally omnipresent Holocaust representations, both in the title itself and when he described the rhetoric he employed as "imitations of other people's speech."[60] According to Stefan Maechler, Dössekker generated his story from memories of his own childhood, from testimony of actual child survivors, and particularly from media representations of the Holocaust.[61] Among the vast number of media products from which Dossekker recycled historical details, Maechler stressed the significance of

Eberhard Fechner's 1984 TV documentary *Der Prozess* (The Trial) about the trial of the Majdanek SS guards.[62] He argued that the historical facts about the camp in *Fragments* were taken straight out of Fechner's documentary, including "the miserable water supply, the dog kennels, the plague of lice, the crematorium with its iron dampers, the women's barracks, the 'children's quarantine' on Field 5."[63] Dössekker also borrowed from the documentary that prisoners were whipped, that children had no toilets and were taken away in roundups, that the camp personnel were corrupt, that there was a roundup and murder of all 18,000 Jewish prisoners on November 3, 1943, and that the only possibility of surviving Majdanek was via the few transports to Auschwitz.[64] Maechler furthermore argued that ideas from William Niederland's 1980 study on the long-term consequences of Nazi persecution and concentration camp imprisonment were obliquely reflected in *Fragments*.[65]

However, most significant for its plot structure and graphic depictions of brutality was Jerzy Kosinski's horror kitsch fantasy *The Painted Bird*, which Dössekker read in the late 1960s. In both texts, the protagonist is a small boy who is separated from his family, experiences violence so horrific that he temporarily loses his voice but magically survives, "a frail child, and yet a superhero."[66] Both boys spend time at an orphanage after the war, both tell of plagues of rats and of children standing in pools of excrement. *Fragments* furthermore echoes the core structure of disconnected episodes based on supposedly fragmentary memory and the sophisticatedly constructed but nonsensical pretense of narrating the past from the naïve perspective of the child. This strategy, which effectively conflates the subject positions of experiencing and narrating self, not only serves to melodramatically juxtapose the absolute innocence of childhood to the ultimate evil of Nazism, but also justifies the lack of historical specifics regarding time and place beyond the vague setting of Poland during the Holocaust.[67] Dössekker may even have followed Kosinski's method for transforming lived reality into narrative form. His German translation of *The Painted Bird* includes an afterword in which Kosinski argued that "objective reality acquires" only "a secondary importance" and the writer therefore "makes use of it only to the extent to which it is already accommodated in the universe created by his imagination" and hence he "takes from outside himself only what he is capable of creating in his imagination."[68] According to Kosinski, experiences are fit into molds of the imagination "which simplify, shape and give them an acceptable emotional clarity" and thus "the remembered events become a fiction, a structure made to accommodate certain feelings."[69] Although his notion that "if memories have a truth, it is more an emotional than an actual one"[70] has since acquired cultural prominence in the belief that feeling-truth trumps fact-truth,[71] Kosinski describes the process of transforming lived experience into fiction. Nevertheless, the genre status both Kosinski and "Wilkomirski" claimed for their texts is that of memoir.

"Wilkomirski's" actual life story is well known by now. Born Bruno Grosjean to an unwed mother in Switzerland in 1941, he moved between several homes, experienced dire poverty, and for several months also the unpredictable violent outbursts of a mentally unstable foster mother. While the physical hardships ended when he was adopted by the affluent Dössekker family in 1945, he described them by recourse to a popular psychology trope as emotionally distant parents. According to the dominant interpretation of his life story, Dössekker translated his difficult childhood via the plot formula of Holocaust survival because, after the Eichmann trial, it became the culturally dominant paradigm for expressing suffering. He engaged in a three-decade-long consumption of historiography, witness accounts, psychological studies about the long-term effects of concentration camp imprisonment, memoirs and novels, documentaries and feature films about the Holocaust, because he believed that "one day it will help me to understand my own history better."[72] After he had read some two thousand books on the subject and twice as many survivor testimonies and repeatedly visited the locations of his imagined childhood (Krakow, Majdanek, Lublin, and Auschwitz in 1972, 1973, and 1993, and Riga in 1994), he supposedly recovered memories of this past with the help of his therapist Monika Matta. Dössekker's delusional belief that he is a Holocaust child survivor named "Binjamin Wilkomirski" was furthermore encouraged by Israeli psychologist Elitsur Bernstein, who became his closest friend in 1979, when he was living in Switzerland, and by Verena Piller, his life partner since 1982.[73] Matta, Bernstein, and Piller thus served as coaxers, empathic interlocutors whose willingness to listen and unquestioning belief in the referential reliability of the supposedly recovered memories elicited their narration, and whose questions and comments, while removed from the written story, effectively co-generated it.[74] Dössekker himself described Piller's role as follows: "I felt the first moment, she was able to create a sort of atmosphere of security and that from the beginning I could tell her first a little bit and then more and more . . . about all my nightmares and where they came from and what I remember. And she had incredible patience and loved to listen, listen again and again."[75] He also credited her with encouraging him to pursue his memories through therapy and writing because she believed they were the cause of his physical illnesses. When he wrote the memoir, he would read each new passage to her and then fax it to Bernstein asking him to confirm the reliability of the memories. Based on the believe-the-victim doctrine of recovered memory discourse, Bernstein validated them by arguing that, if he remembered something, it probably happened. He also read what Dössekker had written for Monika Matta as part of his therapeutic treatment, and both Piller and Bernstein accompanied him on the trips to Krakow, Auschwitz, Majdanek, and Riga.[76]

According to forensic psychologist Ian Joblin, fabricated stories of an exceptional life reflect a sense of inadequacy. Confabulators create a persona who is revered in a given culture in search of legitimacy, self-assurance, and power. Such narratives are not skillfully planned and presented as a complete entity, but rather start on a small scale. Initially, they are only told to a small circle of friends and family. Only if the confabulator is encouraged, or at least not contradicted, in this trial phase, does the story grow and the audience expand. Confabulated life narratives tend to change significantly during the many retellings, not least to cover the inevitable contradictions. According to Joblin, "the more they're rewarded and applauded, the greater the whole schemata of the deception" becomes, and the confabulator's initial sense of inadequacy changes into the other extreme, an equally misguided notion of omnipotence and immunity.[77] Dössekker's transformation into "Wilkomirski" gradually emerged over some forty years. In high school, he told people that he was a refugee from the Baltic area, but only in the mid-1960s, after the Eichmann trial had largely introduced the Holocaust into the public sphere, did he claim Jewish heritage and demonstrate it by wearing a necklace with the Star of David, putting on a yarmulke at home, and placing a mezuzah on his apartment door. However, according to his ex-wife, at that time he called himself Nils Raiskin or something similar, and only in 1972 did he adopt the name Wilkomirski, after seeing a poster of renowned violinist Wanda Wilkomirska during his first trip to Poland. While he claimed that she was his sister and also invented seven other siblings, all of whom died with their mother in a concentration camp, at that time he did not yet consider himself a camp survivor.[78] Of these confabulations, only the name and the notion that his mother died in a concentration camp are reflected in the memoir. Stefan Maechler confirmed Ian Joblin's argument when he suggested that Dössekker's story is so full of contradictions and so poorly grounded in verifiable historical facts that it cannot have been generated as a coldly calculated fraud, as Daniel Ganzfried had initially suggested. According to Maechler, Dössekker's identity as the child Holocaust survivor "Binjamin Wilkomirski" arose "over the course of four decades, unplanned and improvised, with new experiences and necessities constantly woven into it and contradictions arising from a lack of any plan smoothed over, though over time with less and less success."[79]

In addition to his fake memoir, Dössekker also wrote two presentations and co-authored a third with Bernstein on the subject of recovering traumatic childhood memories, which likewise recycled core doctrines of the recovered memory movement that have also entered trauma theory scholarship. They included not only the claim that "traumas from childhood are repressed but continue to have a subconscious effect and create specific psychological symptoms" which "vanish when the repressed memory is made conscious and worked through" but also the nonsensical idea that "the traumatic situation is retained as a photographic copy . . . in the subconscious."[80] And echoing the untenable notion introduced into trauma studies research by controversial psychiatrist

Bessel van der Kolk,[81] Dössekker particularly privileged nightmares as literal re-experiences, and hence the most accurate form of traumatic memory.[82] Both the false memoir and the presentations thus reflected the transition in 1990s psychotherapeutic discourse from a focus on the psychological recovery from empirically confirmed traumatic experiences to the recovery of supposedly repressed memories of hypothesized childhood trauma.[83] His co-generated confabulations of Holocaust survival furthermore manifested the core trauma culture doctrine that truth is subjective and emotional, rather than rational and referential. Dössekker's embrace of a Holocaust victim-cum-survivor identity thus reflects core trauma culture tropes: the significance of victimhood for con-temporary identity construction; the dominant notion that survival constitutes the greatest achievement; the ascription of the rank of hero to the survivor fig-ure; the status of Holocaust survival as the dominant plot paradigm for repre-senting victimhood and suffering; the rise of misery memoirs to preeminent popular literature genre; and the consequent generation of mis lit forgeries. Contrary to the implication in scholarship that explored the "Wilkomirski" affair independently of its context, Bruno Dössekker's recasting of his difficult childhood as a Holocaust fantasy thus constitutes not an exception but rather a paradigmatic embodiment of contemporary culture.

## Laurel Willson's Trauma Tropes

In the course of the "Wilkomirski" scandal, Laurel Willson's impersonation of an imaginary Holocaust child survivor named "Laura Grabowski" was also exposed.[84] In the spring of 1997, Willson began participating in the meetings of a Los Angeles–based group of people who had survived the Holocaust as children. While new members would usually introduce themselves by relating where they were born, how they survived, who in their family survived, and when they came to the States, "Grabowski" talked only about being in emotional pain at her first meeting. Only after two months did she share that she was born around 1941 in Poland, had been at Auschwitz-Birkenau, lived in an orphanage in Krakow afterward, was smuggled into the United States when she was about nine or ten, and adopted by a non-Jewish family.[85] Laurel Willson thus created trauma culture's first known meta-confabulation when, substituting America for Switzerland, she essentially recycled "Wilkomirski's" fake life narrative as her own. "Grabowski" had written to "Wilkomirski" about the impact *Fragments* had had on her as a fellow child survivor, and "Wilkomirski," who regularly inte-grated others' testimonies to shape his own false life narrative, upped the ante even further when he in turn incorporated "Grabowski" into his own fabrication by claiming to remember a girl named Laura from Auschwitz. While her initial letter to "Wilkomirski" had not mentioned that "Laura" had known "Binjamin" in Auschwitz, "Grabowski" not only returned the favor and added this plot twist to her own confabulation, but also extended "Wilkomirski" an invitation to the Los Angeles group of child survivors. When "Wilkomirski" and "Grabowski" met there on April 19, 1998, the two fake survivors generated significant publicity and many a kitsch-sentimental tear. "Wilkomirski" told BBC reporters afterward that he had recognized "Grabowski" instantly by the shape of her face. However, when the two amateur musicians performed an arrangement of the Kol Nidre, the opening prayer for the Yom Kippur evening service, at the gathering, they revealed their lack of even basic knowledge about Jewish religion and tradition.[86]

Laurel Willson further developed her alter ego of Holocaust child survivor "Laura Grabowski" in the virtual reality of the internet. According to Blake Eskin, "the innovations in form brought about by the Web—inexpensive, global distribution of data and inexpensive and pseudonymous electronic dialogue—have put more information at the disposal of the public . . . and made it easier for virtual global communities to develop. This goes for Holocaust deniers as well as for those who could perhaps be called Holocaust seekers, people of various backgrounds with a passionate if sometimes ill-defined affinity for the subject."[87] Willson participated in the online discussion forum at www.holocaust.about.com under the generic handle "child survivor" and posted her poem "We are One" at the same site. She repeated the absurd argument she made in the poem—that everyone who feels like a Holocaust survivor should be considered one—in her post to the H-Holocaust e-mail list on January 24, 1999: "I think we need to be sensitive to all who consider themselves as survivors of the Holocaust. . . . For myself, the Holocaust is about individual suffering. . . . And if some call themselves survivors who are not survivors in any sense of the word, does this upset the whole survivor movement? I think not."[88] Both, the e-mail and the poem's last line—"none of us are any less or any more than our Holocaust siblings"—not only reflect the preeminence of Holocaust survivor status but also inadvertently reveals that the author is actually not a Holocaust survivor herself.

However, "Laura Grabowski" was not Willson's first fake victim-cum-survivor alter ego. Before her impersonation of the Holocaust child survivor, she had published a fabricated memoir entitled *Satan's Underground*, under the pseudonym "Lauren Stratford." It narrates "Lauren's" journey through the earthly hell of child abuse and Satan worship into the arms of the Lord, and depicted in gruesome detail her supposed experience of Satanic Ritual Abuse (SRA).[89] Published in 1991, it sold some 140,000 copies, was featured on the *700 Club*, and became a key source for promoting, perpetuating, and validating the American SRA hysteria that peaked in the early 1990s.[90] In 1989, Willson had already published *I Know You're Hurting*, a Christian self-help book for SRA survivors, as "Lauren Stratford." She employed the same pseudonym for her 1993 book *Stripped Naked*, a fake trauma-and-recovery memoir recounting her experience of Multiple Personality Disorder (MPD), which she claims to have suffered as a result of her abuse.

SRA emerged in the mid-1980s, when American psychotherapeutic discourse was dominated by supposedly recovered memories of sexual child abuse that became ever more bizarre. According to Elaine Showalter, with their emphasis on incest, infanticide, forced breeding, cannibalism, devil worship, sadistic torture, and conspiracy, the SRA narratives touched on "the deepest and most frightening taboos and fantasies of our time."[91] Reinforced by horror stories like Ira Levin's bestselling *Rosemary's Baby* and Roman Polanski's film adaptation, and exacerbated by the spectacular yarns of Satan's kingdom, spiritual warfare, and Armageddon generated by the American evangelical movement, the SRA hysteria moved from small town to small town.[92]

MPD "emerged in part as an answer to one of the most vexing questions for recovered memory advocates: how exactly did the child forget the experience of sexual abuse?" Expanding on the dissociation concept, the *Diagnostics and Statistics Manual of Psychiatric Disorders*, which introduced MPD in 1980, hypothesized that the child splits off alters to protect itself and continue to function in everyday life. Some of the alters were believed to remember the abuse while the adult remained unaware of the split-off personalities and hence also of the abuse memories. The task of the therapist was to recover the repressed or dissociated abuse trauma and, over time, integrate it into the patient's memory. However, most psychiatrists who study the complex process of dissociation maintain that MPD is created in the interaction of patient and therapist whose shared belief in the reality of the recovered memories is based on its depiction in mass media products, particularly Flora Rheta Schreiber's bestselling *Sybil* and its movie adaptation. The plot is based on Cornelia Wilbur's extensive psychotherapy with a patient pseudonymously named Sybil, who developed sixteen independent personalities or alters as a consequence of supposed sexual abuse by her mother. Until 1972, less than fifty cases of MPD were known, but after the 1973 publication of *Sybil* had introduced the story paradigm and imagery, MPD quickly become ubiquitous in the United States, and by 1990 more than 20,000 cases had been diagnosed. And while MPD was a solely American phenomenon until 1989, with the globalization of American popular culture it spread to other countries, including New Zealand, Turkey, Germany, and Norway.[93]

Transcripts of SRA therapy sessions show that patients initially report very diverse stories that are only streamlined into to the dominant plot paradigm during the therapeutic process and through the extensive reading of SRA memoirs and self-help books.[94] SRA is thus likewise a therapeutically co-created disorder, and Showalter's summary of the genesis of MPD narratives also pertains to SRA accounts: "We need not assume that patients are either describing an organic disorder or else lying when they present similar narratives of symptoms. Instead, patients learn about diseases from the media, unconsciously develop the symptoms, and then attract media attention in an endless cycle. The human imagination is not infinite, and we are all bombarded by these plot lines every day."[95] For example, in 1994 Ellen Bass and Laura Davis added a chapter on SRA and MPD to the third edition of *The Courage to Heal*, the bestselling self-help book on recovered memories of child abuse. The plot paradigm was also disseminated widely through women's magazines, misery memoirs, and daytime TV talk shows. "Lauren Stratford," for instance, appeared on both *Geraldo* and *Oprah* as an MPD patient in 1988. And a 1993 issue of *Vanity Fair* stated that "all over the country . . . an astonishing number of women are coming forward with similar tales of satanic cults and ritual abuse."[96] They claimed that, as children, they had "been drugged, tortured with cattle prods, branded with branding irons, raped with crucifixes and animal carcasses, . . . buried in coffins with live snakes and dead bodies, . . . tied to crosses and hung upside down for days, . . . forced to kill and eat babies at satanic ceremonies, . . . photographed for child pornographers, and caged by satanic child-prostitution rings that farmed out their tiny victims for further abuse."[97] Advocates argued that the formulaic similarity of SRA tales signified that the phenomenon was real and ubiquitous. However, some three hundred American cases were investigated by the FBI and eighty-four cases in the United Kingdom, all of which were dismissed for complete lack of evidence.[98]

Like Bruno Dössekker, who was known to have "lied always and every day," both "cleverly and . . . stupidly" for "obvious reasons and for no reasons" since his teens[99] and who sampled core representations of Holocaust victimhood to create his compilation of trauma culture tropes, Laurel Willson exhibited a strong tendency to tell tall tales since early adolescence and developed her fake victim identities based on culturally dominant narratives. In fact, a former friend commented about Willson's ever-changing confabulations that "most of the stories Laurel told me about her mom's abuse were taken literally from *Sybil*."[100] When the SRA phenomenon dominated the American media, Willson even befriended various individuals associated with two of the most spectacular cases investigated in 1985, one in Bakersfield, where she was living at the time, and another in Manhattan Beach, also located in Southern California, and she began incorporating SRA into her own fake life narrative.[101]

Some of the countless tall tales Willson had told over the course of some three decades comprise the entirely fabricated plot of *Satan's Underground*. The protagonist is raped at age six by a day laborer at the encouragement of her mother, who also physically abuses her, as payment for his day's work. From then on, she was raped regularly with her parents' approval and even at their instigation, and by age eight "Lauren" had become a pawn in a pornography ring. After her parents divorced, she went to live with her father at age fifteen, but the pornography ring extended even to the state where he lived, and she had to continue to work for them, all the while leading an overtly normal life at school, college, and church. Pornography eventually led to Satan worship and

"Lauren" was forced to participate in ritualistic infanticide. When she refused, she was brainwashed, tortured, and locked in a metal drum with four dead infants that had been sacrificed in Satanic rituals. Subsequently, she participated in such rituals herself, including the one in which one of the three children she had been forced to breed was sacrificed for Satan. The other two children were killed in so-called snuff films. Eventually she fled from the prostitution-cum-SRA ring, moving from city to city, but was always found and threatened that she must remain silent about her experiences. Nevertheless, "Lauren" courageously came forth and testified in her memoir.

While one may wonder how anyone could believe such fantastic horror stories, the same question could be directed at the critics and scholars who not only unanimously believed but venerated with quasi-religious devotion "Binjamin Wilkomirski's" no less fantastic Holocaust-as-horror-fantasy. After all, the latter depicts how "Binjamin" was thrown head-on into a stone wall; locked in a dog kennel where lice and beetles attacked his nose, mouth, and eyes; kicked in the back of the head and sent flying; and climbed out of a pit filled with naked corpses, his foot sinking into "a big white stomach." He described how another child's head was caved in by a ball; a huge, bloody rat burst out of a dead woman's belly; starving infants chewed their frozen fingers down to the bone; and last but certainly not least, little sticks were shoved up boy's penises "as far as they'd go" and then broken off.[102]

As thematically diverse as the plot lines of *Satan's Underground* and *Fragments* are, both texts exhibit a number of similarities, most of which also pertain to the misery memoir genre at large: They "make uninhibited use of a rhetoric of violence" and both "Binjamin" and "Lauren" "are innocent victims of the most horrible crimes but can find no one who will listen."[103] Only as adults do they encounter empathetic interlocutors who enable them to acknowledge their past horrors and present emotional pain. Reflecting the cultural dominance of recovery discourse in the early 1990s, both stories emerged in a therapeutic context: formal therapy and friendship with a therapist in "Wilkomirski's" case and numerous Christian women and couples who befriended and informally counseled "Stratford," one of whom even legally adopted her at age thirty. Both authors asserted that they wrote their respective memoirs because they believed it to be therapeutically beneficial and as testimony to help others with similar experiences. In fact, both have said, using the same cliché verbatim, that they wanted other victims to know "they are not alone."[104] As both texts are nebulous about details—they are missing dates, places, outside events, and even the names of all principal characters—they can only vaguely be placed in a specific historical and geographical context.[105] In *Fragments* this factual vagueness is explained by the nature of early childhood memory and in *Satan's Underground* by the conspiracy theory argument about protecting the author from the SRA ring. Furthermore, reflecting the fact that illness had become a dominant subject in mis lit,[106] both "Wilkomirski" and "Stratford" evoked serious, even life-threatening illnesses in the fabricated life stories they continued to construct after the publication of their fake memoirs.

As "Lauren Stratford," Willson claimed that "her emotional and physical health deteriorated as a consequence of the extreme abuse she had suffered" and that "during one eight-year period she was hospitalized more than forty times."[107] After she reinvented herself as Holocaust survivor "Laura Grabowski," she cast her many supposed illnesses, particularly a rare blood disease, as consequences of the medical experiments performed on her at Auschwitz by none other than Mengele himself. She furthermore reinterpreted the scars on her arms resulting from her self-mutilation as an adolescent from evidence of her abusive parents and SRA to signifying that she had been part of Mengele's experiments. Simulating his simulator, "Wilkomirski" in turn borrowed the notion of having been experimented on by Mengele, the rare blood disease, and the claim that it had been caused by medical experiments at Auschwitz from "Grabowski."

Literary scholarship treats its objects of analysis largely if not entirely as aesthetic entities and thus, not only polarizes popular and highbrow literature, but also essentially ignores as irrelevant both their commodity status in a capitalist market economy and their reception by readers other than scholars. Moreover, it is still widely believed that literary studies scholars should only concern themselves with texts deemed aesthetically superior—which make up the so-called canon—based on unspecified and, given the relative constancy of the canon, apparently historically invariable criteria. The analysis of popular culture is often wrongly conflated with its non-scholarly consumption and, based on the relative structural simplicity and large-scale reception of the mass media, considered intellectually inferior to the study of canonical literature. This misconception furthermore derives from the mistaken presumption that, like canonical literary studies, popular culture scholarship only seeks to understand the artifact itself rather than how it functions as an aesthetic and a commercial entity generated in the complex interaction between production and reception. Because of these institutionally solidified prejudices, literary studies has ignored the significance of mis lit and its forgery, and consequently treated Dössekker's reinvention of himself as Holocaust child survivor "Binjamin Wilkomirski" as a bizarre obscurity, rather than an integral part of a larger cultural trend.

When contextualized in the growing micro-genre of fake misery memoirs, "Wilkomirski's" fabrication of a Holocaust childhood no longer appears as an isolated incident, but rather as a paradigmatic embodiment of popular trauma culture. Like "Defonseca's" and Willson's confabulated victim narratives, the Holocaust fantasies of *The Boy in the Striped Pajamas* and *Life is Beautiful*, and Rosenblat's extension of his actual survival story, "Wilkomirski's" fake memoir was historically impossible and merged the preeminent popular literature sub-ject of child abuse with the canonical genre of Holocaust testimony. And like Vicki Fraginals's invention of "Anthony Godby Johnson" and Laura Albert's creation of "JT LeRoy," Dössekker's alter ego of "Binjamin Wilkomirski" both preceded the memoir and was subsequently expanded beyond the written story. For example, after publication he added the claim that he had been part of medical experiments in Auschwitz and that his many (vastly exaggerated) illnesses were a consequence of these experiments, plot elements he most likely borrowed from "Laura Grabowski." And the latter as well as "Anthony Godby Johnson" and "JT LeRoy" all employed the virtual reality of the internet to develop their fake personas and stories.

All of the imaginary victim narratives discussed in the two concluding chapters of this analysis of popular trauma culture share the subject matter of horrific violence perpetrated on a young child who functions as the embodi-ment of absolute innocence. Although these fabricated accounts of victimhood were generated in diverse contexts, their resemblances indicate that the trauma-and-redemption story paradigm emplotted in melodramatic good-versus-evil conflicts and embodied in the flat characters of innocent victim and evil villain has thoroughly saturated the public sphere.

# Epilogue

## Fantasies of Witnessing

"... a broadening of the term *witness*, as well as similar uses of the terms *memory* and *trauma*, contributes to a wishful blurring of otherwise obvious and meaningful distinctions between the victims and ourselves, and between the Holocaust and our own historical moment."

–Gary Weissman, *Fantasies of Witnessing*[1]

Contemporary everyday life is often experienced as mundane and banal, interchangeable and unoriginal, lacking a deeper meaning or purpose, in short, as an inauthentic simulation rather than the "real thing." The notion of authenticity is thus created by ascribing inauthenticity to ordinary life as its imaginary and ideal alternative, analogous to the idea of paradise emerging from the notion of paradise lost. It is the reification of authenticity that generates "an ontological fiction called the 'real thing.'"[2] As the nostalgia for the "real thing" expresses a longing for something that never actually existed, authenticity constitutes the ever-elusive holy grail of our late-modern era.

As only the personal, emotional, and experiential are considered authentic and real,[3] the memoir and autobiographical texts in general rose to cultural dominance, while fiction, and the novel in particular, were increasingly devalued as inauthentic. However, the maintenance of value depends on a system of polarities.[4] For autobiographical writing, especially the memoir, to retain its value requires the continued reception of fiction, because fiction functions as literary nonfiction's defining Other. Since the preservation of value depends on polarities, it is threatened by simulation because simulation neutralizes polarities.[5] When fictional narratives simulate autobiographical nonfiction, as fake memoirs do, they threaten to eliminate the difference between authenticity and inauthenticity, which has been superimposed onto the distinction between fiction and nonfiction, and hence to eradicate the significant moral capital and commodity value of the memoir genre.

Late-modern culture also gave rise to what Michael Bernstein termed an ideology of the extreme and described as the belief that "the truth lies in the extreme moments which 'ordinary bourgeois life' covers over."[6] Dori Laub, for instance, argued that "the Holocaust experience is a very condensed version of most of what life is about: it contains a great many existential questions, that we manage to avoid in our daily living, often through preoccupation with trivia."[7] They include "the question of facing death; of facing time and its passage; of the meaning and purpose of living; . . . of losing the ones that are close to us [and] the great question of our ultimate aloneness."[8] And Lawrence Langer's "search for the least transformed, least mediated, and therefore truest portrayal of the Holocaust" in his scholarship essentially constitutes "a search for the fundamental truth revealed by the Holocaust,"[9] which "is ultimately about life or being in the world."[10]

However, authenticity is ascribed not only to one's own experience of extremity in the past, as Laub's words suggest, but also and especially to the oxymoronic vicarious experience of other's suffering through the reception of media products—both popular and, in the case of scholars like Langer, highbrow—in the present. In other words, consuming representations of the pain of others is ascribed the capacity to fill "the void left by diminished opportunities to experience the real thing"[11] and, as such, to satisfy the nostalgic longing for that ontological fiction called the "real thing."[12] However, attributing life lessons and some mystical ultimate truth either to the immediate experience of extremity or to the reception of its media portrayal is both absurd and unethical not least because it conflates actual experience, particularly of extreme violence, with the consumption experience of its representation. Bernstein likewise rejected the notion of *in extremis veritas* and aptly argued that our beliefs and values ought to be developed and tested in the routines of everyday life, rather than created through fantasies of vicariously experiencing extremity by consuming media products.[13]

In search of authenticity and answers to what Laub termed "a great many existential questions,"[14] many a late-modern individual consumes the pain of others not only in misery memoirs, daytime TV talk shows, and media representations of violence generally, but also by tourism to places of mass death. In particular, the sites of Nazi concentration camps and of the World Trade Center—misleadingly termed Ground Zero—have become tourist attractions.[15] Dark tourism, as John Lennon and Malcolm Foley termed it,[16] is becoming increasingly popular because places of mass killings, of which Auschwitz is the paradigmatic instance, are ascribed the status of sacred sites. Astutely intuitive for cultural trends, Oprah Winfrey employed Auschwitz's aura of the negative sublime to rebuild her tarnished reputation and the commodity value of her show when she followed her disastrous book club choice of Frey's *A Million Little Pieces* with Elie Wiesel's *Night*, and broadcast their sentimental journey through the campsite on her show. The program offered viewers a kind of package deal in popular trauma culture's ultimate consumer products of authenticity and survival lessons. And invoking the genre of the travelogue, which enables audiences to vicariously experience exotic places in far-away lands from the comfort of home, it also innovated the notion of televisual trauma tourism.

Although the modern-day pilgrims visit places of mass death seeking to obtain a trace of authenticity by extension, they exhibit fantasies of witnessing past extremity as a quasi-religious experience, and thus engage with these sites through the consumption relations paradigmatic for all tourism. In her renowned Holocaust memoir *weiter leben* (*Still Alive*), Ruth Klüger likewise rejected the sacralization of atrocity sites and insisted that they were empirically real places rather than some imaginary dystopia. She proposed the notion of "timescapes" to signify the categorical difference between Auschwitz as a concentration camp and as a tourist site.[17] In search of authenticity, late-modern individuals thus consume the pain of others as trauma-and-redemption plots in mass media products like daytime TV talk shows and misery memoirs, through touristic engagement with sites of mass death, and, most innovatively, by way of such virtual dark tourism as that offered on *The Oprah Winfrey Show*.

John Berger already explored the reception of extremity depictions in his classic 1972 essay "Photographs of Agony" and analyzed what he described as the audience's sense of moral inadequacy in responding to the atrocity photographs that were being published more and more in American newspapers. According to Berger, seeing the depicted suffering gives rise to either despair or indignation, and while "despair takes on some of the other's suffering to no purpose, indignation demands action."[18] However, the atrocities being shown tend to be vastly removed from the everyday reality within which the photographs are published, and, as Luc Boltanski argued, the further away the suffering is, either physically or socio-culturally, the fewer are the possibilities of action open to the spectators.[19] Whether they shrug off their sense of moral inadequacy as only too familiar or give in to purposeless despair, they cannot follow the ethical imperative to relieve the suffering. Moreover, as the photographs are taken as indicative of the general human condition, they accuse nobody and everybody, and the suffering is effectively depoliticized, because its causes—social, political, and economic inequality and injustice, which often culminate in war—are obscured and the victim's pain is cast as an individual tragedy. Even if spectators were able to perceive the larger conflict behind the depicted victim and, moreover, dared to acknowledge that the politics of their own democratically elected government have caused the suffering, Berger rightly admonished that, in the existing political system "we have no legal opportunity of effectively influencing the conduct of wars waged in 'our' name."[20] Rather than give in to the emotional power of the depicted agony, one's reaction ought to be rational and political. Berger advocated confronting our own lack of political freedom as "the only effective way of responding to what the photograph shows," but he realized that precisely the "violence of the photographed moment actually works against this realization," which is why atrocity photographs "can be published with impunity."[21]

Berger's notion that depictions of atrocity give rise to a sense of moral inadequacy among the audience, based on their awareness of the vast discrepancy between the others' suffering and their own comparative comfort, is also implicit in Gary Weissman's discussion of Holocaust representation. However, as Holocaust discourse represents past rather than present suffering, the sense of moral inadequacy does not arise from the inability to ease it. According to Weissman, instead of seeking to understand the genocide as a complex historical event, audiences engage in the oxymoronic persuit of vicariously witnessing the suffering of its victims.[22] And when we "face great difficulty in feeling anything comparable to what we imagine the victims and witnesses of such horrors must have felt," we mistake this as signifying "our own moral inadequacy in responding,"[23] rather than the unethical and nonsensical notion that, to commemorate the pain of others, one must vicariously suffer with and like them. Berger rejected the idea that the audience take on some of the others' suffering and argued that we must instead change the political structures that prevent us from alleviating it. However, a core tenet of American Holocaust commemoration is that the audience must not only suffer (an unethical demand), but that the reception of Holocaust representations must cause suffering approximating that of the victims (an impossible and hence nonsensical commandment). As American Holocaust discourse became paradigmatic for trauma culture at large, the idea that audiences must suffer with, and even as, the victims emerges as the dominant mode of reception advocated—even by authors themselves— for other representations of extremity. American AIDS memoirist Edmund White, for example, advocated that "we want them [the audience] to toss and turn with us, drenched in our night sweats."[24]

The absurd and unethical notion that to commemorate past extremity the audience should vicariously experience their pain is grounded in the fallacious analogy between the experience of the Holocaust and the consumption of its representation created by the vast extension of "witnessing" and "memory" from signifying the former to the latter. The ubiquitous metaphorical uses of these terms and their respective derivatives—including "vicarious witnesses," "secondary witnesses," "retrospective witnesses," "witness's witness," "witnesses by adoption," "witnesses through the imagination," "postmemory," "prosthetic memory," "secondary memory" and "vicarious memory"—facilitates this blurring because their imprecise meanings indicate both the survivors' recall of their lived experiences and the nonwitnesses' familiarity with Holocaust representations.[25] Weissman argued that many scholars, writers, and film makers, including such prominent figures as Steven Spielberg, Claude Lanzmann and Lawrence Langer, conflate the witnesses' experiential and the nonwitnesses' mediated Holocaust knowledge and their respective subject positions in order

to claim the authority of witness testimony for their own Holocaust representations.[26] One may object that they only suggest an oblique analogy between
themselves and the survivor-witness, but whichever qualifier they may employ,
its only function is social—to minimally obscure their impropriety—rather than
semantic. After all, many critics and scholars—who seem unaware that they
engage in appropriative and self-aggrandizing gestures—also frequently omit
the qualifying signifier without, apparently, any change in meaning. Ellen Fine,
for example, reiterates what has become a dominant Holocaust trope, that
"to listen to the witness is to become a witness."[27]

Weissman designated as "nonwitness" everyone for whom the Holocaust
constitutes a core identity marker although they are neither survivors nor do
they have immediate familial ties to survivors.[28] They create what he aptly
called fantasies of witnessing the Holocaust, and argued that nonwitnesses seek
to actualize their fantasies by engaging in literal and metaphorical trauma
tourism through sites, films, or texts.[29] The term thus also stresses the com-
monsensical idea that, while nonwitnesses may read books, watch films, look at
photographs, listen to survivors either in person or through video testimony,
visit museums and memorial sites, they cannot witness the Holocaust, but only
engage with it by way of representations. It should be obvious that these activities categorically differ from the immediate experience of genocidal persecution.[30] Nonsensically seeking to witness the reality of the Holocaust by consuming
its representations, nonwitnesses essentially enact the reception equivalent of
what Dominick LaCapra conceptualized as "writing trauma" and juxtaposed to
"writing about trauma." While the latter mode of representation is dominated
by the interpretative powers of consciousness, the former supposedly allows
the trauma to be externalized from the victim's mind into a narrative, without
the interference of consciousness. However, the trauma is said not to be embodied in the text's present signifiers, but rather in its absences and silences.
LaCapra follows Cathy Caruth's empirically unsustainable idea that such a
re-presentation of trauma can communicate it so that the reader of this
oxymoronic unmediated trauma narrative can experience it in its literal totality.[31]
It is this nonsensical literal experience of another's trauma by way of its
supposedly unmediated re-presentation that nonwitnesses desire with regard
to the Holocaust. They seek to read trauma rather than read about trauma,
because only the latter would enable them to "feel the horror" that some imaginary composite figure of all Holocaust victims suffered and "to perceive that
reality *as a reality*," rather than as a representation.[32] While this is epistemologically impossible, nonwitnesses nevertheless exhibit a nostalgic longing for such
an unmediated experience of the Holocaust. As Daniel Schwarz wrote about his
own vision, which he dubiously attributes to an unspecified "we," in his study of
Holocaust representation in canonical literary texts, "in our nightmares, we are
deported and suffer the horrors of these camps."[33] However, while he depicts

this fantasy of witnessing the Holocaust as a nightmare, one may reinterpret it as a dream about something that is as much, if not more, desired than it is dreaded or feared. Not only may the title of his monograph, *Imagining the Holocaust*, constitute a telling Freudian slip, but he continues his vision with a sentence that seems to express not only a nightmarish dread, but also an almost nostalgic longing for the past he did not experience and can thus only imagine: "I dream of myself within shtetls, camps and confined circumstances, as a participant in the very world I am writing about."[34]

Weissman restricts the realm of his analysis to American culture, and, while he mentions in passing that nonwitnesses are primarily but not solely Jewish, he does not explore why any gentile would engage in Holocaust fantasies. German gentile nonwitnesses in particular occupy a complex subject position that differs from that of either Jewish or other non-Jewish nonwitnesses. Fantasies of witnessing the Holocaust are prominently enacted in Katharina Hacker's semi-autobiographical novel *Eine Art Liebe* (A Love of Sorts).[35] Published in 2003 by the renowned Suhrkamp Verlag, the novel retells in fictional form Saul Friedlander's memoir *Quand vient le souvenir* (*When Memory Comes*).[36] It intertwines this with a second plot line, set in mid-1990s Israel, about a young German woman, the first-person narrator of the novel and alter-ego of the author, into a post-Holocaust platonic love story of sorts. Having come to Israel as a student, the narrator befriends Friedlander's alter ego, Moshe Fein, and learns of his past as a hidden child in France, through their conversations over the course of several years. While Hacker's literary "piggy-backing" upon Friedlander's famous memoir may indicate a lack of imagination and a questionable effort to acquire literary laurels partly based on someone else's fame, an intertextual reading with Italian-German artist Daniela Comani's *Ich war's. Tagebuch 1900–1999* (*It Was Me. Diary 1900–1999*) allows a more complex understanding of Hacker's novel.

Comani's project exists in three versions, a sixty-six minute audio installation, a booklet, and a three-by-six meter digital print on vinyl.[37] The diary of sorts consists of 365 brief entries of significant events in twentieth century world history, which are separated only by the respective dates, ranging from January 1st to December 31st. While the days follow chronologically, the years from 1900 to 1999 are random and omitted from the text itself, though they are provided in an appendix. The title phrase evokes its negation in the ironic title of Hermann van Harten's theater project *Ich bin's nicht, Hitler ist's gewesen* (It Wasn't Me, Hitler Did It),[38] and likewise rejects the apologetic German stance with regard to Nazi crimes. However, in the text itself the depicted events expand temporally and geographically far beyond the Third Reich, and the subject position of the unnamed first-person narrator also varies between perpetrator and victim and between active participant and passive observer. The text begins as follows: "January 1st. I founded the Communist Party of Germany in

Berlin. January 2nd. Berlin. I was able to take insight into my Stasi files.[39] January 3rd. Today I announced the foundation of the dictatorship in Rome. [. . .] January 7th. At the end of a 50-day expedition I have reached the South Pole. January 8th. Memphis, USA. In a sound studio, I made a recording at my own cost: the single 'That's All Right Mama,' which I intend to give my mother for her birthday."[40] The narrative thus alternates, not only between the years of the twentieth century and various national histories, but also between core events in political, social, and cultural history. And Comani's use of the first person throughout the text indicates that she imagines herself as the core protagonist, and thus the ultimate eyewitness of twentieth-century history.

Expanding Weissman's concept beyond fantasies of witnessing the Holocaust from the victim-cum-survivor's perspective to principle events of the twentieth century and a narrative perspective that also incorporates perpetrators and bystanders, Comani could be said to have generated a nonwitness's fantasy of witnessing twentieth century world history. However, within the first few lines, Comani's text deconstructs the hyperrealism it invokes by its genre designation of diary and its structure evocative of medieval annals and signals its fantasy status and hence the author's subject position as a self-conscious nonwitness.

Hacker's reimagining of Friedlander's Holocaust memoir as part of a novel whose second protagonist is a fictionalized alter ego of herself can also be considered an attempt to imagine herself into history. Moreover, in a brief author's note at the end of the book, Hacker writes that she sought to understand a past of which she has no memory through the imagination, in order to create a personal connection to this part of history. She thus inadvertently describes herself as a nonwitness and her novel as fantasy of witnessing. Hacker's semi-autobiographical narrator does not exhibit Comani's self-conscious nonwitness status and furthermore ignores the complexities of a German gentile imagining herself as the testimony-enabling interlocutor of Friedlander's alter ego. However, she neither imagines herself into the Holocaust past, as Daniel Schwarz did, nor superimposes it onto the present, as Norma Rosen, Vanessa Ochs, Aviva Cantor, and Lesley Brody did in their Holocaust fantasies.[41] In creating a fictional alter ego who listens to the testimony of Friedlander's doppelganger, Hacker's novel may even constitute a covert reply to Paul Celan's famous, although increasingly platitudinous, notion that "nobody bears witness to the witness."[42] Hacker's attempt to envisage herself into collective Holocaust memory through her fictional double is nevertheless ethically questionable. It not only blurs the boundaries between the categorically distinct subject positions of witness and nonwitness but it also partially overwrites and erases the historical testimony of Friedlander's memoir, because in the readers' minds both texts will inevitably merge into one composite story. Last but not least, in treating Friedlander's life story as if it constituted part of the public realm—freely available to all who see it fit to use for their own ends—Hacker's novel essentially dispossesses him of the ownership of his testimony.

However, the ultimate gentile Holocaust nonwitness is Bruno Dössekker.[43] While Hacker sought to establish a personal connection to the Holocaust by generating a fantasy of witnessing the testimony of Friedlander's fictional alter ego in the present, Dössekker imagined himself into an ahistorical past by generating the ultimate Holocaust fantasy. His choice of a Holocaust survivor as his alter ego and the fact that his delusional life story was widely believed despite its improbability indicates the extent to which the public sphere is saturated with Holocaust tropes. Moreover, while the fact that Dössekker imagined himself as a child survivor was necessitated by his age, it also indicates that, intuitively perceptive of cultural trends, he merged the story paradigm of Holocaust survival, which had generated popular trauma culture's core set of characters and dominant plot structure, with the primary mis lit subject of child abuse.

Although the genocide of European Jewry remains a dominant topic in American popular culture, particularly in commercial cinema, child abuse is increasingly replacing the Holocaust as the paradigmatic embodiment of evil because it is a far less historically specific subject matter. Beyond *Fragments*, this trend was reflected in the mis lit fakes and alter egos of "Anthony Godby Johnson" and "JT LeRoy," generated by Vicki Fraginals and Laura Albert.

Popular trauma culture is, then, embodied and disseminated in a wide range of cultural artifacts: trauma-and-recovery narratives televised on first-generation TV talk shows and their camp parody on trash talk programs; misery memoirs and their fakes depicting child abuse and the Holocaust survival of children as stories of suffering-and-redemption; dark tourism to pseudo-sacred sites of mass death and its simulation in the virtual reality of television. What these mass media products share is the formulaic representation of extremity as good-versus-evil melodrama, embodied in the flat characters of victim-cum-survivor and perpetrator, which culminates in happy endings of recovery and redemption and incites kitsch sentiment as the dominant mode of reception. Milan Kundera wrote that "kitsch excludes everything from its purview which is essentially unacceptable in human existence."[44] By representing the pain of others as second-tear inducing kitsch, it can thus not only function as entertainment, and therefore a marketable commodity, but it can also be audaciously ubiquitous in the public sphere as its consumers seek only to revel in their own sentimental arousal, rather than to eliminate the depicted suffering. Its emplotment as kitsch thus makes the represented extremity invisible in a political sense, and, beyond all else, it is this that makes selling the pain of other as mass media commodities unethical.

# NOTES

## INTRODUCTION

1. Nancy K. Miller and Jason Tougaw, "Introduction: Extremities," in *Extremities: Trauma, Testimony, and Community* (Urbana: University of Illinois Press, 2002), 2.

2. For discussions of the Eichmann trial as a cultural and media event see Annette Wieviorka, *The Era of the Witness* (Ithaca: Cornell University Press, 2006) and Jeffrey Shandler, "The Man in the Glass Box: Watching the Eichmann Trial on American Television," in *Visual Culture and the Holocaust*, ed. Barbie Zelizer (New Brunswick: Rutgers University Press, 2000), 91–110.

3. Wieviorka, *Witness*, 31.

4. Susan Sontag, *Regarding the Pain of Others* (New York: Picador, 2003).

5. Adam Shatz, "Oprah's New Mess," *Los Angeles Times* (18 Jan. 2006), para. 2.

6. Shatz, "Mess," para. 3.

7. John Beech, "Genocide Tourism," in *The Dark Side of Travel: The Theory and Practice of Dark Tourism*, ed. Richard Sharpley and Philipe Stone (Bristol, UK: Channel View Publications, 2009), 207–223.

8. The DVD of the special, produced by Harpo Productions and distributed through http://oprahstore.oprah.com, displays the oddly fragmented title: *Oprah / Auschwitz Death Camp / Elie Wiesel* with each line printed in a different font and separated by being underlined with stylized barbed wire. The show's special status was marked by being filmed entirely on location, and thus without the presence of a studio audience, and by limited commercial interruption. While the typical division of the *Oprah Winfrey Show* into eight segments was replaced by four longer ones and the number of commercial slots thus cut in half, they were doubled in length. The special thus reflects the regular ratio of 48 minutes show time and 12 minutes advertising, which ensured that TV stations who buy the syndicated show could seamlessly insert the special into the regular programming slot and provided them with equal amounts of salable commercial space.

9. Cited in Shatz, "Mess," para. 5.

10. Roger Luckhurst, *The Trauma Question* (New York: Routledge, 2008), 133.

11. Naomi Seidman, "Elie Wiesel and the Scandal of Jewish Rage," *Jewish Social Studies* 3, 1 (1996), 2.

12. Phillip Lopate, "Resistance to the Holocaust," *Tikkun* 4, 3 (1989), 56.

13. John Lennon and Malcolm Foley, *Dark Tourism: The Attraction of Death and Disaster* (Andover, UK: Thomson Learning, 2004); see also Sharpley and Stone, *Travel*, 3–22.

14. Wieviorka, *Witness*, 119–120; Tim Cole, *Selling the Holocaust: From Auschwitz to Schindler: How History Is Bought, Packaged, and Sold* (New York: Routledge, 2000), 7, 186.

15. Shatz, "Mess," para. 5, citing film critic J. Hoberman.

16. Peter Novick, *The Holocaust in American Life* (Boston: Mariner, 2000), 197, 239.

17. Cathy Caruth, ed., *Trauma. Explorations in Memory* (Baltimore: Johns Hopkins University Press, 1995); Cathy Caruth, *Unclaimed Experience: Trauma, Narrative, and History* (Baltimore: Johns Hopkins University Press, 1996); and Shoshana Felman and Dori Laub, *Testimony: Crises of Witnessing in Literature, Psychoanalysis and History* (New York: Routledge, 1992) are the most influential studies in trauma theory. Their exclusive focus on canonical literature and film has become paradigmatic in trauma studies scholarship, see for instance Deborah Horwitz, *Literary Trauma: Sadism, Memory, and Sexual Violence in American Women's Fiction* (Albany: SUNY Press, 2000); Nicola King, *Memory, Narrative, Identity. Remembering the Self* (Edinburgh: Edinburgh University Press, 2000); Anne Whitehead, *Trauma Fiction* (Edinburgh: Edinburgh University Press, 2004); E. Ann Kaplan, *Trauma Culture: The Politics of Terror and Loss in Media and Literature* (New Brunswick: Rutgers University Press, 2005). Only Roger Luckhurst has acknowledged the ubiquity of trauma, victimization, and suffering in popular culture and sought to integrate it into an analysis of trauma in canonical representations. See particularly his "Traumaculture" [sic], *New Formations* 50 (2003), 28–47; "The Science-Fictionalization of Trauma: Remarks on Narratives of Alien Abduction," *Science Fiction Studies* 15, 1 (1898), 29–52; and *The Trauma Question*.

18. Since trauma theory scholarship is virtually without influence on the notion of trauma generated in contemporary culture, because its reception is limited to the discursive space of the academic ivory tower like that of most research, its complex and extensive arguments will not be integrated into the discussion here. For detailed critiques of postmodern trauma theory see Ruth Leys, *Trauma: A Genealogy* (Chicago: University of Chicago Press, 2000); Wulf Kansteiner, "Genealogy of a Category Mistake. A Critical Intellectual History of the Cultural Trauma Metaphor," *Rethinking History* 8, 2 (2004), 193–221; Wulf Kansteiner and Harald Weilnböck, "Against the Concept of Cultural Trauma," in *Cultural Memory Studies: An International and Interdisciplinary Handbook*, ed. Astrid Erll and Ansgar Nünning (Berlin: de Gruyter, 2008), 229–240; Harald Weilnböck, "'The Trauma Must Remain Inaccessible to Memory': Trauma Melancholia and Other (Ab-)Uses of Trauma Concepts in Literary Theory," www.eurozine.com/articles/2008-03-19-weilnbock-en.html (accessed 08/01/2009); and my own article, "Irresponsible Nonsense: An Epistemological and Ethical Critique of Postmodern Trauma Theory," which is currently under review at *Memory Studies*.

19. Bruno Latour, *Science in Action: How to Follow Scientists and Engineers through Society* (Cambridge: Harvard University Press, 1987), 108, 201.

20. Max Horkheimer and Theodor Adorno, "The Culture Industry: Enlinghtenment as Mass Deception," in *Dialectic of Enlightenment* (Stanford: Stanford Univerisity Press, 2007), 120–167; Martha Woodmansee, "Toward a Genealogy of the Aesthetic: The German Reading Debate of the 1790s," *Cultural Critique* 11 (1988/89), 208.

21. For related discussions of affinities between talk shows and Holocaust video testimony see Wieviorka, *Witness*, 96–144; and my article on "Testimonial Talk between Daytime TV Talk Shows and Holocaust Video Testimony," currently under review at *The Journal of Popular Culture*.

## PART ONE    POPULAR TRAUMA CULTURE

1. James Young, *Writing and Rewriting the Holocaust: Narrative and the Consequences of Interpretation* (Bloomington: Indiana University Press, 1988), 118.

2. Jacob Heilbrunn, "Telling the Holocaust Like It Wasn't," *New York Times* (11 Jan. 2009), 5.

3. Nancy K. Miller and Jason Tougaw, "Introduction: Extremities," in *Extremities: Trauma, Testimony, and Community* (Urbana: University of Illinois Press, 2002), 3.

4. Lauren Berlant, "Poor Eliza," *American Literature* 70, 3 (1998), 657.

## CHAPTER 1    HOLOCAUST TROPES

1. Peter Novick, *The Holocaust in American Life* (Boston: Mariner, 2000), 178.

2. Gary Weissman, *Fantasies of Witnessing: Postwar Efforts to Experience the Holocaust* (Ithaca: Cornell University Press, 2004), 26.

3. Novick, *Holocaust*, 207.

4. Ibid., 226.

5. Cited in ibid., 227.

6. Ibid., 227.

7. Cited in ibid., 227.

8. Ibid., 229.

9. Ibid., 230.

10. Tim Cole, *Selling the Holocaust: From Auschwitz to Schindler: How History Is Bought, Packaged, and Sold* (New York: Routledge, 2000), 16.

11. Norman Finkelstein, *The Holocaust Industry: Reflections on the Exploitation of Jewish Suffering.* (London: Verso, 2001).

12. Cole, *Selling*, 73.

13. Nancy K. Miller and Jason Tougaw, "Introduction: Extremities," in *Extremities: Trauma, Testimony, and Community* (Urbana: University of Illinois Press, 2002), 3.

14. A. O. Scott, "Never Forget. You're Reminded," *New York Times* (23 Nov. 2008), AR1.

15. Jacob Heilbrunn, "Telling the Holocaust Like It Wasn't," *New York Times* (11 Jan. 2009), 5.

16. Winslet made the remark prior to her role in *The Reader*; cited in Scott, "Reminded," AR1.

17. Philip Roth, *Operation Shylock* (New York: Vintage, 1993), 133.

18. Cole, *Selling*, 186.

19. Ibid., 7.

20. Ibid., 186.

21. Annette Wieviorka, *The Era of the Witness* (Ithaca: Cornell University Press, 2006), 119–120.

22. Cole, *Selling*, 186.

23. Roland Barthes, *Mythologies* (New York: Hill and Wang, 1972), 143.

24. Ibid., 143.

25. Ibid., 149.

26. Finkelstein, *Industry*, 3.

27. If uniqueness were not an epistemological impossibility, it would make the event irrelevant for both historiography and collective memory, because it would constitute a *sui generis* entity and, as such, would not be relatable to any other event, and indeed remain incomprehensible.

28. The paradoxical nature of such Wieselesque Holocaust mysticism has not only been embraced as the dominant mode of argument in some Holocaust studies scholarship, but also and especially in the trauma theory of Cathy Caruth, Shoshana Felman, and Dori Laub.

29. Novick, *Holocaust*, 234.

30. Cited in ibid., 234.

31. Cited in ibid.

32. Cited in Wieviorka, *Witness*, 117.

33. Cited in Cole, *Selling*, 13.

34. Michael Berenbaum cited in Cole, *Selling*, 14.

35. Novick, *Holocaust*, 16.

36. John Mowitt, "Trauma Envy," *Cultural Critique* 46 (2000), 294.

37. Novick, *Holocaust*, 170–203, 207–238; Cole, *Selling*, xii–xiii.

38. Novick, *Holocaust*, 15.

39. Christopher Lasch, *The Minimal Self: Psychic Survival in Troubled Times* (New York: W. W. Norton, 1984), 125. The chapter "The Dancer and the Angel of Death: How Did Anyone Survive the Holocaust?" in journalist and best-selling novelist Ben Sherwood's *The Survivors Club: The Secrets and Science that Could Save Your Life* (New York: Grand Central Publishing, 2009) indicates that the trend that began in the 1970s continues through the first decade of the new millennium.

40. This notion is also central to a rather different mode of Holocaust reception reflected in the Eastern European discourse of antifascism, see for instance, Anne Rothe, "The Third Reich and the Holocaust in East German Official Memory," in *Comparative Central European Holocaust Studies*, ed. Louise Vasváry and Steven Tötösy de Zepetnek (West Lafayette: Purdue UP, 2009), 79–94.

41. Novick, *Holocaust*, 13.

42. Cole, *Selling*, 176.

43. Phillip Lopate, "Resistance to the Holocaust," *Tikkun* 4, 3 (1989), 56.

44. Novick, *Holocaust*, 13.

45. Philip Gourevitsch, "Behold Now Behemoth," *Harper's Magazine* (July 1993), 56.

46. Karyn Ball, "Introduction: Trauma and its Institutional Destinies," *Cultural Critique* 46 (2000), 41.

47. Alyson Cole, *The Cult of True Victimhood: From the War on Terror to the War on Welfare* (Berkeley: University of California Press, 2007), 106–107.

48. Cited in James Young, *Writing and Rewriting the Holocaust: Narrative and the Consequences of Interpretation* (Bloomington: Indiana University Press, 1988), 128.

49. Cited in Weissman, *Fantasies*, 119.

50. Young, *Writing*, 118.

51. Ibid., 119.

52. Ibid., 127–131.

53. Lopate, "Resistance," 56, his italics.

54. Emil Fackenheim, George Steiner, Richard Popkin, Elie Wiesel, "Jewish Values in the Post-Holocaust Future: A Symposium," *Judaism 3* (1967), 266–299.

55. Ibid.; Jean-Michel Chaumont, *Die Konkurrenz der Opfer: Genozid, Identität, und Anerkennung* (Lüneburg: zu Klampfen), 98.

56. Well known among Holocaust scholars is the story that Raul Hilberg had great difficulty finding a publisher for his dissertation, which he subsequently expanded to the about two thousand pages of his seminal three-volume *The Destruction of European Jews*. It was only published in 1961 and only by a small, independent press, Quadrangle Books. Prior to Hilberg's study, there had only been two monographs on the history of the Holocaust, Leon Poliakov's *Harvest of Hate* (1954) and Gerald Reitlinger's *The Final Solution* (1953). See John Cox, "Raul Hilberg: In Memoriam," *Journal of Jewish Identities* 1, 2 (July 2008), 1–6.

57. Novick, *Holocaust*, 197.

58. Ibid., 9.

59. Ibid., 195.

60. Lopate, "Resistance," 61.

61. Ibid., 56.

62. Chaumont, *Opfer*, 105.

63. Finkelstein, *Industry*, 47, his italics.

64. Ian Buruma, "The Joys and Perils of Victimhood," *New York Review of Books* (8 Apr. 1999), www.nybooks.com/articles/525 (accessed 3/3/2008), 3.

65. Novick, *Holocaust*, 191–194. Unlike in American culture, where the uniqueness claim led to the macabre competition among minorities about who suffered most, in Western Europe it led to competition between former political prisoners of the resistance and Jewish victims, see Chaumont, *Opfer*.

66. Novick, *Holocaust*, 195.

67. Cited in Wieviorka, *Witness*, 103. Wiesel's mistaken claim that the term "ghetto" was applied from the Holocaust ghettos to the American inner city reflects the centrality of the Holocaust to his understanding not only of world history but also and especially of Jewish history. According to Julius Lester, the word "ghetto" comes from the Italian term "getto," which designates an iron foundry, because it "was first used to describe the section of Venice where Jews were segregated from gentiles in the sixteenth century," and which was located next to the iron foundry. See Julius Lester, "The Lives People Live," in *Blacks and Jews: Alliances and Arguments*, ed. Paul Berman (New York: Delacorte Press, 1994), 165.

68. Novick, *Holocaust*, 191–192.

69. Marita Sturken, *Tourists of History: Memory, Kitsch, and Consumerism from Oklahoma City to Ground Zero* (Durham: Duke UP, 2007), 28.

70. Geoffrey Hartman, "Tele-Suffering and Testimony in the Dot Com Era," in Zelizer, *Visual*, 120.

71. Novick, *Holocaust*, 195.

72. Tova Reich, My *Holocaust* (New York: Harper Collins, 2007), 43.

73. Novick, *Holocaust*, 195.

74. Reich, *Holocaust*, 247.

75. Novick, *Holocaust*, 6–7.

76. Buruma, "Victimhood," para. 14.

77. Cole, *Selling*, 12.

78. Novick, *Holocaust*, 202.

79. Buruma, "Victimhood," para. 19.

80. Jacob Neusner, "A 'Holocaust' Primer," in *In the Aftermath of the Holocaust*, ed. Jacob Neusner (New York: Garland, 1993), vol. 2, 978.

81. In Tova Reich's satire *My Holocaust*, the minor but important figure Arlene severely criticizes both practices. She argues that "'this back-to-the-shtetl heritage nostalgia trip is obscene; these grand tours of the death camps are grotesque'" (24). And when her daughter is twinned with a Holocaust child victim at her bat mitzvah, she considers this practice as "gruesome, morbid, a form of child abuse" (20). For a scholarly critique of school trips by Israeli adolescents to death camp memorials see Tom Segev, *The Seventh Million: The Israelis and the Holocaust* (New York: Hill and Wang, 1994), 487–507.

82. Novick, *Holocaust*, 190–191.

83. Ibid., 11, 202.

84. Weissman, *Fantasies*, 5, 20, 26–27.

85. Alain Finkielkraut, *The Imaginary Jew* (Lincoln: University of Nebraska Press, 2006), 36.

86. Daniel Schwarz, *Imagining the Holocaust* (New York: St. Martin's, 1999), 5–6.

87. Ibid.

88. Buruma, "Victimhood," para. 4.

89. Ibid.

90. Cited in Michael Bernstein, *Forgone Conclusions: Against Apocalyptic History* (Berkeley: University of California Press, 1994), 54.

91. Ibid.

92. Rosen cited in ibid.

93. Vanessa Ochs, "Not in My Backyard," *Tikkun* 8 (July–August 1993), 55.

94. Aviva Cantor, *Jewish Women/Jewish Men* (San Francisco: Harper, 1995), 390.

95. Leslie Brody, "Introduction," *Daughters of Kings: Growing Up as a Jewish Woman in America*, ed. Leslie Brody (Boston: Faber and Faber 1997), 17.

96. Finkielkraut, *Imaginary*, 32.

97. Zygmunt Bauman, "The Holocaust's Life as a Ghost," *Tikkun* 13 (July–August 1998), 36.

98. Bernstein, *Apocalyptic*, 85.

99. Finkielkraut, *Imaginary*, 34.

100. Bauman, "Ghost," 36–7.

101. Bernstein, *Apocalyptic*, 55.

102. Ibid., 86

103. Ibid., 87–88.

104. Ibid., 54.

105. George Steiner "In Extremis," in *The Cambridge Mind* (Cambridge: Cambridge University Press, 1976), 305.

106. Finkielkraut, *Imaginary*, 32.

107. Steiner, "In Extremis," 305.

108. Finkielkraut, *Imaginary*, 26.

109. Ibid., 31.

110. Bauman, "Ghost," 34.

## CHAPTER 2      VICTIM TALK

1. Peter Schneider, *Couplings* (Chicago: University of Chicago Press, 1998), 102.

2. Ian Hacking, "Making Up People," in *Reconstructing Individualism: Autonomy, Individuality, and the Self in Western Thought*, ed. T. C. Heller et al. (Stanford: Stanford University Press, 1986), 236.

3. Ibid., 228–230.

4. Ian Hacking, "The Making and Molding of Child Abuse," *Critical Inquiry*, 17, 2 (1991), 254.

5. Hacking, "Making Up People," 223.

6. Ian Hacking, *Rewriting the Soul: Multiple Personality and the Sciences of Memory* (Princeton: Princeton University Press, 1995), 21.

7. Hacking, "Making and Molding," 254.

8. Martha Minow, "Surviving Victim Talk," *UCLA Law Review*, 40 (1993), 1411.

9. Susan Sontag, *Regarding the Pain of Others* (New York: Picador, 2003), 99.

10. Joseph Amato, *Victims and Values: A History and Theory of Suffering* (New York: Praeger), 186.

11. Ibid., xix.

12. Ibid., xxii.

13. Ibid., 186.

14. For a genealogy of PTSD see Allan Young, *The Harmony of Illusions: Inventing Post-Traumatic Stress Disorder* (Princeton: Princeton University Press, 1995); Roger Luckhurst, "Traumaculture" [sic], *New Formations* 50 (2003), 29–33; and Roger Luckhurst, *The Trauma Question* (New York: Routledge, 2008), 59–76.

15. Peter Novick, *The Holocaust in American Life* (Boston: Mariner, 2000), 274.

16. Amato, *Victims*, 48.

17. Bernhard Giesen, *Triumph and Trauma* (Boulder: Paradigm, 2004), 46.

18. Giesen, *Triumph*, 46

19. Sontag, *Pain*, 40.

20. Anthony Giddens, *Modernity and Self-Identity: Self and Society in the Late Modern Age* (Cambridge: Polity, 1991), 164–169.

21. Amato, *Victims*, 175.

22. Ibid., x.

23. Minow, "Surviving," 1415–1416.

24. Ibid., 1427.

25. Michael Bernstein, *Forgone Conclusions: Against Apocalyptic History* (Berkeley: University of California Press, 1994), 93.

26. Minow, "Surviving," 1427, 1433.

27. Ibid., 1416.

28. Elaine Showalter, *Hystories: Hysterical Epidemics in Modern Culture* (New York: Columbia University Press, 1997), 4.

29. Novick, *Holocaust*, 153.

30. Zygmunt Bauman, "The Holocaust's Life as a Ghost," *Tikkun* 13 (July–August 1998), 35.

31. Today, such "recovered" memories are largely agreed to constitute therapeutically co-generated fantasies. See Richard Ofshe and Ethan Waters, *Making Monsters: False Memories, Psychotherapy, and Sexual Hysteria* (New York: Charles Scribner's Sons, 1994).

32. Amato, *Victims*, 157.

33. Luckhurst, *Question*, 34–49.

34. Amato, *Victims*, 157.

35. A. B. Yehoshua, *Between Right and Right* (Garden City: Doubleday, 1981). I altered the translation by replacing "amoral" with "immoral."

36. Bauman, "Ghost," 36.

37. Ibid.

38. Amato, *Victims*, 196.

39. Minow, "Surviving," 1430–1431.

40. Ibid.

41. Ibid.

42. Alyson Cole, *The Cult of True Victimhood: From the War on Terror to the War on Welfare* (Berkeley: University of California Press, 2007), 175.

43. Amato, *Victims*, 157.

44. Cole, *Cult*, 38.

45. Minow, "Surviving," 1430–1431.

46. Bauman, "Ghost," 35.

47. Cited in Novick, *Holocaust*, 8.

48. Amato, *Victims*, xxiii.

49. Charles Sykes, *A Nation of Victims: The Decay of American Character* (New York: St. Martin's, 1992); Robert Hughes, *Culture of Complaint: The Fraying of America* (New York: Oxford University Press, 1993).

50. For extensive references see Cole, *Cult*, 184–185.

51. Alan Dershowitz, *The Abuse Excuse: And Other Cop-Outs, Sob Stories, and Evasions of Responsibility* (Boston: Little, Brown, 1994).

52. Cole, *Cult*, 22, 27.

53. Ibid., 5.

54. Ibid.

55. Ibid., 6.

56. Ibid., 5.

57. Ibid., 22.

58. Ibid., 133.

### CHAPTER 3    AMERICAN SURVIVORS

1. These are the last lines of Polish-Jewish journalist and writer Hanna Krall's story "The One from Hamburg," *Chicago Review* 3/4 (2000), 131–138. Thanks to Alina Klin for bringing this story to my attention.

2. Alyson Cole, *The Cult of True Victimhood: From the War on Terror to the War on Welfare* (Berkeley: University of California Press, 2007), 17.

3. Emil Fackenheim, George Steiner, Richard Popkin, and Elie Wiesel, "Jewish Values in the Post-Holocaust Future: A Symposium," *Judaism* 3 (1967), 288; Jean-Michel Chaumont, *Die Konkurrenz der Opfer: Genozid, Identität, und Anerkennung* (Lüneburg: zu Klampfen), 108.

4. Donald Downs, *More than Victims: Battered Women, the Syndrome Society, and the Law* (Chicago: University of Chicago Press, 1996), 49.

5. Cited in Christopher Lasch, *The Minimal Self: Psychic Survival in Troubled Times* (New York: W. W. Norton, 1984), 119.

6. Annette Wieviorka, *The Era of the Witness* (Ithaca: Cornell University Press, 2006), 1–24.

7. Ibid., 86.

8. Ibid., 71.

9. Hannah Arendt, *Eichmann in Jerusalem: A Report on the Banality of Evil* (New York: Penguin 1963), 224.

10. Lucy Dawidowicz, *A Holocaust Reader* (New York: Behrman House, 1976), 11–12.

11. Peter Novick, *The Holocaust in American Life* (Boston: Mariner, 2000), 274.

12. Elie Wiesel, "The Holocaust as Literary Inspiration," in *Dimensions of the Holocaust*, ed. Elie Wiesel et al. (Chicago: Northwestern University Press, 1990), 7.

13. Cited in Novick, *Holocaust*, 201.

14. Cited in Gary Weissman, *Fantasies of Witnessing: Postwar Efforts to Experience the Holocaust* (Ithaca: Cornell University Press, 2004), 48.

15. Cited in Wieviorka, *Witness*, 116.

16. Wieviorka, *Witness*, 113.

17. Ibid., 139.

18. Ibid., 134.

19. Ibid., 135.

20. Cited in ibid., 135.

21. Alexander von Plato, "Geschichte ohne Zeitzeugen? Einige Fragen zur 'Erfahrung' im Übergang von Zeitgeschichte zur Geschichte," in *Zeugenschaft des Holocaust: Zwischen Trauma, Tradierung, und Vermittlung*, ed. Michael Elm and Gottfried Kößler (Frankfurt: Campus, 2007), 151–152.

22. Wulf Kansteiner, *In Pursuit of German Memory: History, Television, and Politics after Auschwitz* (Athens: Ohio University Press, 2006), 324.

23. James Young, "Parables of a Survivor," *New Leader* (18 Dec. 1995), 17.

24. Fackenheim et al., "Values," 288; cited in Chaumont, *Opfer*, 108 and Wieviorka, *Witness*, 102–103.

25. Wieviorka, *Witness*, 110–111.

26. Ibid., 98, 115.

27. Ibid., 110–111.

28. Ibid., 115.

29. Chaumant, *Opfer*, 104–105.

30. Ibid., 228.

31. Cited in Lasch, *Minimal*, 119. Although Des Pres overtly rejects the notion of employing camp life as an analogy to the "predicament of modern man in 'mass society,'" Lasch (119) argues that the trend of his analysis reinforces such comparisons.

32. Tova Reich, *My Holocaust* (New York: Harper Collins, 2007), 17.

33. Lasch, *Minimal*, 112.

34. Ibid., 16–17.

35. Ibid., 61–62.

36. Downs, *Victims*, 49.

37. See Katie Roiphe's scathing review of over a dozen incest novels "Making the Incest Scene," *Harper's Magazine* 291 (Nov. 1995), 65, 68–71 and part three of this book, on misery memoirs.

38. Ian Buruma, "The Joys and Perils of Victimhood," *New York Review of Books* (8 Apr. 1999), www.nybooks.com/articles/525 (accessed 3/3/2008), 7.

39. The summary is based on an analysis of the first seven episodes.

40. Zygmunt Bauman, "The Holocaust's Life as a Ghost," *Tikkun* 13 (July–August 1998), 34.

41. "The Survivor," dir. by Larry Charles, *Curb Your Enthusiasm: The Complete Fourth Season* (HBO Video, 2005).

## CHAPTER 4      TRAUMA KITSCH

1. Milan Kundera, *The Unbearable Lightness of Being* (New York: Harper Perennial, 1991), 251.

2. Clement Greenberg, for example, dichotomizes kitsch and high art in his classic 1939 essay "Avant-Garde and Kitsch," in *Clement Greenberg: The Collected Essays and Criticism* (Chicago: University of Chicago Press, 1986), vol. 1, 5–22.

3. Sam Binkley, "Kitsch as a Repetitive System: A Problem for the Theory of Taste Hierarchy," *Journal of Material Culture* 5 (2000), 133; Marita Sturken, *Tourists of History: Memory, Kitsch, and Consumerism, from Oklahoma City to Ground Zero* (Durham: Duke University Press, 2007), 19.

4. Binkley, "Kitsch," 133.

5. Ibid., 134.

6. Ibid., 140–141.

7. Avishai Margalit, "The Kitsch of Israel," in *Views in Review: Politics and Culture in the State of the Jews* (New York: Farrar Straus Giroux, 1998), 215–216.

8. Ibid., 215.

9. Luc Boltanski, *Distant Suffering: Morality, Media, and Politics* (Cambridge: Cambridge University Press, 1999), 92.

10. Binkley, "Kitsch," 145.

11. Ibid.

12. Margalit, "Israel," 208; Sturken, *Tourists*, 22.

13. Boltanski, *Suffering*, 21.

14. Margalit, "Israel," 208.

15. Anthony Giddens, *The Consequences of Modernity* (Stanford: Stanford University Press, 1990), 17, 21–29.

16. Binkley, "Kitsch," 135.

17. Ibid., 135–136.

18. Cited in Sturken, *Tourists*, 284.

19. Sturken, *Tourists*, 284.

20. Barbara Ehrenreich, "Welcome to Cancerland," *Harper's Magazine* 303, 1818 (2001), 53.

21. Sturken, *Tourists*, 285.

22. Peter Brooks, *The Melodramatic Imagination: Balzac, Henry James, Melodrama, and the Mode of Excess* (New Haven: Yale University Press, 1976), 14.

23. Ibid., 19–20.

24. Ibid.

25. Ibid.

26. Ibid.

27. Ibid., 14–15.

28. Ibid., 16–17.

29. Ibid., 17.

30. Nancy K. Miller and Jason Tougaw, "Introduction: Extremities," in *Extremities: Trauma, Testimony, and Community* (Urbana: University of Illinois Press, 2002), 4; James Young, *Writing and Rewriting the Holocaust: Narrative and the Consequences of Interpretation* (Bloomington: Indiana University Press, 1988), 118.

## PART TWO    TELEVISION

1. Michael Ignatieff, "Is Nothing Sacred? The Ethics of Television," in Michael Ignatieff, *The Warrior's Honor: Ethnic War and the Modern Conscience* (New York: Henry Holt, 1997), 11.

2. Philip Auslander, *Liveness: Performance in Mediatized Culture* (New York: Routledge, 2008), 2.

3. Jane Shattuc, "The Oprahfication of America: Talk Shows and the Public Sphere," in *Television, History, and American Culture: Feminist Essays*, ed. Mary Beth Haralovich and Lauren Rabinovitz (Durham: Duke University Press, 1999), 168.

4. Vicki Abt and Mel Seesholtz, "The Shameless World of Phil, Sally and Oprah: Television Talk Shows and the Deconstructing of Society." *Journal of Popular Culture* 28, 1 (Summer 1994), 173.

5. Andrew Postman, "Introduction to the Twentieth Anniversary Edition." in *Amusing Ourselves to Death: Public Discourse in the Age of Show Business*, by Neil Postman (New York: Penguin, 2006), xiv. According to Kenneth Gergen, "the average American television set runs for seven hours per day." See Kenneth Gergen, *The Saturated Self: Dilemmas of Identity in Contemporary Life* (New York: Basic Books, 1991), 54. The significant discrepancy between both citations might be resolved if we assume that Gergen included but Postman excluded the hours when the TV set was running in the background but audiences were not particularly watching the program.

6. Abt and Seesholtz, "Shameless," 172.

7. Gergen, *Self*, 57.

8. Elaine Showalter, *Hystories: Hysterical Epidemics in Modern Culture* (New York: Columbia University Press, 1997), 207.

9. Christine Quail, Kathalene Razzano, and Loubna Skalli, *Vulture Culture: The Politics and Pedagogy of Daytime Television Talk Shows* (New York: Peter Lang, 2005), 23.

10. Ibid.

11. Ibid.

12. Jane Shattuc, *The Talking Cure: TV Talk Shows and Women* (New York: Routledge, 1997), 51.

13. Elisabeth Birmingham, "Fearing the Freak: How Talk TV Articulates Women and Class," *Journal of Popular Film and Television* 28, 3 (2000), 134.

14. Linda Alcoff and Laura Gray-Rosendale, "Survivor Discourse: Transgression or Recuperation?" in *Getting a Life: Everyday Uses of Autobiography*, ed. Sidonie Smith and Julia Watson (Minneapolis: University of Minnesota Press, 2001), 211, 213.

15. Janice Peck, "The Mediated Talking Cure: Therapeutic Framing of Autobiography in TV Talk Shows," in *Life*, ed. Smith and Watson, 151.

16. Ibid., 148.

17. Ibid., 152.

### CHAPTER 5    TALKING CURES

1. Wendy Kaminer, *I'm Dysfunctional, You're Dysfunctional: The Recovery Movement and Other Self-Help Fashions* (Reading, MA: Addison-Wesley Publishing, 1992), 30, 32.

2. Eva Moskowitz, *In Therapy We Trust: America's Obsession with Self-Fulfillment* (Baltimore: Johns Hopkins University Press, 2001), 261.

3. Patricia Priest, *Public Intimacies: Talk Show Participants and Tell-All TV* (Cresskill, NJ: Hampton Press, 1995), 11.

4. Moskowitz, *Therapy*, 260.

5. Julie Manga, *Talking Trash: The Cultural Politics of Daytime TV Talk Shows* (New York: New York University Press, 2003), 27.

6. Moskowitz, *Therapy*, 262.

7. Deborah Lupton, "Talking About Sex: Sexology, Sexual Difference, and Confessional Talk Shows," *Genders* 20 (1994), 45.

8. Ken Plummer, *Telling Sexual Stories: Power, Change, and Social Worlds* (New York: Routledge, 1995), 54.

9. Jane Shattuc, *The Talking Cure: TV Talk Shows and Women* (New York: Routledge, 1997), 85.

10. Moskowitz, *Therapy*, 269.

11. Shattuc, *Cure*, 85.

12. Ibid., 39.

13. Ibid., 96.

14. Christine Quail, Kathalene Razzano, and Loubna Skalli, *Vulture Culture: The Politics and Pedagogy of Daytime Television Talk Shows* (New York: Peter Lang, 2005), 68.

15. Moskowitz, *Therapy*, 266.

16. Shattuc, *Cure*, 85.

17. Ibid.

18. Moskowitz, *Therapy*, 266.

19. Ibid., 265.

20. Ibid., 266.

21. Ibid., 263–265.

22. Ibid., 262.

23. Ibid., 262.

24. Manga, *Trash*, 31.

25. Marilyn Matelski, "Jerry Springer and the Wages of Fin-Syn: The Rides of Deregulation and the Decline of TV Talk," *Journal of Popular Culture* 33, 4 (2000), 67.

26. Shattuc, *Cure*, 25.

27. Title cited in Moskowitz, *Therapy*, 268.

28. Shattuc, *Cure*, 15.

29. Ibid., 120.

30. Moskowitz, *Therapy*, 279.

31. Janice Peck, "The Mediated Talking Cure: Therapeutic Framing of Autobiography in TV Talk Shows," in *Getting a Life: Everyday Uses of Autobiography*, ed. Sidonie Smith and Julia Watson (Minneapolis: University of Minnesota Press, 2001), 142.

32. James Nolan, *The Therapeutic State: Justifying Government at Century's End* (New York: New York University Press, 1998).

33. Norman Fairclough, *Language and Power* (London: Longman, 1989), 226–228.

34. Moskowitz, *Therapy*, 277.

35. Michel Foucault, *Madness and Civilization: A History of Insanity in the Age of Reason* (New York: Vintage Books, 1973).

36. Peck, "Talking," 142.

37. Shattuc, *Cure*, 120.

38. Mimi White, *Tele-Advising: Therapeutic Discourse in American Television* (Chapel Hill: University of North Carolina Press, 1992), 23.

39. Moskowitz, *Therapy*, 259; Priest, *Intimacies*, 4.

40. Moskowitz, *Therapy*, 247–248.

41. Shattuc, *Cure*, 111–112.

42. Peck, "Talking," 143.

43. Priest, *Intimacies*, 105–122.

44. Cynthia Davis, "B(e)aring It All: Talking About Sex and Self on Television Talk Shows," in *Confessional Politics: Women's Sexual Self-Representation in Life Writing and Popular Media*, ed. Irene Gammel (Carbondale: Southern Illinois University Press, 1999), 148.

45. Peck, "Talking," 143.

46. Ibid., 144.

47. Shattuc, *Cure*, 119.

48. Peck, "Talking," 143.

49. Elisabeth Birmingham, "Fearing the Freak: How Talk TV Articulates Women and Class," *Journal of Popular Film and Television* 28, 3 (2000), 135.

50. Ibid., 138; Kathleen Lowney, *Baring Our Souls: TV Talk Shows and the Religion of Recovery* (New York: deGruyter, 1999), 55.

51. Philip Gassell, ed., *The Giddens Reader* (Stanford: Stanford University Press, 1993), 29.

52. Cited in Birmingham, "Fearing," 135.

53. The standard English translation of Kant's essay is "An Answer to the Question: What is the Enlightenment" in Immanuel Kant, *Practical Philosophy*, transl. and ed. by

Mary Gregor (Cambridge: Cambridge University Press, 1999). I also relied on http://www.english.upenn.edu/~mgamer/Etexts/kant.html (accessed 03/02/2010).

54. Gassell, *Giddens*, 29.

55. Jethro Lieberman, *The Tyranny of the Experts: How Professionals Are Closing the Open Society* (New York: Walker, 1970).

56. Ibid., 9.

57. Quail et al., *Vulture*, 49–50.

58. Peck, "Talking," 140.

59. Nolan, *Therapeutic*, 8.

60. Ibid.

61. Moskowitz, *Therapy*, 255.

62. Shattuc, *Cure*, 99

63. Cited in Elaine Showalter, *Hystories: Hysterical Epidemics in Modern Culture* (New York: Columbia University Press, 1997), 156.

64. Quail et al., *Vulture*, 48.

65. Ibid., 49.

66. Michel Foucault, *The History of Sexuality*, vol. 1 (New York: Pantheon, 1978), 58–68.

67. Ibid., 61–62.

68. Ibid., 62.

69. Ibid., 60.

70. White, *Tele-Advising*, 313.

71. Foucault, *Sexuality*, 61.

72. Ibid., 68.

73. Kathleen Lowney (*Baring*, 83) similarly argued that "the person-categories of victim and victimizer become blurred. Both suffering and the infliction of suffering become condensed into just one thing—needing to change through therapy."

74. Foucault, *Sexuality*, 59.

75. Ibid., 62.

76. Ibid., 59.

77. Shattuc, *Cure*, 130.

78. Foucault, *Sexuality*, 59.

79. Ibid., 59.

80. Ibid., 66.

### CHAPTER 6    TRAUMA CAMP

1. Jerry Springer on *Larry King Live* 05/08/1998, cited in Julie Manga, *Talking Trash: The Cultural Politics of Daytime TV Talk Shows* (New York: New York University Press, 2003), 159–160.

2. Jane Shattuc, *The Talking Cure: TV Talk Shows and Women* (New York: Routledge, 1997), 162.

3. Patricia Priest, *Public Intimacies: Talk Show Participants and Tell-All TV* (Cresskill, NJ: Hampton Press, 1995), 185.

4. Elisabeth Birmingham, "Fearing the Freak: How Talk TV Articulates Women and Class," *Journal of Popular Film and Television* 28, 3 (2000), 136–137.

5. Cited in Bernard Timberg, *Television Talk: A History of the TV Talk Show* (Austin: University of Texas Press, 2002), 177.

6. Eva Moskowitz, *In Therapy We Trust: America's Obsession with Self-Fulfillment* (Baltimore: Johns Hopkins University Press, 2001), 269.

7. Timberg, *Talk*, 175. Although the taped episode never aired, the murder was reported widely in the press and, according to Birmingham ("Fearing," 133), the show experienced its highest ratings in its wake.

8. Cited in Timberg, *Talk*, 181.

9. Shattuc, *Cure*, 155.

10. Ibid., 163.

11. Ibid., 180.

12. Camp parody was also explicitly invoked in talk show spoofs. According to Shattuc (*Cure*, 164), *Talk Soup* "premiered on the 'E' network in 1993 as a tongue-in-cheek, late-night digest of the most outrageous moments from the day's shows. The initial host, Greg Kinnear, established the show's humor; he played for wry laughs with his pseudoserious commentary laced with icy irony." And "in December 1995, *Night Stand* premiered as a spoof of talk shows, with a buffoon host and programs such as 'Teenage Hardbody Prostitutes' and 'Sexaholics: The Problem, the Cure and Where to Meet Them.'" The fact that Jerry Springer appeared on the latter show is a further indication that camp parody is the dominant reception invited by trash talk programs.

13. Moskowitz, *Therapy*, 267.

14. Shattuc, *Cure*, 153.

15. According to Shattuc (*Cure*, 153), one rating point represents 959,000 households.

16. Timberg, *Talk*, 181.

17. Marilyn Matelski, "Jerry Springer and the Wages of Fin-Syn: The Rides of Deregulation and the Decline of TV Talk," *Journal of Popular Culture* 33, 4 (2000), 63.

18. Jo Tavener, "Media, Morality, and Madness: The Case Against Sleaze TV," *Critical Studies in Media Communication* 17, 1 (2000), 63.

19. Moskowitz, *Therapy*, 266.

20. Jason Mittell, "Television Talk Shows and Cultural Hierarchies" *Journal of Popular Film and Television* 31, 1 (2003), 43.

21. Timberg, *Talk*, 143.

22. Matelski, "Springer," 67.

23. Shattuc, *Cure*, 147.

24. Timberg, *Talk*, 177.

25. Shattuc, *Cure*, 148.

26. Moskowitz, *Therapy*, 269.

27. Shattuc, *Cure*, 148.

28. Cited in ibid., 151–152.

29. Timberg, *Talk*, 180.

30. Shattuc, *Cure*, 159.

31. Tavener, "Sleaze," 64.

32. Shattuc, *Cure*, 138.

33. Tavener, "Sleaze," 64.

34. Shattuc, *Cure*, 138, 142; Timberg, *Talk*, 176.

35. Moskowitz, *Therapy*, 267.

36. Between 1989–90 and 1996 there were fifteen shows in national syndication (Moskowitz, *Therapy*, 267; Shattuc, *Cure*, 1997, 2, 149). The number rose to nineteen in the 1996–97 season (Manga, *Trash*, 33). Shattuc (*Cure*, 153) provides the daily TV schedule in the Boston area for November 1995, according to which viewers could watch talk shows back-to-back Monday through Friday from 9 A.M. to 5 P.M. with three shows running parallel at 9 A.M., 10 A.M., and 11 A.M. and two simultaneous shows at 3 P.M. Fox also showed nightly re-runs of its six shows back-to-back from 11 P.M. through 4 A.M. with competition in the 2 A.M. slot from another channel.

37. Moskowitz, *Therapy*, 269.

38. This analysis borrows eclectically from various discussions of camp in ways that can neither do justice to their complexity nor necessarily reflect what the respective authors would consider their core ideas. For instance, it expands on Susan Sontag's brief mention of camp as a mode of reception, even though she predominantly locates camp in object characteristics. And it largely omits the complex discussion of whether and to what extent camp is necessarily and exclusively a queer concept, as Moe Meyer (*Camp*, 5) asserts when he defines it as "the total body of performative practices and strategies used to enact queer identity" and argues that the function of camp "is the production of queer social visibility." Furthermore, while Meyer argues that camp is imbued with the politically progressive potential to challenge the hetero-normative status quo and Sontag considers it as a purely aesthetic and hence apolitical concept, I suggest that in the context of daytime talk shows the camp-parodic mode of reception is not only politically acquiescing but socially oppressive and exploitative. See Moe Meyer (ed.), *The Politics and Poetics of Camp* (New York: Routledge, 1999); Susan Sontag, "Notes on Camp," in *Against Interpretations and Other Essays* (New York: Picador, 2001), 275–292.

39. Only artifacts can be (interpreted as) camp. Natural objects (not transformed into cultural artifacts by removing them from their natural context) can never be camp, because they lack the intentionality of human creation, and the camp-defining insider meaning cannot be ascribed to them.

40. Sontag, "Notes," 285.

41. Meyer, *Camp*, 13.

42. Andrew Ross, "Uses of Camp," *Yale Journal of Criticism* 2, 2 (1988), 5.

43. Ibid., 10.

44. Meyer, *Camp*, 15.

45. Sontag, "Notes," 277, Sontag's italics.

46. Ibid., 292.

47. Jane Feuer, "Reading *Dynasty*: Television and Reception Theory," *South Atlantic Quarterly* 88, 2 (1989), 447–448. According to Feuer, in neither gay nor mainstream culture did a camp reception preclude spectators from alternating between viewing *Dynasty* as camp parody and in a mode of suspended disbelief. Feuer furthermore argues analogously to Meyer that "camp is not a property of a text" or cultural artifact at large, but rather "exists in the nature of the activations." Like Sontag, though, she cautions that "not just any text can be camped, and *Dynasty* certainly facilitates the process" (Feuer, "Reading," 448).

48. Timberg, *Talk*, 181.

49. Sontag, "Notes," 290.

50. Ibid., 276.

51. Christine Quail, Kathalene Razzano, and Loubna Skalli, *Vulture Culture: The Politics and Pedagogy of Daytime Television Talk Shows* (New York: Peter Lang, 2005), 79.

52. Cited in Priest, *Intimacies*, 197.

53. Priest, *Intimacies*, 102–103.

54. Their comments were thus cited anonymously in Priest (*Intimacies*, 102–103). In addition to the fact that all talk show producers refused to assist Priest in contacting former guests—she essentially had to employ strategies of investigative journalism to find them—the fact that guests have to sign legal documents prohibiting critical comments may explain why Priest's monograph on *Donahue* participants has remained the only book-length empirical study on the experience of talk show guests.

55. Sontag, "Notes," 290.

56. Meyer, *Camp*, 11.

57. Chuck Kleinhans, "Taking Out the Trash: Camp and the Politics of Parody," in *Camp*, ed. Moe Meyer, 195.

58. Sontag, "Notes," 279.

59. Stuart Hall, *The Hard Road to Renewal* (London: Verso 1988), cited in Shattuc, *Cure*, 21.

60. For instance, Gloria-Jean Masciarotte, "C'mon Girl: Oprah Winfrey and the Discourse of Feminine Talk," *Genders* 11 (1991), 81–110.

61. Cited in Quail et al., *Vulture*, 76.

62. Umberto Eco, "The Frame of Comic 'Freedom,'" in *Carnival*, ed. Thomas Seboek (Berlin: Mouton, 1985), 6; see also Quail et al., *Vulture*, 77.

63. Andrea Stulman Dennett, "The Dime Museum Freak Show Reconfigured as Talk Show," in *Freakery: Cultural Spectacles of the Extraordinary Body*, ed. Rosemarie Garland Thomson (New York: New York University Press, 1996), 318.

64. Kathleen Lowney, *Baring Our Souls: TV Talk Shows and the Religion of Recovery* (New York: deGruyter, 1999), 11–12.

65. Robert Bogdan, *Freak Show: Presenting Human Oddities for Amusement and Profit* (Chicago: University of Chicago Press), 1988.

66. Dennett, "Dime," 318.

67. Birmingham, "Fearing," 136, summarizing Dennett, "Dime," 315.

68. Dennett, "Dime," 316.

69. Birmingham, "Fearing," 137.

70. Ibid., 138.

71. Shattuc, *Cure*, 161.

72. Ibid.

73. Ibid.

74. Birmingham, "Fearing," 136–137.

75. Ibid.

76. Ibid., 137.

77. Shattuc, *Cure*, 141.

78. Quail et al., *Vulture*, 107.

79. Shattuc, *Cure*, 174.

### PART THREE    POPULAR LITERATURE

1. Leigh Gilmore, *The Limits of Autobiography: Trauma and Testimony* (Ithaca: Cornell University Press, 2001), 16.

2. Susan Rubin Suleiman, "Problems of Memory and Factuality in Recent Holocaust Memoirs: Wilkomirski/Wiesel," *Poetics Today* 21, 3 (2000), 551.

3. Michael Bernstein, *Forgone Conclusions: Against Apocalyptic History* (Berkeley: University of California Press, 1994), 47.

4. Ibid.

5. Ibid., 51.

6. Ibid., 47.

7. Ibid.

8. Susan Sontag, *Regarding the Pain of Others* (New York: Picador, 2003), 26–27.

9. Suleiman, "Factuality," 551.

10. Bernstein, *Apocalyptic*, 48.

11. Dorrit Cohn similarly describes fiction as a "nonreferential narrative" in *The Distinction of Fiction* (Baltimore: Johns Hopkins University Press, 1999), 9.

12. Sidonie Smith and Julia Watson, "Definitions," in *Getting a Life: Everyday Uses of Autobiography*, ed. Sidonie Smith and Julia Watson (Minneapolis: University of Minnesota Press, 2001), 1.

13. Philippe Lejeune, *The Autobiographical Pact* (Minneapolis: University of Minnesota Press, 1989).

14. Wiesel cited in Stefan Maechler, *The Wilkomirski Affair: A Study in Biographical Truth* (New York: Schocken Books, 2001), 214.

### CHAPTER 7    SELLING MISERY

1. Julia Glass, "Truer Than Fact," *New York Times* (11 Feb. 2006), 1.

2. Nancy K. Miller, *But Enough About Me: Why We Read Other People's Lives* (New York: Columbia University Press, 2002), 1.

3. Martin Amis, *Experience* (London: Jonathan Cape, 1999), 6.

4. James Bradley, "Stealing Memory's Thunder," *The Australian* (4 June 2008), 13.

5. Leigh Gilmore, *The Limits of Autobiography: Trauma and Testimony* (Ithaca: Cornell University Press, 2001), 16.

6. Steve Almond, "Liar, Liar, Bestseller on Fire," *Boston Globe* (6 Mar. 2008), A11.

7. Ibid.

8. Tim Adams, "Feel the Pain," *Observer* (29 Jan. 2006), 4–5.

9. Benjamin Kunkel, "Misery Loves a Memoir" *New York Times* (16 July 2006), 27.

10. Ibid.

11. Ibid.

12. Bradley, "Thunder," 13.

13. Michael Bernstein, *Forgone Conclusions: Against Apocalyptic History* (Berkeley: University of California Press, 1994), 87–88.

14. Christopher Lasch, *The Culture of Narcissism: American Life in an Age of Diminishing Expectations*, (New York: W.W. Norton, 1991), 17.

15. Richard Sennett, *The Fall of Public Man* (New York: W. W. Norton, 1992), 265.

16. Russell Smith, "Publishers Are Just as Guilty as the Likes of Frey," *The Globe and Mail* (Canada) (19 Jan. 2006), R1.

17. Sam Leith, "Misery Memoirs Like *Ugly* by Constance Briscoe Make Pornography of Personal Pain," *Daily Telegraph* (England) (19 Nov. 2008), 21.

18. Cited in Matthew Shaer and Terese Mez, "Memoirs: Whose Truth—And Does It Matter?" *Christian Science Monitor* (9 May 2008), 16.

19. Adams, "Pain," 4–5.

20. Tim Martin, "The Fake Memoir Has a Fine Literary Tradition Behind It," *Daily Telegraph* (England), (8 Mar. 2008), 30.

21. Ed West, "Is This the End for the Misery Memoir?" *Daily Telegraph* (England) (5 Mar. 2008), 31.

22. Leith, "Pornography," 21.

23. West, "End," 31.

24. India Knight, "Our Taste for All This Misery Lit Makes Ugly Reading," *Sunday Times* (England) (23 Nov. 2008), 20.

25. Martin, "Fake," 30.

26. West, "End," 31; see also Knight, "Ugly," 20.

27. Adams, "Pain," 4–5.

28. Ibid.

29. Ibid.

30. Knight, "Ugly," 20.

31. Adams, "Pain," 4–5; West, "End," 31.

32. [Anonymous], "Literature of Lying," *The Independent* (England) (5 Mar. 2008), 18.

33. Other misery memoirs published in the 1990s and deemed aesthetically mid- to high-brow include Jean-Dominique Bauby, *The Diving Bell and the Butterfly*; Linda Cutting, *Memory Slips*; Silvia Fraser, *My Father's House*; Sandra Gilbert, *Wrongful Death*; Lucy Grealy, *Autobiography of a Face*; Kay Redfield Jamison, *An Unquiet Mind*; Mary Karr, *The Liar's Club*; Susanna Kaysen, *Girl, Interrupted*; Caroline Knapp, *Drinking: A Love Story*; Nancy Raine, *After Silence*; Lauren Slater, *Prozac Diary*; William Styron, *Darkness Visible*; and Tobias Wolff, *In Pharaoh's Army*. See Gilmore, *Autobiography*, 2–3 (note 7).

34. Leith, "Pornography," 21.

35. Knight, "Ugly," 20.

36. Adams, "Pain," 4–5.

37. West, "End," 31.

38. Ibid.

39. Adams, "Pain," 4–5.

40. Fidelma Maher and Tiffany Bakker, "Pop Tart—Have You Noticed . . . Misery is the New Celebrity," *Sunday Telegraph Magazine* (Australia) (9 April 2006), 10.

41. Leith, "Pornography," 21.

42. The commercial success of novel and film adaptation and the fact that it was followed at number four by another Holocaust novel, Markus Zusak's *The Book Thief* about a girl who saved books from being burnt in the Third Reich and shared them with a Jewish man in hiding, indicates that despite the rise of child abuse to the trauma-and-redemption plot *du jour*, Holocaust kitsch still has significant selling power.

43. [Anonymous], "Children's Best Sellers: Paperback Books," *New York Times* (3 May 2009), BR 20.

44. While the texts were not all written in German, they are sold in German translation in the German-language market which they thus both reflect and influence: Francis Bok, *Flucht aus der Sklaverei* (Cologne: Bastei Lübbe, 2004); Inci Y., *Erstickt an euren Lügen* (Munich: Piper, 2007); Nina Merian, ed., *Wir ließen die Heimat zurück* (Augsburg: Weltbild, 2007); Ralph Georg Reuth, ed., *Deutsche auf der Flucht* (Augsburg: Weltbild, 2007); Michael Martensen, *Im Himmel kann ich Schlitten fahren* (Freiburg: Herder, 2006); Michael Schophaus, *Im Himmel warten Bäume auf dich* (Munich: Droemr Knaur, 2007); Marlene John, *Sag' mir, wer ich bin* (Munich: Heyne, 2007); Jane Elliott, *Ausgeliefert* (Augsburg: Weltbild, 2007); and Agnes Sassoon, *Überlebt* (Augsburg: Weltbild, 2007).

45. Kali Tal, *Worlds of Hurt: Reading the Literatures of Trauma* (Cambridge: Cambridge University Press, 1996), 182.

46. James Bone, "Black Gangland Author Was Writing Wrongs," *The Times* (England) (5 Mar. 2008), 43.

47. Leith, "Pornography," 21.

48. Bone, "Wrongs," 43.

49. Ibid.

50. Ibid.

51. Ibid.

52. Ibid.

53. Leith, "Pornography," 21.

54. Ibid.

55. Knight, "Ugly," 20.

56. Leith, "Pornography," 21.

57. Knight, "Ugly," 20.

58. Adams, "Pain," 4–5.

59. [Anonymous], "Emotional Untruths," *Boston Globe* (14 Jan. 2006), A14.

60. Martha Woodmansee, "Toward a Genealogy of the Aesthetic: The German Reading Debate of the 1790s," *Cultural Critique* 11 (1988–1989), 208.

61. Ibid., 207.

62. Susan Sontag, *Regarding the Pain of Others* (New York: Picador, 2003), 41.

63. Ibid., 99; her italics.

64. Bernstein, *Apocalyptic*, 91.

65. Ibid., 54.

66. Ibid., 19.

67. Ibid., 92, his italics.

68. Ibid.

69. Dolf Zillmann, "The Psychology of the Appeal of Portrayals of Violence," in *Why We Watch: The Attractions of Violent Entertainment*, ed. Jeffrey Goldstein (Oxford: Oxford University Press, 1998), 182.

70. Ibid., 183.

71. Ibid., 183, 185.

72. Jeffrey Goldstein, "Why We Watch," in Goldstein, *Watch*, 215.

73. Zillmann, "Violence," 185.

74. Dolf Zillmann, "The Logic of Suspense and Mystery," in *Responding to the Screen: Reception and Reaction Processes* ed. Jennings Bryant and Dolf Zillmann (New York: Routledge, 1991), 291.

75. Ibid., 292.

76. Dolf Zillmann, "Television Viewing and Physiological Arousal," in Bryant and Zillmann, *Screen*, 103.

77. Ibid., 107; see also Jeffrey Goldstein, "Introduction," in Goldstein, *Watch*, 3.

78. Dolf Zillmann, "Empathy," in Bryant and Zillmann, *Screen*, 140–141.

79. Zillmann, "Violence," 182.

80. Cited in Zillmann, "Violence," 190.

81. Zillmann, "Violence," 189.

82. Ibid., 200.

83. Cynthia Hoffer and Joanne Cantor, "Perceiving and Responding to Mass Media Characters," in Bryant and Zillmann, *Screen*, 64–65.

84. Ibid.

85. Joanne Cantor, "Fright Responses in Mass Media Representations," in Bryant and Zillmann, *Screen*, 177.

86. Hoffer and Cantor, "Characters," 84–85.

87. Zillmann, "Violence," 200–201.

88. Goldstein, "Watch," 220.

89. Zillmann, "Violence," 203.

90. Ibid., 204.

91. Ibid., 186–187.

92. Ibid., 199, 210–211.

## CHAPTER 8    FAKE SUFFERING

1. Benjamin Kunkel, "Misery Loves a Memoir" *New York Times* (16 July 2006), 27.

2. Cited in James Bradley, "Stealing Memory's Thunder," *The Australian* (4 June 2008), 13.

3. K. K. Ruthven, *Faking Literature* (Cambridge: Cambridge University Press, 2001), 2–16.

4. Ibid., 127.

5. Ibid., 60.

6. Ibid., 171.

7. Ibid., 31.

8. Ibid., 44.

9. Ibid., 43.

10. H. M. Paull, *Literary Ethics* (London: T. Butterworth, 1928).

11. Ralph Keyes, *The Post-Truth Era: Dishonesty and Deception in Contemporary Life* (New York: St. Martin's, 2004), 154–159.

12. Martin Arnold, "Making Books: In Fact, It's Fiction," *New York Times* (12 Nov. 1998), 1.

13. Keyes, *Post-Truth*, 163.

14. Cited in Graeme Hammond, "The Great Pretenders," *Sunday Telegraph* (Australia) (12 May 2002), 22.

15. Benjamin Redford, *Media Mythmakers: How Journalists, Activists, and Advertisers Mislead Us* (Amherst, NY: Prometheus Books, 2003), 165–166; Hammond, "Pretenders," 22.

16. Henry Louis Gates, Jr., "Authenticity, or the Lesson of Little Tree" *New York Times Book Review* (24 Nov. 1991), 1.

17. Ibid.

18. Ruthven, *Faking*, 78.

19. Tim Martin, "Non-Jewish, Not Raised By Wolves," *Daily Telegraph* (England) (8 March 2008), 30.

20. Ruthven, *Faking*, 24–28.

21. Ibid., 30. For a more detailed discussion of fake Aboriginal texts see ibid., 31–32.

22. Maureen Dowd, "Oprah's Bunk Club," *New York Times* (28 Jan. 2006), A1.

23. Motoko Rich, "A Family Tree of Literary Fakers," *New York Times* (8 Mar. 2008), B7.

24. Dowd, "Bunk," A1.

25. Ruthven, *Faking*, 192.

26. Ibid., 78.

27. Andy McSmith, "Literature of Lying: The Cover is Blown on Yet Another Tall Story," *The Independent* (England) (5 March 2008), 18.

28. Larry Rohter, "Tarnished Laureate," *New York Times* (15 Dec. 1998). The article was reprinted in *The Rigoberta Menchú Controversy*, ed. Arturo Arias (Minneapolis: University of Minnesota Press, 2001), 58–65.

29. Rohter, "Tarnished," 59.

30. Lynn Walford, "Truth, Lies, and Politics in the Debate over Testimonial Writing: The Cases of Rigoberta Menchú and Binjamin Wilkomirski" *Comparatist: Journal of the Southern Comparative Literature Association* 30 (2006), 115.

31. See, for example, Claudia Ferman, "Textual Truth, Historical Truth, and Media Truth," in *Controversy*, ed. Arias, 156–170; W. George Lovell and Christopher H. Lutz, "The Primacy of Larger Truths," in *Controversy*, ed. Arias, 171–197.

32. Motoko Rich, "Lies and Consequences: Tracking the Fallout of (Another) Literary Fraud," *New York Times* (5 March 2008), E2.

33. Shelley Gare, "Africa's War Child," *Weekend Australian* (19 Jan. 2008), 15.

34. Ibid., 15.

35. Mary Louise Pratt, "*I, Rigoberta Menchú* and the 'Culture Wars,'" in *Controversy*, ed. Arias, 29–48.

36. Motoko Rich, "Gang Memoir, Turning Page, Is Pure Fiction," *New York Times* (4 Mar. 2008), 2.

37. Cited in James Bone, "Black Gangland Author Was Writing Wrongs," *The Times* (England) (5 Mar. 2008), 43.

38. Mimi Read, "A Refugee from Gangland," *New York Times* (28 Feb. 2008), F1.

39. William Shaw, "Shocking Tales of Life in the Ghetto . . . with a Twist," *Sunday Telegraph* (England) (16 Mar. 2008), 4; See also Clark Hyot, "Fooled Again," *New York Times* (16 Mar. 2008), WK12.

40. Rich, "Gang," A1.

41. Rich, "Lies," E1; Hyot, "Fooled," WK12.

42. Shaw, "Ghetto," 4.

43. Ibid.

44. Steve Almond, "Memoir as Fiction? Not so Fast," *Boston Globe* (22 Jan. 2006), E7.

45. David Carr, "How Oprahness Trumped Truthiness," *New York Times* (30 Jan. 2006), I.

46. Tim Adams, "Feel the Pain," *The Observer* (England) (29 Jan. 2006), 4–5.

47. Edward Wyatt, "Several Million Little Dollars," *New York Times* (12 Mar. 2006); Mark Peyser cites 3.5 million sold copies in "The Ugly Truth," *Newsweek* (23 Jan. 2006), 62.

48. Sara Ivy, "Biting the Hand, But Then Later Feeding Its Owner," *New York Times* (30 Jan. 2006), C8.

49. Ibid.

50. Edward Wyatt, "Author Is Kicked Out of Oprah Winfrey's Book Club," *New York Times* (27 Jan. 2006), A1.

51. Edward Wyatt, "Treatment Description in Memoir Is Disputed," *New York Times* (24 Jan. 2006), E1.

52. Randy Kennedy, "My True Story, More or Less, and Maybe Not at All," *New York Times* (15 Jan. 2006), I; Edward Wyatt, "Questions for Others in Frey Scandal," *New York Times* (28 Jan. 2006), 7; Almond, "Memoir," E7.

53. Wyatt, "Questions," 7.

54. Wyatt, "Club." A1.

55. Wyatt, "Frey," E1.

56. At the same time, *A Million Little Pieces* was still at number 20 on the hardcover list while the sequel, *My Friend Leonard*, released shortly before the scandal, was number four on the hardcover list.

57. Gary Weissman, *Fantasies of Witnessing: Postwar Efforts to Experience the Holocaust* (Ithaca: Cornell University Press, 2004), 28–88; Naomi Seidman, "Elie Wiesel and the Scandal of Jewish Rage," *Jewish Social Studies* 3, 1 (1996), 1–19.

58. Wyatt, "Frey," E1.

59. Almond, "Memoir," E7.

60. A similar note has been added to *My Fried Leonard*. See Dwight Garner, "Inside the List," *New York Times* (12 Feb. 2006), I.

61. Wyatt, "Club," A1.

62. Rich, "Lies," 2.

63. Maureen Dowd, "Oprah's Bunk Club," *New York Times* (28 Jan. 2006), A1.

64. The sales numbers reported by Shahnahan (700,000 copies) and Iley (more than two million) vary significantly, but might be explained by the ten-month time difference between their articles. See Mark Shanahan, "Too Close To Home," *Boston Globe* (28 Mar. 2006), C1; Chrissey Iley, "You Couldn't Make Up My Toxic Childhood," *Sunday Times* (England) (28 Jan. 2007), 3.

65. Iley, "Toxic," C1.

66. Sebastian Shakespeare, "Plundering the Pathos of their Past," *The Evening Standard* (England) (30 Jan. 2007), 13.

67. Cited in Dowd, "Bunk," 1.

68. Ruthven, *Faking*, 150.

69. Herman Kelly, *Kathy's Real Story: A Culture of False Allegations Exposed* (Dublin: Perfect Press, 2007).

70. Ed West, "Is This the End for the Misery Memoir?" *Daily Telegraph* (England) (5 Mar. 2008), 31.

71. Ibid.

72. Stephen McGinty "No, You Couldn't Make That Up—But Memoir Writers Sometimes Do" *The Scotsman* (28 Sept. 2006), 29.

73. West, "End," 31.

74. Hammond, "Pretenders," 22; www.snopes.com/inboxer/hoaxes/kaycee.asp (accessed 05/25/2009).

75. Redford, *Mythmakers*, 166–167.

76. Hammond, "Pretenders," 22.

77. Ibid.

78. Susan Kurosawa, "Too Smart for Skeptical Viewers," *The Australian* (24 Oct. 2002), B26.

79. Jay Weissberg, "The Calling Game," *Variety* (8 Oct. 2007), 59.

80. Wyatt, "Frey," E1.

81. Daniel Mendelsohn, "Stolen Suffering," *New York Times* (9 Mar. 2008), 3.

82. Susan Rubin Suleiman, "Problems of Memory and Factuality in Recent Holocaust Memoirs: Wilkomirski/Wiesel," *Poetics Today* 21, 3 (2000), 546.

83. Ruth Klüger, "Kitsch ist immer plausibel," *Süddeutsche Zeiung* (30 Sept. 1998), cited in Stefan Maechler, *The Wilkomirski Affair: A Study in Biographical Truth* (New York: Schocken Books, 2001), 280–281.

84. Ibid.

85. Maechler, *Affair*, 281.

86. Tad Friend, "The Ghost Writer," *Independent on Sunday* (England) (24 Mar. 2002), 18–22. This is a slightly shortened version of Tad Friend "Virtual Love: People Became Obsessed with a Boy's Tale of Suffering and Redemption. Then They Wanted to Meet Him," *The New Yorker* (26 Nov. 2001). The *New Yorker* version was reprinted, entitled "The Electrifying True Story Behind *The Night Listener*," as an appendix to Armistead Maupin, *The Night Listener* (New York: Harper Perennial, 2006), 4–28.

87. Cited in John Patterson "Out There," *The Guardian* (England) (14 Sept. 2006), 14.

88. Jean Baudrillard, *Seduction* (New York: St. Martin's, 1990), 155. See also Philip Auslander, *Liveness: Performance in Mediatized Culture* (New York: Routledge, 2008), 116.

## CHAPTER 9     FORGING CHILD ABUSE

1. Cathrine Bennett, "Oh No, Not Another Psychopathic Nun," *The Observer* (England) (9 Mar. 2008), 31.

2. Cited in Philip Gourevitch, "Behold Now Behemoth: The Holocaust Memorial Museum," *Harpers Magazine* (July 1993), 65.

3. Elaine Showalter, *Hystories: Hysterical Epidemics in Modern Culture* (New York: Columbia University Press, 1997), 166.

4. Ian Hacking, "The Making and Molding of Child Abuse," *Critical Inquiry*, 17, 2 (1991), 267.

5. Libby Brooks, "False Memoir Syndrome: Trauma Hucksters' Lies Must Be Exposed, But Autobiographers Deserve Some Creative License," *The Guardian* (20 Mar. 2008), 40.

6. Simon Caterson, "All Memoirs Are Very Unreliable," *Weekend Australian* (12 Apr. 2008), 28.

7. H. C. Kempe et al., "The Battered Child Syndrome," *Journal of the American Medical Association* 181, 1 (1962), 17–24.

8. Hacking, "Making and Molding," 267–269.

9. Ibid., 267.

10. Louise Armstrong, *Rocking the Cradle of Sexual Politics: What Happened When Women Said Incest* (Reading, MA: Addison-Wesley, 1994), 78.

11. According to Hacking ("Making and Molding," 276), "touching" constitutes by far the most frequent instance of sexual child abuse, for instance, of the 291 cases reported in Minnesota in one year, only 8 involved intercourse, 39 the vaguely phrased "indecent liberties," and the remainder "touching."

12. Showalter, *Hystories*, 149.

13. Ibid., 150.

14. Ibid., 152. On the so-called Memory Wars over the veracity of "recovered" memories see Showalter, *Hystories*, 144–158; Frederic Crews, *The Memory Wars: Freud's Legacy in Dispute* (New York: Granata, 1995); Elisabeth Loftus and Katherine Ketcham, *The Myth of Repressed Memory: False Memories and Allegations of Sexual Abuse* (New York: St. Martin's, 1994).

15. Judith Herman, *Trauma and Recovery: The Aftermath of Violence from Domestic Abuse to Political Terror* (New York: Basic Books, 1997), 144.

16. Showalter, *Hystories*, 149.

17. Ibid., 149–150.

18. See Richard Ofshe and Ethan Watters, *Making Monsters: False Memories, Psychotherapy, and Sexual Hysteria* (New York: Charles Scribner's Sons, 1994) for a thorough critique of "recovered" memory. Their discrediting analysis of the three most-cited empirical studies that supposedly proved the verity of "recovered" memories is summarized in Showalter, *Hystories*, 148–149.

19. Dagmar von Hoff, for instance, provides a twelve-page bibliography of contemporary Western European and American literature and films that employ the incest motif. See Dagmar von Hoff, *Familiengeheimnisse: Inzest in Literatur und Film der Gegenwart* (Cologne: Boehlau, 2003), 377–388.

20. Marlene Kruck, for example, lists nineteen books for children and approximately eighty books for young adult readers on sexual child abuse published in German. See Marlene Kruck, *Das Schweigen durchbrechen: Sexueller Missbrauch in der deutschsprachigen Kinder- und Jugendliteratur* (Berlin: Lit Verlag, 2006).

21. Katie Roiphe, "Making the Incest Scene," *Harper's Magazine* 291 (Nov. 1995), 65, 68–71.

22. Ibid., 67.

23. Ibid., 69.

24. Ibid, 68.

25. Showalter, *Hystories*, 158.

26. Cited in ibid., 166.

27. Ibid.

28. Roiphe, "Incest," 65.

29. Ibid., 67–68.

30. Showalter, *Hystories*, 167.

31. Cited in ibid., 91; Freely's italics.

32. Ibid., 151; Donald Downs, *More than Victims: Battered Women, the Syndrome Society, and the Law* (Chicago: University of Chicago Press, 1996), 49.

33. Amy Curtis-Webber, "Not Just Another Pretty Victim: The Incest Survivor and the Media," *Journal of Popular Culture* 28, 4 (1995), 38.

34. Ibid.

35. Hacking, "Making and Molding," 255.

36. Dolf Zillmann, "Television Viewing and Physiological Arousal," in *Responding to the Screen: Reception and Reaction Processes* ed. Jennings Bryant and Dolf Zillmann (New York: Routledge, 1991), 112.

37. Ibid.

38. Ibid., 113.

38. See the earlier section on "Consuming Violence" in chapter 7 for a more detailed discussion of employing research on audience reception of screen violence conducted in media studies for the analysis of the reception of misery memoirs.

40. As false memoirs only simulate the autobiographical trinity of author, narrator, and protagonist, I distinguish these subject positions linguistically. In all probability, "Anthony Godby Johnson" only existed as a confabulation, and was impersonated by two women, first by Vicki Fraginals, who created the character and wrote the fake misery memoir, and, when Fraginals no longer maintained the character she had created, by Lesley Karsten. Moreover, each of them not only impersonated "Tony" but also his respective maternal caretaker in countless phone conversations, e-mails, and internet chats. Except in quotes, I distinguish the respective subject positions as follows: I refer to the women who impersonated "Tony" in the semi-public sphere of virtual reality and, in Vicki Fraginals's case, as the author of the false memoir by their actual full or last names as Vicki Fraginals and Lesley Karsten. In their impersonation of "Tony's" maternal caretakers, they are designated by their first names in quotation markes as "Vicki" and "Lesley." I refer to the fake author-narrator of *A Rock and a Hard Place* as "Anthony Godby Johnson" and to the narrator and protagonist of the false memoir and of his numerous prior and subsequent conversations in virtual reality for about a decade as "Tony."

41. Tad Friend, "The Electrifying True Story Behind *The Night Listener*," in Armistead Maupin, *The Night Listener* (New York: Harper Perennial, 2006), 9–10.

42. Cited John Cornwall, "The Ghost Writer," *The Weekend Australian* (20 April 2002), R01.

43. Armistead Maupin, "Adapting *The Night Listener* to the Screen," in Maupin, *Night*, 33.

44. Cited in Michelle Ingrassia, "The Author Nobody's Met," *Newsweek* (21 May 1993), 63.

45. Friend, "Electrifying," 27.

46. Tad Friend, "The Ghost Writer," *Independent on Sunday* (England) (24 Mar. 2002), 22.

47. Friend, "Electrifying," 6.

48. Ibid., 7.

49. Ken Plummer, *Telling Sexual Stories: Power, Change, and Social Worlds* (New York: Routledge, 1995), 20.

50. Ingrassia, "Author," 63.

51. Cited in Meg Cox, "Crown Publishers Denies Boy's Book on AIDS Is Hoax," *Wall Street Journal* (25 May 1993), B5.

52. Cited in Friend, "Electrifying," 7.

53. Ibid.

54. Ingrassia, "Author," 63.

55. Friend, "Electrifying," 11.

56. Ingrassia, "Author," 63.

57. Friend, "Electrifying," 11, 13–14.

58. Ben Macintyre, "Hoax Claims Sparks Debate on Praised Book by AIDS Boy," *The Times* (England) (27 May 1993).

58. Leslie Dreyfous, "Tony's Heart: The Story of an Extraordinary Boy's Rebirth," Associated Press (11 Apr. 1993). For another laudatory review see Kim Painter, "Tony's Story: Love Prevails Over Abuse," *USA Today* (10 May 1993), 1D.

60. Cornwall, "Ghost," R01.

61. Friend, "Electrifying, 13.

62. Cornwall, "Ghost," R01.

63. I will refer to characters in the fake memoir in quotation marks analogous to those used for "Tony" to indicate the false claim of their indexicality and to distinguish these solely imaginary figures from actual people with whom they interact in sometimes confusing ways. For instance, Vicki Fraginals created the character of "Vicki" in the memoir and impersonated her prior to and after its publication in the many conversations with Armistead Maupin, Paul Monette, Jack Godby and many others in the virtual reality of telephone and e-mail. Moreover, she also invented an imaginary husband, "Earnist Johnson," who appears in the text as well as in "Vicki's" and "Tony's" virtual communication and who disappears from both after a likewise imaginary divorce.

64. Friend, "Electrifying," 14.

65. Ibid.; Benjamin Redford, *Media Mythmakers: How Journalists, Activists, and Advertisers Mislead Us* (Amherst, NY: Prometheus Books, 2003), 174; Edward Helmore and Cathy Galvin, "Hoax Claim Sets Off Row on Aids Victim's Book," *Sunday Times* (England) (30 May 1993).

66. Cited in Friend, "Electrifying," 6.

67. Macintyre, "Hoax," n.p.

68. Ingrassia, "Author," 63.

69. Cited in Friend, "Electrifying," 28.

70. Ibid., 10.

71. Ibid., 28.

72. Anthony Godby Johnson, *A Rock and a Hard Place* (New York: Signet, 1994), 95–96.

73. Cornwall, "Ghost," R1.

74. Friend, "Electrifying," 14–15.

75. Cornwall, "Ghost," ROI.

76. Ibid.; Friend, "Electrifying," 17.

77. Friend, "Writer," 22.

78. Friend, "Electrifying," 23–25.

79. Ibid., 6.

80. I will again differentiate the individual who wrote the texts and/or impersonated the imaginary boy (Laura Albert and Savannah Knoop) from the character ("JT") and the author of the books ("JT Leroy" or "LeRoy").

81. Cited in Alan Feuer, "At Trial, a Writer Recalls an Alter Ego that Took Over," *New York Times* (21 June 2007), BI.

82. Ibid.

83. In 2008, Savannah Knoop published her own memoir *Girl Boy Girl: How I Became JT LeRoy*. However, it primarily chronicles "JT's" interaction with celebrities rather than providing an account of how Knoop, a college drop-out bussing tables even after she began impersonating "JT," managed to simultaneously live two such different lives. According to Courtney Sullivan, Knoop "can't seem to decide whether she's a willing participant or a hapless victim, so she paints Albert as both co-conspirator and manipulative mastermind." See J. Courtney Sullivan, "Nonfiction Chronicle," *New York Times* (30 Nov. 2008), 19.

84. Tony Allen-Mills, "Is He Really She? Hoax Riddle of Cult US Novelist," *Sunday Times* (England) (16 Oct. 2005), 23; Laura Barton "Who's the Boy/Girl?" *The Guardian* (England) (4 Jan. 2006), 10; Luke Crisell, [no title], *The Observer Magazine* (6 Mar. 2005), 12.

85. Cited in Alan Hickman, "Raccoon Penis Bones for Sale: The Spin on J.T. LeRoy," *Philological Review* 29, 1 (2003), 87.

86. Michele Magwood, "Twisted Line between Reality and Fantasy," *Sunday Times* (South Africa) (1 July 2007), 16; Motoko Rich, "A Family Tree of Literary Fakers," *New York Times* (8 Mar. 2008), B7.

87. David Segal, "Nothing but the Truth: The Author of a Hoax Insists Her Creation Is No Fraud," *Washington Post* (21 June 2007), C1.

88. G. Beato, "Boy Toy," *Washington Post* (26 Aug. 2001), T7.

89. [Anonymous], "Best-Selling Writers Take the Flak as Facts Turn to Fiction," *Irish Times* (12 Jan. 2006), 13.

90. Cited in Hickman, "Bones," 89.

91. Cited in Alan Feuer, "Going to Court Over Fiction by a Fictitious Writer," *New York Times* (15 June 2007), BI. According to Feuer, Albert was convicted of fraud in 2007 and ordered to pay $116,000 in damages and $350,000 in legal fees to Antidote Films as the jury found that she had "strayed beyond the normal limits of pseudonymous invention." Unlike the film adaptation of *Sarah*, for which production had not yet begun when Albert and Knoop's impersonation was exposed and which was subsequently abandoned, *The Heart Is Deceitful Above All Things* had been adapted before the scandal broke. It "received a shockingly rough ride at Cannes" and its few American reviews unanimously panned the film. The *Hollywood Reporter*, for instance, called it "a grueling, cinematic excretion." The *Washington Post* commented that it was written and directed by Italian actress Asia Argento—daughter of horror B-movie director

Dario Argento, who starred in several of her father's films and also plays the female lead of Sarah in *The Heart Is Deceitful Above All Things*—"primarily as a showcase for her Courtney Love impersonation" and "reeks of a project desperate for edgy credibility, from its too-cool supporting cast," including Peter Fonda, Winona Ryder, and Marilyn Manson, "to its gay-gothic coming-of-age plot." However, a number of reviews, most of them in leading British newspapers, were predominantly laudatory. See [Anonymous], "No Cure for a Broken 'Heart,'" *Washington Post* (14 Apr. 2006), T31; Steven Rose, "Wild Child," *The Guardian* (England) (8 July 2005), 8; Stephanie Theobald, "She's Smokin'," *Sunday Times* (England) (26 June 2005), 10; Nick Roddick, "Kiss and Sell," *Evening Standard* (England) (23 June 2005), A4; Luke Crisell, [no title], *The Observer Magazine* (England) (6 Mar. 2005), 12; Geoffrey MacNab, "Something Wild," *The Independent* (England) (4 June 2004), 11.; Chris Sullivan, "JT LeRoy: Primal Scream," *The Independent* (England) (9 July 2005), 14, 16.

92. Feuer, "Court," B1.

93. Ibid.

94. Russell Smith, "Publishers Are Just as Guilty as the Likes of Frey," *The Globe and Mail* (Canada) (19 Jan. 2006), R1.

95. Ibid.

96. Alan Feuer, "Jury Finds 'JT LeRoy' Was Fraud," *New York Times* (23 June 2007), B1.

97. Segal, "Truth," C1.

98. Cited in Barton, "Boy/Girl," 10.

99. Cited in Magwood, "Line," 16.

100. Hickman, "Bones," 85–96; Woody Wilson, "Tradition and Travesty in JT LeRoy's *Sarah* and *The Heart Is Deceitful Above All Things*," *Journal of Appalachian Studies* 9, 2 (2003), 415–432.

101. Wilson, "Tradition," 415.

102. Ibid., 417.

103. Hickman, "Bones," 86.

104. Feuer, "Court," B1.

105. Hickman, "Bones," 94.

106. Ibid., 91.

107. David Segal, "A Novelist's Novelist: Is the Acclaimed JT LeRoy Just a Character Himself?," *Washington Post* (13 Oct. 2005), C01.

108. Feuer, "Jury," B1.

109. Warren St. John, "A Literary Life Born of Brutality," *New York Times* (4 Nov. 2004), 1.

110. Peaches Geldof, "My Phantom Friend," *Sunday Telegraph* (19 Feb. 2006), 24.

111. St. John, "Brutality," 1.

112. Ed Siegel, "Unpleasantville in Books, Plays, and Songs, America Is Getting Creepier—and More Interesting," *Boston Globe* (26 Aug. 2001), L1.

113. Barton, "Boy/Girl," 10.

114. Segal, "Novelist," C1.

115. Jessica Callan, Eva Simpson, and Suzanne Kerins, "Michael Stipe Infatuated with JT LeRoy," *The Mirror* (4 June 2002), 16.

116. St. John, "Brutality," 1.

117. Segal, "Novelist," C1.

118. St. John, "Brutality," 1.

119. Ibid.

120. Alberto Mobilio, "Shell Shock," *New York Times* (27 Feb. 2005), 1.

121. Steven Beachy, "Who Is the Real JT LeRoy? A Search for the True Identity of a Great Literary Hustler," *New York Magazine* (10 Oct. 2005).

122. St. John, "Brutality," 1.

123. Warren St. John, "Figure in JT LeRoy Case Says Partner Is Culprit," *New York Times* (7 Feb. 2006), E1.

124. Feuer, "Trial," B1.

125. Ibid.

125. Ibid.

127. Ibid.

128. Segal, "Truth," C1.

129. St. John, "Figure," E1.

130. Maupin, "Adapting," 28, his italics.

131. Gill Pringle, "My Tallest Tale of Them All," *The Independent* (England) (15 Sept. 2006), 9.

132. Beato, "Toy," T07.

## CHAPTER 10     SIMULATING HOLOCAUST SURVIVAL

1. Stefan Maechler, *The Wilkomirski Affair: A Study in Biographical Truth* (New York: Schocken Books, 2001), 273.

2. Jesse McKinley, "The Truth About Jerzy May Never Be Known," *New York Times* (14 Jan. 2001), 1.

3. Gary Weissman, *Fantasies of Witnessing: Postwar Efforts to Experience the Holocaust* (Ithaca: Cornell University Press, 2004), 80.

4. Cited in Weissman, *Fantasies*, 68.

5. Andrew Gross and Michael Hoffman, "Memory, Authority, and Identity: Holocaust Studies in Light of the Wilkomirski Debate," *Biography* 27, 1 (2004), 34.

6. "The Sunday Times Bestseller of the Year," *Sunday Times* (England) (21 Dec. 2008), 42.

7. A. O. Scott, "Never Forget. You're Reminded," *New York Times* (23 Nov. 2008), AR1.

8. Jacob Heilbrunn, "Telling the Holocaust Like It Wasn't," *New York Times* (11 Jan. 2009), 5.

9. James Christopher, "Making Innocence of the Monstrous," *The Times* (England) (11 Sept. 2008), 16.

10. See, for instance, Saul Friedlander, *Probing the Limits of Representation: Nazism and the 'Final Solution'* (Cambridge: Harvard University Press, 1992).

11. John Boyne, "Through the Eyes of Suffering Children," *The Times* (England) (21 Jan. 2006), 7.

12. Ibid.

13. Cited in Scott, "Reminded," AR1.

14. India Knight, "Our Taste for All This Misery Lit Makes Ugly Reading," *Sunday Times* (England) (23 Nov. 2008), 20.

15. Ted Rall, "The Real Sham Is Her Taste," *National Post* (Canada) (31 Jan. 2009), WP12.

16. Elisabeth Day, "When One Extraordinary Life Story is Not Enough," *The Observer* (England) (15 Feb. 2009), 6.

17. Ibid.; Tom Leonhard, "Holocaust Love Memoir Is Exposed as a Fraud," *Daily Telegraph* (England) (29 Dec. 2008), 12.

18. Graeme Hammond, "The Great Pretenders," *Sunday Telegraph* (Australia) (12 May 2002), 22.

19. [Anonymous], "Holocaust 'Love Story' Exposed as a Fake," *New Zealand Herald* (30 Dec. 2008), n.p.

20. Day, "Extraordinary," 6.

21. Stephen McGinty, "No, You Couldn't Make That Up—But Memoir Writers Sometimes Do" *The Scotman* (28 Sept. 2006), 29.

22. Andy McSmith, "Literature of Lying: The Cover is Blown on Yet Another Tall Story," *The Independent* (England) (5 March 2008), 18; see also Simon Caterson, "All Memoirs Are Very Unreliable," *Weekend Australian* (12 Apr. 2008), 28; and David Mehegan, "Den of Lies," *Boston Globe* (1 Mar. 2008), C1.

23. Rall, "Sham," WP12.

24. Lawrence van Gelder, "Holocaust Memoir Turns Out to be Fiction," *New York Times* (8 Mar. 2008), 1.

25. McSmith, "Lying," 18.

26. Mehegan, "Den," C1.

27. McSmith "Lying," 18; Caterson, "Unreliable," 28.

28. McSmith, "Lying," 18.

29. Ibid.

30. Henryk Broder, "Verliebt in eine tote Kobra" *Der Spiegel* 50 (9 Dec. 1996) http://www.spiegel.de/spiegel/print/d-9133130.html (accessed 08/25/2010).

31. While literary criticism on *Fragments* largely refers to the author, the narrator, and the protagonist as Binjamin Wilkomirski—ironically creating the trinity of identity paradigmatic for autobiographical writing that fake memoirs precisely do not exhibit but seek to simulate—I again differentiate these three subject positions linguistically. Except in quotes, I refer to the person who fabricated the memoir by his actual full or last name (Bruno Dössekker). The text's author-narrator as well as the author as public persona is signified by the author's pseudonymous full or last name in quotation marks ("Binjamin Wilkomirski") to indicate both the author's false claim to be a Holocaust child survivor and the fact that readers and other interlocutors believed it and interacted with him accordingly. And lastly, I refer to the narrated self or protagonist by the pseudonymous first name, likewise in quotation marks ("Binjamin") to distinguish author-narrator and protagonist.

32. Maechler, *Affair*, 119.

33. Ibid., 92.

34. Ibid., 114.

35. Cited in Philip Gourevitch, "Behold Now Behemoth," *Harper's Magazine* (July 1993), 60.

36. Cited in Jörg Lau, "Ein fast perfekter Schmerz," *Die Zeit* (17 Sept. 1998), 66.

37. Jay Geller, "The Wilkomirski Case: *Fragments* or Figments?" *American Imago* 59, 3 (2002), 343.

38. Maechler, *Affair*, 73–76.

39. Ibid., 118.

40. Cited in Blake Eskin, *A Life in Pieces: The Making and Unmaking of Binjamin Wilkomirski* (New York: W.W. Norton), 33.

41. Jörg Lau ("Schmerz," 66) cites Fromma Zeitlin's seminar at Princeton. Jay Geller ("Figments," 343–365) writes that he used *Fragments* in his Holocaust courses at Vanderbilt University for two years, was planning to teach it again in fall 1998, and had even invited "Wilkomirski" to present the ideas on recovering childhood memory he had developed with Elitsur Bernstein, only to find out about a month before the planned visit about Daniel Ganzfried's accusation that *Fragments* is a fake.

42. Weissman, *Fantasies*, 212.

43. Cited in Maechler, *Affair*, 116.

44. Lau, "Schmerz," 66.

45. Maechler, *Affair*, 114.

46. Cited in Maechler, *Affair*, 114.

47. Eskin, *Pieces*, 69.

48. Tova Reich, My *Holocaust* (New York: Harper Collins, 2007), 177–178.

49. Maechler, *Affair*, 118.

50. Philip Gourevitch, "The Memory Thief," *The New Yorker* (14 June 1999), 52.

51. Maechler, *Affair*, 134.

52. Lynn Walford, "Truth, Lies, and Politics in the Debate over Testimonial Writing: The Cases of Rigoberta Menchú and Binjamin Wilkomirski" *Comparatist: Journal of the Southern Comparative Literature Association* 30 (2006), 113–121.

53. Weissman, *Fantasies*, 212.

54. K. K. Ruthven, *Faking Literature* (Cambridge: Cambridge University Press, 2001), 173.

55. Cathy Caruth, ed., *Trauma: Explorations in Memory* (Baltimore: Johns Hopkins University Press, 1995); Cathy Caruth, *Unclaimed Experience: Trauma, Narrative, and History* (Baltimore: Johns Hopkins University Press, 1996).

56. Weissman, *Fantasies*, 213.

57. Michael Bernard-Donals, "Beyond the Question of Authenticity: Witness and Testimony in the *Fragments* Controversy," *PMLA* 116, 5 (2001), 1302–1315.

58. Susan Rubin Suleiman, "Problems of Memory and Factuality in Recent Holocaust Memoirs: Wilkomirski/Wiesel," *Poetics Today* 21, 3 (2000), 552.

59. Ibid.

60. Binjamin Wilkomirski, *Fragments: Memories of a Wartime Childhood* (New York: Schocken Books, 1996), 5.

61. Maechler, *Affair*, 196–203.

62. Ibid., 59, 63–67.

63. Ibid., 243.

64. Ibid., 244.

65. William Niederland, *Folgen der Verfolgung: Das Überlebendensyndrom Seelenmord* (Frankfurt: Suhrkamp, 1980).

66. Maechler, *Affair*, 212.

67. Ibid., 212–213.

68. Cited in Maechler, *Affair*, 242.

69. Ibid.

70. Ibid.

71. Ralph Keyes, *The Post-Truth Era: Dishonesty and Deception in Contemporary Life* (New York: St. Martin's, 2004), 207.

72. Cited in Gourevitch, "Thief," 56.

73. Maechler, *Affair*, 61/2, 67.

74. Ken Plummer, *Telling Sexual Stories: Power, Change, and Social Worlds* (New York: Routledge, 1995), 20.

75. Cited in Maechler, *Affair*, 62.

76. Maechler, *Affair*, 82–92; Gourevitch, "Thief," 59.

77. Cited in Hammond, "Pretenders," 22.

78. Maechler, *Affair*, 237.

79. Ibid., 269.

80. Cited in Maechler, *Affair*, 252.

81. Bessel van der Kolk et al., "Nightmares and Trauma: A Comparison of Nightmares After Combat with Lifelong Nightmares in Veterans" *American Journal of Psychiatry* 141 (1984), 187–190. For a critique of van der Kolk's research see Ruth Leys, *Trauma: A Genealogy* (Chicago: University of Chicago Press, 2000), 229–265.

82. Maechler, *Affair*, 250.

83. Elaine Showalter, *Hystories: Hysterical Epidemics in Modern Culture* (New York: Columbia UP, 1997), 144–158.

84. Apart from quotations, I differentiate again between the confabulating individual, the author-narrator, and the protagonist of the fabricated story. However, Laurel Willson created two distinct misery narratives. Following the respective pseudonyms she chose, I thus refer to the author-narrator of her Satanic Ritual Abuse story as "Lauren Stratford" or "Stratford" and its protagonist as "Lauren" while I designate the author-narrator of her fake Holocaust story as "Laura Grabowski" or "Grabowski" and its protagonist as "Laura."

85. Eskin, *Pieces*, 96.

86. Ibid., 101–102.

87. Blake Eskin, "Holocaust Seekers Online: A Tangled Web," *Forward* (17 March 2000), n.p.

88. Cited in Eskin, "Seekers," n.p.

89. Bob Passantino, Gretchen Passantino, and John Trott, "Lauren Stratford: From Satanic Ritual Abuse to Jewish Holocaust Survivor," www.cornerstonemag.com/features/iss117/lauren.htm (accessed 05/20/2009). See also Bob Passantino, Gretchen Passantino, and John Trott, "Satan's Sideshow: The True Lauren Stratford Story," www.cornerstonemag.com/features/iss090/sideshow.htm (accessed 05/20/2009).

90. Passantino et al., "Holocaust," para 1; Maechler, *Affair*, 206.

91. Showalter, *Hystories*, 174.

92. Ibid., 173.

93. Ibid., 9–10, 160–170.

94. Ibid., 180.

95. Ibid., 6.

96. Leslie Bennetts, "Nightmares on Main Street," *Vanity Fair* (June 1993), 45.

97. Ibid.

98. Showalter, *Hystories*, 173.

99. Cited in Gourevitch, "Thief," 65.

100. Cited in Passantino et al., "Sideshow," para. 51.

101. Passantino et al., "Sideshow," para. 60–74.

102. Wilkimirski, *Fragments*, 17, 41–42, 55, 60, 71, 79, 86; see also Weissman, *Fantasies*, 214.

103. Maechler, *Affair*, 209.

104. Ibid., 210.

105. Passantino et al., "Sideshow," para. 5.

106. Roger Luckhurst, "Traumaculture" [sic], *New Formations* 50 (2003), 36–39.

107. Passantino et al., "Sideshow," para. 14.

## EPILOGUE

1. Gary Weissman, *Fantasies of Witnessing: Postwar Efforts to Experience the Holocaust* (Ithaca: Cornell University Press, 2004), 20.

2. K. K. Ruthven, *Faking Literature* (Cambridge: Cambridge University Press, 2001), 149, 169.

3. Richard Sennett, *The Fall of Public Man* (New York: W. W. Norton, 1992), 259.

4. Philip Auslander, *Liveness: Performance in Mediatized Culture* (New York: Routledge, 2008), 116; Jean Baudrillard, *Seduction* (New York: St. Martin's, 1990), 155.

5. Auslander, *Liveness*, 116; Baudrillard, *Seduction*, 155.

6. Michael Bernstein, *Forgone Conclusions: Against Apocalyptic History* (Berkeley: University of California Press, 1994), 91.

7. Dori Laub, "Bearing Witness, or the Vicissitudes of Listening" in Shoshana Felman and Dori Laub, *Testimony: Crises of Witnessing in Literature, Psychoanalysis, and History* (New York: Routledge, 1992), 72.

8. Ibid.

9. Weissman, *Fantasies*, 132.

10. Ibid., 137.

11. Jeffrey Goldstein, "Why We Watch," in *Why We Watch: The Attractions of Violent Entertainment* ed. Jeffrey Goldstein (Oxford: Oxford University Press, 1998), 217.

12. Ruthven, *Faking*, 169.

13. Bernstein, *Apocalyptic*, 84, 89; Weissman, *Fantasies*, 78.

14. Laub, "Witness," 72.

15. Marita Sturken, *Tourists of History: Memory, Kitsch, and Consumerism from Oklahoma City to Ground Zero* (Durham: Duke University Press, 2007), 165–218; James Young, *The Texture of Memory: Holocaust Memorials and Meaning* (New Haven: Yale University Press, 1994).

16. John Lennon and Malcolm Foley, *Dark Tourism: The Attraction of Death and Disaster* (Andover, UK: Thomson Learning, 2004); see also Richard Sharpley and Philipe Stone (eds.) *The Darker Side of Travel: The Theory and Practice of Dark Tourism* (Bristol, UK: Channel View Publications, 2009), 3–22.

17. Ruth Kluger, *Still Alive* (New York: Feminist Press, 2003), 67–68.

18. John Berger, "Photographs of Agony," in *About Looking* (New York: Pantheon, 1980), 38.

19. Luc Boltanski, *Distant Suffering: Morality, Media, and Politics* (Cambridge: Cambridge University Press, 1999), 23.

20. Berger, "Agony," 40.

21. Ibid.

22. Weissman, *Fantasies*, 92.

23. Ibid., 209.

24. Cited in Ian Buruma, "The Joys and Perils of Victimhood," *New York Review of Books* (8 Apr. 1999), www.nybooks.com/articles/525 (accessed 3/3/2008), para. 8.

25. Weissman, *Fantasies*, 92.

26. Ibid., 136–137.

27. Ellen Fine, *Legacy of Night: The Literary Universe of Elie Wiesel* (Albany: SUNY Press, 1992), 9.

28. Weissman, *Fantasies*, 5, 20.

29. Ibid., 4.

30. Ibid., 20.

31. Dominick LaCapra, *Writing History, Writing Trauma* (Baltimore: Johns Hopkins University Press, 2001), 186.

32. Weissman, *Fantasies*, 27, his italics.

33. Daniel Schwarz, *Imagining the Holocaust* (New York: St. Martin's, 1999), 5.

34. Ibid.

35. Katharina Hacker, *Eine Art Liebe* (Frankfurt: Suhrkamp, 2005).

36. Saul Friedlander, *When Memory Comes* (New York: Farrar Straus Giroux, 1999).

37. Daniela Comani, *Ich war's. Tagebuch 1900–1999 (Frankfurt am Main: Revolver Archiv, 2007).* The large-scale digital print was part of an exhibition at the Kunst-Werke Berlin e.V. from November 18, 2007 to January 13, 2008. See the bilingual German/English exhibition catalogue *History Will Repeat Itself. Strategien des Reenactment in der zeitgenössischen (Medien)kunst und Performance*, ed. by Imke Arns and Gabriele Horn (Bönen, Westfahlen: Druckverlag Kettler, 2007), 82–83. The booklet, which is available in the German original as well as in Italian and English translation, is the most accessible version and available through the artist's web site www.danielacomani.net.

38. http://www.freietheateranstalten.de (accessed 03/08/2010).

39. The term *Stasi* is the informal abbreviation for *Staatssicherheit*, the East German secret police. Their files were largely preserved after unification and any German on whom the Stasi compiled information has the right to read their files.

40. Daniela Comani, *It Was Me. Diary 1900–1999 (Frankfurt am Main: Revolver Archiv, 2007),* 1.

41. See the critique of vicarious Holocaust victimhood in chapter 1 for the discussion of Rosen, Ochs, Cantor, and Brody.

42. "Aschenglorie/Ash-aureole," in *Selected Poems of Paul Celan*, transl. by John Felstiner (New York: W. W. Norton, 2001), 260.

43. Weissman, *Fantasies*, 213.

44. Milan Kundera, *The Unbearable Lightness of Being* (New York: Harper Perennial, 1991), 248.

# INDEX

Amato, Joseph, 24, 27, 28, 29
anti-victimists, 23, 29–31
atrocity photographs, 84, 95, 160–161
Auschwitz: as metonymy or metaphor, 15, 17, 34; setting of *The Boy in the Striped Pajamas*, 140; setting *of Fragments*, 148, 149; setting of Laurel Willson's false life story, 151, 156, 157; setting of *My Holocaust*, 17; setting of *Night*, 137; setting *of Oprah Winfrey Show Special*, 2, 3, 115, 159; setting of *Survival in Auschwitz*, 146
authenticity, 18, 43, 57, 65, 78, 84–85, 87, 102, 111, 144, 158–160
autobiographical pact, 81, 86, 101–112, 137

Baudrillard, Jean, 112
Bauman, Zygmunt, 19–21, 27–29
Beah, Ishmael, *A Long Way Gone*, 104–105
Berger, John, 160–161
Bernstein, Michael, 19–20, 26, 29, 84–85, 89, 95, 158–159
Binkley, Sam, 43, 44
Boltanski, Luc, 43, 44, 160
*Boy in the Striped Pajamas, The* (novel by Boyne; film dir. Herman), 10, 42, 91, 114, 136–140
Boyne, John, 10, 138–140
Burroughs, Augusteen, *Running with Scissors*, 88, 108
Buruma, Ian, 17, 18, 39

camp (mode of representation), 5, 50, 58, 60, 71–78, 80, 82, 113, 165, 182n38, 182n47
child abuse: in Anthony Godby Johnson's fake memoir, 108, 112, 122–123, 125–126, 128, 130; ethics of representation, 89; in fake misery memoirs, 108–109, 111–113, 105, 114, 152–154, 156; genealogy, 4–5, 28, 114–122; and Holocaust memory, 45–46, 136, 138–139, 143, 157, 165; in JT LeRoy's fake auto-fiction, 130–131, 134–135; and kitsch, 121, 138–139; in misery memoirs, 6, 46, 83–84, 88–93, 165, 190–194; recovered memory of, 27, 66, 118–119; on talk shows, 52, 56–58, 77
Cole, Alyson, 29, 30, 32
Cole, Tim, 10, 11, 14
confession, 55–57, 60–61, 65–69, 71, 89

dark tourism, 2–3, 49, 159–160, 162, 165
Defonseca, Misha, 6, 116, 126, 136–138, 141–144, 156
*Diagnostics and Statistics Manual*, 24, 65, 153
Donahue, Phil. See *Phil Donahue Show*
Dössekker, Bruno. See Wilkomirski, Binjamin
*DSM. See Diagnostics and Statistics Manual*

Eichmann trial on television, 1–5, 7, 12, 15, 22, 39, 49, 50, 59, 136, 149–150
embeddedness, 44

"Final Solution," 1, 3. *See also* Holocaust discourse, American
Finkelstein, Norman, 10, 12, 17
Finkielkraut, Alain, 18–21
forgeries (literary), 6, 86, 116, 99–113, 122, 142. *See also* Johnson, Anthony Godby; Wilkomirski, Binjamin; Willson, Laurel
Foucault, Michel, 22, 67–69
Frank, Anne, 7, 10, 12, 15, 24, 33, 136
Freud, Sigmund, 28, 33, 96, 116, 121, 124, 136
Frey, James, *A Million Little Pieces*, 2–3, 88, 100, 106–108, 111, 130
Friedlander, Saul, 6, 163–165
Friend, Tad, 112, 123, 125–126, 128–129

ghetto, 171n67
Giddens, Anthony, 44, 64, 66
Godby Johnson, Anthony. See Johnson, Anthony Godby
Grabowski, Laura, 138, 151–157, 199n84

Hacker, Katharina, 6, 163–165
Holocaust discourse, American: and authenticity, 159; and American values, 12–13, 50, 78, 88; and child abuse, 115–116, 122, 136; child victims in, 136–143, 162, 164; and Christianity, 3, 25, 34, 95, 137; ethics, 28; examples, 9–11; and Jewish identity, 7, 17–21; hereditary victim claims, 17–21, 162, 164; and historical knowledge, 11, 34–35, 59, 65; *Holocaust* miniseries, 36, 42; and kitsch, 3, 19, 36, 42, 112, 114–115, 139–140, 142, 146, 148, 186n42; lessons, 3, 11–14, 28, 38, 170n39; melodramatic plot structure, 11; as myth, 11–12; as narrative paradigm, 2, 7, 8, 47, 49, 115, 136;

# ABOUT THE AUTHOR

**ANNE ROTHE** is assistant professor of German at Wayne State University in Detroit.

Lightning Source UK Ltd.
Milton Keynes UK
UKOW05f1812061114

241235UK00001B/64/P